THE HONOURABLE BEAST

THE HONOURABLE BEAST

A Posthumous Autobiography

John Dexter

NICK HERN BOOKS
London

A Nick Hern Book

The Honourable Beast first published in 1993
by Nick Hern Books Limited, 14 Larden Road, London W3 7ST

Copyright © 1993 Riggs O'Hara and the Estate of
John Dexter
Excerpts from *Peter Hall's Diaries* by
Peter Hall, edited by John Goodwin
(Hamish Hamilton, 1983) copyright ©
Petard Publications Ltd, 1983 reproduced
by permission of Hamish Hamilton Ltd

Thanks are also due to Clive Merrison for
extracts from his diary of the rehearsals
of *The Party*

A CIP catalogue record for this book is available
from the British Library

ISBN 1 85459 039 1

Typeset by Deltatype Ltd, Ellesmere Port, Cheshire
Printed in Great Britain by The Bath Press, Avon

1000 716 241

Contents

Publisher's Note

Every effort has been made to contact the owners of copyright material reproduced in this volume. Apologies are offered in advance for any unauthorised usage.

List of Illustrations

For Riggs
and for
George and Jocelyn and John
Diana
Joan and Maggie
Alec and Gambon and Hopkins
Larry
Sting
and all those who are
Knock, Knock, Knock, Knock/
Knocking at the door

Introduction

A book about John Dexter had to be a book about work. As he said in a note I found, 'To work to live to live to work. We all come to the theatre to be in love with our work. If we do not, we had better settle for the lesser road, to work to live.'

Over the long period of our time together I had saved everything I could: letters, notes, memos, etc.; and after toying with ideas of coffee-table books and picture books of his productions, the fall at 4 a.m. of two books from a shelf led me to the obvious conclusion that since I had all the information I must make a book of it. The two books were the first volume of *The Lisle Letters* and *The Letters of Evelyn Waugh*.

Through the encouragement of virtually everyone we knew, I set about trying to peddle the wares, but where? Everyone who knew anyone who they thought could help called me, called them and fixed appointments with publishers. Through the suggestion of Kathleen Tynan, Howard Brenton, Tariq Ali and David Aukin, I decided on Nick Hern, and the greatest compliment I can pay him is that he understood the idea and trusted me to do a book telling the story of John's Life and Work through the use of his own words.

Nick suggested bringing Lyn Haill into the team, and the three of us would meet once a week and go through letters and transcribed notes, finding various bits of paper with observations. But still no real form emerged.

I decided to take two productions and tell their story. One that no one really wanted to do, which became a success, *Dialogues of the Carmelites* by Poulenc at the Metropolitan Opera House, and the other an obvious success, especially after the rediscovery and definitive production of *Pygmalion, Man and Superman*, which never got on. I put them together and gave them to Lyn and Nick to read. (They responded immediately and told me to go on.) The shape became easier to contemplate but still difficult to see. I found my personal involvement made it almost impossible to carry on. In effect I was reliving my life as well. The present had become the past and vice versa. I needed help. Someone to perform for or to force me to be objective, and to approach it as a project.

Along came Andrew Weale. I was about to start a play with a group of young actors, arranged by Trish Pierce, and at the first meeting I asked if anyone would like to help with my book. Andrew said yes, and I waited to see if he meant it and would turn up, and if he would be of any help. Help is too small a word to describe what I had lucked into. Andrew is an Oxford graduate, a Classics scholar, a drama school graduate, a professional actor, a singer of classical music and a proof reader in his spare time. It was perfect. He set about immersing himself in the Life and Work of John Dexter and by the end knew him as well as I did. I could not and would not have done it without him.

The question of whether to incorporate John's background and childhood was resolved when I found this note; 'Tell the story of the work until now, and if the past or the personal come into it that's OK as long as they illuminate the present.' Again a sign, a direction to follow.

As you can see, everywhere I went, everything I read, every notebook, diary, etc. led me in the same direction. I just followed along. Even the title was an accident. Jameson Keane, John's godson, who had lived with us for many years, is a painter, and when John was in hospital working on *Moscow Gold*, he needed Jamie to draw out his ideas for a set to be sent to Josef Svoboda, whom he wanted as designer. Jamie as usual was late. John said from his hospital bed, 'He's a beast.' Me defending said, 'You're a beast too.' Then I paused and said, 'But an honourable one'. It seemed the only title to use.

What a difficult experience this book has been for me, but something kept pushing me on. The support and enthusiasm of everyone, plus something else I found of John's: 'Behind the work of any creative artist there are three principal wishes. The wish to make something, the wish to perceive something either in the external world of the sense or the internal world of feeling, and the wish to communicate these perceptions to others . . .

Those who have no interest in communication do not become artists, they become mystics or mad men.'

Riggs O'Hara

1

The Toy Theatre

How to look forward without looking back.

Forward looking journal.

Keep a working journal. Do not look back too much – only as far as is needed to see forward. Swim every day.

A record of a year's work is a discipline I have not before attempted and even if it is finally unprintable at least there will be a record of the pleasure and pains of being a Stage Director at a time when the craft is so much accused of every crime from favouritism to petty theft, sometimes correctly, sometimes not.

To begin a working journal at the moment at which a commitment is made to a text is a discipline I have not before attempted but it may at least break the tendency of many years, which has been to avoid discussion at a personal level of the working process. It could also help me clarify for myself the effects of ill health, background, education and experience which have contributed to whatever craft I have. It may also be an act of hubristic over-confidence which I shall live to regret, but as my career seems to have been, to a very large extent, a confidence trick executed by a very unconfident trickster whose aim was sometimes to be a magician, I am running true to form.

The best and most exhilarating days for a sixty-one year old apprentice magician, working in the eighties, are those following the arrival of a new and unsolicited script which, from the first page, sometimes from as much as the title and the cast list, forces the attention and which, by the final page, has called up a pleasurable commitment, excitement and joy at the same time. David Hwang's play M. Butterfly is such a play. I read it at a time when plans for my New Theatre Company were active and suggested possibilities beyond anything I had so far envisaged and which will, with David Hwang's play, dominate, to some extent, this journal and avoid the biographical and reminiscent anecdotes to which in rehearsal I am so inclined.

Digression on the Art of Directing might sustain an academic thesis. I am not the man for a thesis, but a journal perhaps will allow me to indulge myself. After all, whose time am I wasting but my own? David Hwang's play is well worth reporting to a journal in detail. But how can I explain my directorial response to it unless I can recall those early productions-without decor-at the Royal Court Theatre in Sloane Square? And how can I explain them without some reference to the rigours of twice nightly weekly rep, which has left one permanent scars and can provoke strong words.

Quote – Robert Atkins to Emlyn Williams: Listen, you bloody Welsh pit pony, we open on Monday, so I think you'd better know it by Friday because you're on on Saturday matinée. So get the coal dust out of your eyes, and back to the studying.

Or equally hasty emotional ones.

Quote – Tell Mr Hwang I could begin rehearsal next week. I don't want to wait 'til September.

If weekly twice-nightly repertory has provoked bad habits – and it certainly has – it also produced an urgent need in me as an actor to get on my feet on a Tuesday, avoiding the furniture, and sometimes learn most of the text by Monday. And as a director, it did give awareness of the immense confidence a player feels when his footwork is secure. For example Esmé Percy to Robert Stephens in the foyer: 'Learn to tap – it's all in the footwork.' And Jacques Charron to Albert Finney in the sixties: 'Comedy is in the feet – Comédie est dans le foots.' What is true of comedy is true for tragedy (and David Hwang's play is both). David Hwang's play demands nimble footwork, God knows, and careful planning. Hence my desire to make a ground plan after only three readings, even if we do not open until a Monday next September.

A ground plan, a sense of the space demanded, a zero from which the designer can fly away or above: M. Butterfly began as all the others began. But does it begin? I have heard almost nothing for almost a week and the usual paranoias have set in. No call. They don't want me. I am difficult, British, homosexual, expensive – and whilst I can, with modified rapture, admit to the first three charges, the last is deeply wounding. So my melo-dramatic response is to make a ground plan to show how economical it can be to engage me. But more significantly it is a wonderfully enjoyable time with a script as good as this.

December has been a wonderful month, apart from a false

Spring in the garden, even though the promised Arts Council investment to the New Theatre Company is likely to be withdrawn.

Let me clarify the situation for myself by writing it down: A few weeks ago I offered the services of the NTC to the Malvern Festival for an unusual production of *Portraits* by William Douglas Home. My producer, Henry Sherwood, took up my suggestion that we might calculate and offer ourselves to investors around the provinces with a long term view to reviving the Malvern Festival and using it for the work in mind for the company (bearing in mind the word company is used very loosely, it being an uncontracted group of old and new colleagues who would like for a time to work together and hopefully earn a decent living, at the same time avoiding direct subsidy with all its attendant problems). These problems, in this really false spring, are the only chill of this very mild December. I came back from the arts panel of the above Council with a request to see the script of *Portraits* and have the costing plans. At which point David Hwang's play came into my hands, sent by Mr Ostrow in New York.

Hence this journal – an attempt to focus my thinking about where I am, where I have been and where I am going, and maybe by indirection to find some new directions out.

After several years of quite severe illness, it seems about time to find an easier way of using the craft I have, than I have achieved in the past. To manage this focus and speculate on why I made things so difficult for so long is to waste time at this point, and distracts me from the best of all antidotes to the snares of subsidy and the bores of bureaucracy – namely two new plays, one by an established author (Douglas Home) and the other by David Hwang.

The Douglas Home play is in the hands of the designer and I can give no more help until he is ready to see me. If the David Hwang play takes over the journal (and leaves the New Theatre Company to take care of itself until April, at least as far as the written word is concerned) it is because *Portraits* is clear in my head, almost cast. The creative, and therefore, it is to be presumed, interesting part of this record is over. The rest is hard graft from the first day of rehearsal with the players.

M. Butterfly presents a cultural and sexual collision between the East and the West, technically constructed to respond to all the illusion of the anti-illusionist theatre I have pursued since I found myself without scenery in Sloane Square. But how I got to Sloane Square, and in what emotional and physical state, will require a digression into biography which will at least take my pen away from professional paranoia that only a call from New York can cure.

During the rehearsals for *Chips with Everything*, on the square at Chelsea Barracks, I remember standing with George Devine years after we first met in 1956, when he had just founded the English Stage Company and taken me on as an inexperienced director. We were shivering in the cold and somewhere between laughter and tears as we remembered grandparents (of which George had his share) and tried to vie grandfather stories.

Both my father and grandfather were amateur painters. A stormy seascape in thickly painted oils by my grandfather dominated his seldom used drawing room, whilst at our home in Derby there was a watercolour of the ruined Town Hall at Ypres, meticulously painted by my father whilst recovering from shrapnel wounds received in 1917 – which eventually killed him in 1957. This skill with pen and brush was not, however, part of my inheritance, as we were to discover when I began to paint scenery for my own toy theatre.

My grandmother was altogether a remarkable person, whom alas I never got to know as well as I would have liked. Her one-line tutorials stayed with me and developed my resistance to academic facts and figures, leaving plenty of space for my parents to fill with a love of music and theatre which they happily shared with me, from the first toy theatre to the piano lessons given up in despair after a few years.

If the way I work is the result of my life, then the Smiths (my mother's family) and Dexters have a lot to answer for. I had forgotten how consistent my running away from school had become. To run away from education, when that is the thing I remember wanting most, was a problem long before masturbation (that came later with the Boy Scouts!). Maybe the miseries of school and the splendours of the latter made the mixture unstable later on. At school I never remember play as anything other than running about, and yet according to Auntie Nellie, even at three, when taken on one of those Christmas rides in a department store, I was not concerned at all with the present given at the end by Father Christmas, but with how the ride worked. At three I had made a toy theatre. (That can't be right. 1. I have no manufacturing skill. 2. I couldn't even read.) I wonder? Would things have been different had I been brought up in London. Yes, but that doesn't matter.

On my mother's side there were the Jockeys, as they were referred to by my paternal grandparents. Her family was large, wild and (to me) wonderful. Out of the money, in the public bar and in trouble, except when winning races which happily they did for a long time. Not, however, when I was young. They were always mentioned by my father's parents as objects to be pitied and their tendencies in me were to be guarded against at whatever cost, even to the degree of sending me to a preparatory school to prevent contamination, taking the first of many false steps in the direction of Sloane Square.

The preparatory school left me unprepared for anything, least of all the elementary school in which my parents placed me, having discovered that my knowledge of the multiplication table was as rudimentary then as it is now, and that my spelling was in the same category. A breach began to open between myself and the no doubt pleasant groves of academe. Only words, no figures, made any sense to me. I began from a new beginning by finding my prep school good manners a distinct handicap, leading to cissy-dom, a suspicion enhanced by total inability to play games of any kind except storytelling which, on wet afternoons behind the goal posts, I would do. And in doing so, knew the pleasure of a captive audience. I began to indulge in dramatisations, using my mother's copies of *Play Pictorial* for ideas and the struggle between doing what I enjoyed and what I ought to be doing began. Homework or Toy Theatre. The struggle was unequal. It still is, but at that time it was an intolerable strain on everyone from parents to grand-parents and teachers.

Time has lessened its strain on the teachers and is lessening it on me. The strain on my parents never lessened and only for a few years were the rewards shared. My debt cannot be repaid. My father was brought up by rod and rule to better himself, my mother to enjoy herself. They were a perfect match to everyone except my grandparents and for a long time, at least until I went into the army, I seemed to be the battleground. Only now can I guess what this must have cost my parents. I, on the other hand, sailed in these troubled waters happily, as long as the lights in the toy theatre worked.

The toy theatre, operated by my father, was an escape from school work and from the tensions at home and of course the beginning of theatre as a magic escape route, a feeling which has never left me, even if most of the best work I have done has been an attempt to bring audiences face to face with the real world about them.

Before Sloane Square in '56, escape was enough. But the toy theatre began to push school, scholarship, grammar school and all formal education beyond the bounds of what would be possible for someone whose concentration was limited except when the small blue velvet curtain rolled up, to my father's accompaniment on the piano. The music – usually Lehár, Sullivan, Verdi – was from that point the first aid to magic (and still is the greatest aid). I discovered what, in view of my abilities as a scene painter, was the most magic the entertainment offered. At school (on sports day) the stories were invented. At home they were put upon the stage and any higher educational possibilities vanished.

By school-leaving age I was a Boy Scout with a passion for an Entertainment Badge, a patrol leader's stripe, and a bicycle, making it possible to force my theatrical ambitions upon my patrol by writing intolerable one act plays by Emlyn Williams out of Shaw – by me. All trace of these has been obliterated. If only all mistakes at that stage could have given me as much pleasure, I might, in later years, have taken in more of my father's gentility and less of his father's acerbity. Having neatly laid all my most obvious faults at my grandfather's door, I can now feel free to claim virtues from my father, concealed as they were in a Puritan look and manner. From my mother I inherited the greatest life enhancement of all – a wonderful indolence which enables me to do absolutely nothing with great pleasure, whilst at the same time living with the profligacy of a drunken jockey.

My father had not much more love for the Jockeys than his parents had, brought up as he had been to work and improve himself. But his way of improving me did not agree with theirs as, for example, when he made me stand outside the Drill Hall watching people pour into the Hall. 'I know you should be at your homework, but I want you to remember tonight. There's a great man playing in there: Rachmaninov.'

I did remember, and not only Rachmaninov, for it happened that in front of the Drill Hall, and immediately behind us, stood the Methodist Chapel and Hall which became the Scout Hall and then, by coincidence, the home of the first repertory theatre in Derby, in which I had the good fortune to begin to realise that acting was not for me.

It is not surprising that I remember Rachmaninov with such romanticism whenever I need to remember (as I do at this time) just what those early years were like, if the craft of direction is to get into these pages at all. It was a small stage in a small town that began to reveal my inadequacies as an actor – doubts which were increased from time to time, as when a Candida stared at my flies as I tried to concentrate on Marchbanks without checking to see if they were open and destroying my velvet smooth illusion of romantic despair, so carefully rehearsed for all of four days. Or when I first discovered the joys of heavy character make-up to hide behind. Beards, wigs, grease paint and poses to put Olivier to shame. Week after week, from Priestley to Christie, and every now and then Shaw (at which point Shaw's stage directions gave me directions toward the skills needed to become a theatre craftsman), the performances I gave more and more convinced me I had neither the breath nor the bearing of an actor. I learned that much, but from the stage directions much more, and from that time my thoughts turned towards producing or directing plays, and away from embarrassing myself and the public. Later I discovered Shaw's rehearsal technique was much like that which operated in weekly rep.

I began to feel professional enough to experiment with amateurs on my return from an unglamorous period of service in the army, which concluded with an encounter with polio, caught in Egypt whilst playing the juvenile lead in *Quiet Weekend*.

I had, prior to this, been happily trooping around the Middle East, passing myself off as a now professional actor, based on my previous experience in the church hall, startling several thousand soldiers of the South African army in Leptis Magna by the sheer bravura of my performance in *Night Must Fall*. Getting the bird back home in *Hay Fever* at Derby rep was nothing in comparison, but as I began to walk again in England, my hard won battlefield expertise was forced on many willing and sometimes unwilling groups of amateurs. These rehearsals were the background to a long, slow process of recovery, and with a pension of seven-and-six a week and a bicycle, I began to enjoy a delayed adolescence at the age of twenty-three. The emotional and sexual scars have healed but the pleasures of these three summers and winters remain. Reading, writing, and getting money.

Helped by understanding from my father who, still carrying shrapnel from the First World War, recalled trying to adjust himself to disability and the civilian world at the same time, and listened to the plans and always supported them, however improbable and unprofitable. Of all forms of theatre, the amateur is the most disheartening when it fails to please the box office – as he came to see for three years whilst my form of university continued to operate – as well as my legs.

Eventually some financial stability arrived in a regular and highly respectable engagement with the role of P. C. Brydon in *The Archers*. I combined this with a teacher's course at the Central School of Speech.

In this indolent time, the only other regular income I had was derived from the pension and whatever one-week engagements I could pick up. This could barely support the grandstand tastes, so I made do with sleeping rough and standing room, and very happily with Wolfit and Gielgud at Stratford, trekking back reluctantly to Derby to do a 'special' week in rep to pay for it and my keep at home.

It was during a special week that I first met John Osborne, who was responsible for the first major change in my understanding of the craft I needed to exercise. We shared a room and grumbled about the management, agents, the West End, and the state of our auditions. I read his plays, he listened to my gossip with his wife of the time [Pamela Lane], in an atmosphere quite unlike that which his play of the period suggested.

In 1956 Sloane Square may have been beginning to swing into the sixties style. If it was, the movement failed to register to any great degree with me. King's Road and the Chelsea Palace, Au Père de Nico and the English Stage Company workshops I remember vividly, but very little else. The Beautiful People were beginning to make themselves beautiful to indifferent eyes, occupied as they were by a mountain of scripts to be read at five shillings a time. Thoughts of Granville Barker and GBS in the rehearsal room above the theatre – and Ellen Terry. The past was more interesting than the future which seemed very uncertain.

George Devine worked rather like an analyst sitting behind a patient, reflecting you and effacing himself; questioning you, until you came up with your own solution, but never imposing a solution of his own. So that, apart from one's awareness afterwards of his methods, one had no awareness of him beyond a few scrapings of his pipe.

I was at that time almost totally unlettered and, of the group at the Court, the one with whom he had least background in common. His conversation always prodded me into knowing myself, without (until the last couple of years) telling me much about himself.

I suppose he was my university and every production weekend I find myself trying to imagine what his notes would be and how he would deliver them. There is part of him walking about in me, and I can glimpse it in moments of crisis, but recall him in tranquillity, I cannot – and I do not think he ever intended that one should be able to do so.

The analyst remains behind the chair and reflects and responds, and you'd need to be another analyst to try and pin him down.

Between my first and last memories of George Devine, lies an odd history of two non-communicators having to communicate. At the first there was the grandfatherly severity of manner befitting the Director of the Old Vic School, and at the last a steely mane of white hair, the inevitable smelly pipe and sometimes equally smelly green shirt blouse, bottomed out with baggy grey flannels and lady's high-heeled shoes for a part in John Osborne's *A Patriot for Me*. ('I don't know how the bloody hell women manage in these things.') The first meeting in an office above the Old Vic, later to be occupied by Messrs Jacobi, Brett, Pickup, usually in states of convulsed hysterics, compared to which my strained nerves on a cold spring morning were as nothing. Two secretaries, having discussed the whereabouts of GBS (George Bernard? I thought) and assessed that he was in conference with GD, asked me to wait at the stage door, which would have been a pleasure had I not been so nervous. Ten minutes standing in the most exciting stage door I had ever passed through did serve to send me in to my interview in a totally overawed frame of mind. My record was not impressive – weekly rep and no degree of any kind. Our second meeting, at an audition, was equally unproductive.

Eventually, though, I went to work at the Royal Court. I arrived in Sloane Square devoid of any coherent theatrical philosophy beyond a philosophy of compromise, engineered by the desire for any employment at all in any theatre which could be a permanent home in which I could be of some use. In the early years I felt much under the wicked sway of the University Wits with whom George was happy and in whose company he felt most at home. But for the first months, I was alone with the scripts – and the audition files, from which I neatly extracted my own: 'Nice little chappie, not greatly talented. Looks like Noguchi. GD.'

(Advice about royalties: 'If I'd had even a half per cent from my production of *Rebecca*, who knows what would have happened to me.' 'Yes, George, but what would have happened to Sloane Square?' 'Someone else, boy; someone else, there's always someone else.')

To begin with, rehearsals, preparation and books. At first our conversations were always about work, wood, canvas, nuts and bolts, and through this starved language we began to communicate. When my theory and language became inaccurate, he would say with a shake of the mane and a chew on his pipe: 'You'd better show me, if you can, on a Sunday. You're hopeless at theory and I haven't got the time to waste listening.'

After my first production-without-decor, in which I began to work for and with a minimum of everything except acting talent, George began to talk more easily on technical matters and slowly our officer-to-NCO dialogue developed.

'Well, Corporal, why don't you want to be an officer?'

''Cause I want to be with the men, sir.'

'Well, Staff Sergeant, can you throw a line over a lead in one?'

'Yes, Colonel, if the men can, I can.'

Because of George I came to know Arnold Wesker and Jocelyn Herbert and, through them, came to know him as he did me. And in some such manner, the production of Arnold Wesker's play *The Kitchen* came into being, and with it the clarification of all theory.

'Dear John, have you gone mad? How many plates?'

'Not more than a thousand, after that it's Jocelyn's old sheets and some trestles and two weeks' rehearsal.'

'Shall we see the Dexter hand?'

'With a bit of luck and Robert Stephens in the lead.'

'Well, you'd better get on with it.'

I went to Arnold with the news and on a joyful afternoon in St James' Park, we studied all the interludes and began to learn by how much less is better. The sheer pleasure of this work was shattered by my father's sudden death 'from wound received in 1917'.

The news was given to me by Lindsay Anderson, who had walked from the Royal Court to Robert Stephens' house where we were as usual conducting a late night post mortem into the play. The company ran the rehearsals for a few days as I dealt with family problems and my own sense of loss and failure. When I returned, the opening was postponed and I flung myself into the rehearsals with a fury which, whilst it allayed my grief, did nothing much to reduce the actors' tensions. Fortunately, they were mostly old friends and superb technicians, so that through the use of a whistle and swearing, they were able to invent mimes of culinary acts that would have been the envy of Robert Carrier. 'Twenty-four cod balls, six more fish, Rita.' And only with knives, forks and plates. Without all these elements, this organisation of chaos would not have been possible.

It was, for me, a first exercise in an economy which produced a style that relied totally on the imagination of the actors, and even more of the audience. This exercise continued and culminated for me years later at the Old Vic in the Waterloo Road with *A Woman Killed with Kindness*, with of course the designer who has always guided my best work, Jocelyn Herbert. If Sloane Square was my university then Jocelyn was Dean to George's crusty and revered Senior Tutor. The other undergraduates, Anderson, L. and Gaskill, W. became, and still are, friends. This will explain why Sloane Square and its environs have for me all the sentimental value most people lavish on the world of Brideshead, in spite of the fact that our casts were considerably less well-dressed and mannered than the friends of Sebastian Flyte – though none the less drunk, doped and dissolute in life-style.

George was the only man I know who could help without interfering. Justice had to be earned; which made it more appreciated when you got it. All of us wanted his approval very much. If you could prove your belief in a play, then you would get your production. But he did believe you should be able to defend anything with your mouth. He never held a disaster against you if it was something that had gone right to the extreme. What he couldn't bear was a disaster that stayed in the middle.

Before first rehearsal, he assembled the cast for an opening talk on the play. 'I like to get all that out of my system, and then be prepared to scrap the lot of it.'

I like to scrap too, but not to change my position in front of people. It's hard enough keeping people's confidence anyway without setting them a false objective.

George died in 1965; and during rehearsals of Wesker's *The Old Ones* at the Court in 1972, I encountered a difficult passage in the text and instinctively turned to shout a question to the now vacant seat in the upper circle. I said afterwards: 'Your head always turns round to where he used to be. It still does.'

When I joined the Royal Court, Jocelyn Herbert was one of the staff painters and our conversations were largely practical; she talked my language, which was more than most people there did. I saw Ionesco's *The Chairs* which she designed, and had watched her in the workshop, and then I asked her to do *Purgatory*.

I came from weekly rep where you have a limited number of flats which are painted and overpainted until the paint flakes off, so the design ideas at the Court were new to me. I wanted to get away from naturalism and realism. I did two Sunday night productions-without-decor: *Yes and After*, with a stripped-down stage, and *The Kitchen*, and these pointed me in the direction of provoking the audience to think for themselves and use their imagination.

The difference between working with Jocelyn and another designer is the 'rightness' of everything. One never has the feeling that she is trying to impose her design personality on a play – that, of course, comes through anyway – nor is she trying to make a design statement. The design is always at the service of the play. If Jocelyn likes what I'm doing, it's reassuring. If she doesn't, I question what I've done.

Notes on productions at the Court:

The Kitchen: For Sunday night productions at the Court, some of the responsibility and weight was taken off you. Everyone knew there wasn't going to be scenery, so you could chance something like *The Kitchen*. You could risk doing with nothing.

The way of using the lights for *The Kitchen* came at the beginning, with the idea of one big lamp hanging over the top. That's where the idea of using an overhead grid came from. We had 8 Pagents, which are the best for getting an overhead beam that you can control. Turning on the light was the best way of turning on an oven.

Chips with Everything: I knew the drilling would be paramount. It was at the heart of the play. I remembered National Service and that drilling was miserable.

Purgatory: The play called for a window, and a door, and that's what we did. It was an absolutely simple relationship. Jocelyn came up with a very simple structure which worked for me. I'd got two people on stage for twenty minutes, and I needed the tree as a separate place from the centre where people could sit down.

Roots: The *Roots* model was perfect. The only thing I said was that I always wanted to be aware of the space outside, the emptiness of it. As the play was about Dusty Wesker (Arnold's wife), Jocelyn felt the need to go to Norfolk, Dusty's home and the setting of the play, and I needed *not* to go but to stay and work with the text.

Real time and natural time are both at the service of theatrical time when you're doing a play, so the placing of *Roots* was very simple. Jenny Beales had to fry liver and onions – it was a practical problem of how long it needed to cook and serve and eat it. Practical problems were about all you had time to solve, and in solving those in that sort of play, you tend to discover the play itself.

There was so much tension going on that Jocelyn's was just another wave on the shore. It was incredibly tense. It was at that time quite an unusual play for the audience to put up with. It's all very different now that *Roots* is a set text for schools. The Royal Court originally turned it down because both Tony Richardson and George thought it wasn't right.

Chicken Soup With Barley: By setting it in a basement we helped to convey some sort of submerged society. It intensified the family feeling, and the constant coming and going of people, coming from one home to visit another, something which doesn't happen any more. We did two weeks' talking, looking at the ground plans, playing with bits of cardboard. We had to 'sort out the plumbing', the geography of the place. You do that with any play, no matter how abstract.

I'm Talking About Jerusalem was more difficult than *Roots* or *Chicken Soup With Barley*, and needed much more light and space. I think in a way it was the most beautiful piece of design in the Trilogy because it opened out the space much more than the other two.

Diary:
1962. George and Jocelyn were parked in front of the Royal Court in George's prize possession, an Alvis. I went up to the window:

  'Larry's asked me to go to the National.'
  GD: 'Are you going to do it?'
  'Well . . .'
  GD: 'It's what you've been trained for, Sergeant.'
  'Well, not without William.'
  GD: 'Who, then, will take on this place?'

And with this question, George came to the central problem as usual. If the NT were to drain the Court of actors and writers as it seemed to be doing to his directors, it would mean that he would have to continue in harness. He died, to our greatest loss a few years later.

2

NT – '63–'67

I live, and always have, on a commitment to talent. A director is a servant of talent, not its master.

We've all been victims of economy. The English were facing economic problems in the theatre and the opera from war time onward. So the tradition of putting less on stage and suggesting more is something we all grew up with. If we went to see *Romeo and Juliet* we were visually trained not to expect half of Verona on the stage. Because materials were at a premium, everything had to be made out of something else, and designers and directors had to find simpler ways of doing things. In that process the English theatre found a style of design that it would not have found otherwise, and really theatre was stronger than it had been in the past. We just had to find some way of making the repertoire survive the pressure of the economy.

My aesthetic, if there is one, has always been survival.

We work in what many people consider a luxury art and, moreover, at a time of world economic recession, but when we consider the life-enhancing possibilities of the work we do, we have, I think, no choice but to continue. I have been lucky in my career in the guidance given by men like George Devine and Laurence Olivier: men for whom economic and practical budgeting was as fascinating as the act of creation itself. I hope I shall never lose this influence, which has taught me to place intuition above theory and pragmatism beyond philosophy. We need intuition and instinct which cannot be learnt and practicality which can; these, combined with a sound sense of the value of money, are enough with which to begin.

I suppose it's because I'm questioning myself. Having done the Methodist church, the Church of England, the Catholic church, and one or two other side religions as well fairly intensively between the ages of 17 and 27, I've found that it all comes back to oneself, that the solution (if you're ever going to find it) to what, why, how one spends one's time doing something as seemingly meaningless as theatre, is a question of faith, belief in that object itself, in theatre as religion. But you can't say 'I believe in theatre as religion' unless there's some kind of religious force driving you, and I wish I knew what it was. Because it means that each play you come to, you want just to examine that. Every play is a working out of some personal problem for the director just as much as for the author. You don't agree to do the play unless it relates to something you feel about, and the object of doing it is to search out what your religion is, exactly. That's why I look for writers who live a bit dangerously with the theatre. I think it's still greater than I know, and I still have further to travel. We're still searching for a means of blinding Oedipus over and over again, we're still searching for moments when someone wants to rip out from his consciousness the fact that he's the unseeable. Very few dramatists want to deal with that because it's so dangerous. You can so easily be accused of pretention or imitativeness or derivativeness. Those are the people I love – those who walk a tightrope.

Othello, 1964.

I'll never forget the first reading of *Othello*. You can criticise the performance until you're black in the face, but that first reading made the hair on the back of the neck stand up, it was so extraordinary. I started the day by giving my usual chat to the company. When I had finished, Larry made an apologetic announcement: 'I promise you it'll never be as bad again', and then proceeded to do the entire performance. And he was quite right, for in that first reading he paced himself for the whole monumental play, just to see what the reach was going to be. There are very few examples now for actors to watch of that magnitude of skill. We're not talking now about sensitivity, spirit, but just sheer physical and vocal skill, taking this great wodge and making sense of it.

'Sir can put more energy into one line than the rest of you can put into a whole scene. Your generation's coming off badly. You'll have a lot to answer for!'

If Paul Scofield played Othello, it would be all right. He could play Othello or Lear nine times a week . . . But Larry can only play it twice a week because he puts so much emotional intensity into it.

Casting Maggie Smith as Desdemona.
Nobody wants her. I do. A strong-willed mature woman who's been around and knows what she wants. She wants that big black man. Isn't everyone tired of pretty blonde ingénue Desdemonas?

I said to Jocelyn, 'I think there's a tower, a bare stage, a sky and one bench.' That's where I started from. I don't know why a tower. Jocelyn doesn't ask me to explain why I feel a play needs something.
  She originally designed a floor which would have been a massive focus point, made from real wood, which took the light superbly. When we tried it, it wasn't possible to get the panels of the floor to match and Larry got his bare feet caught. It was a loss, but it was technically impossible so we replaced it with a cloth. The title of the play is 'Othello', and if Othello was going to get his feet trapped, then the floor had to go, which Jocelyn was the first to realise.

'Yes, I know; but how?' A desperate voice emerging from Othello's head when, after a perfect performance, I congratu-lated him in unusually fulsome terms in the Lilian Baylis room. I could no more give a logical explanation of the 'how' behind that famous performance he had just given than I can explain the mysteries of the rehearsal process. So the important and necessary 'How' will always be a mystery. The ten-week rehearsal period contained much mystery. It was first and foremost a thrilling time, but a slow, painful discovery of the job, place, pace and time for each scene. For example the first entrance of Othello, still and silent, carrying a flower from Desdemona's bridal spray, had been the subject of many canteen lunches.
  'A white flower perhaps, Larry?'
  'A red rose please, the audience to hush.'
  'Certainly, if you want her to have been deflowered.'
  'Horticultural pedant, pass the toast.'

Eventually this entrance gave rise to one of the many intuitive, instructive mysteries which in its sheer theatricality gave me a great shiver of pleasure.

'Johnny, my dear, my entrance –'

'Yes,' with a sinking heart.

'Wonderful, so simple, so easy, gives me breathing time, but I wonder dare I suggest.' (Discussing himself as Miss Worthington).

'Anything as long as you don't saw the arm too much thus or thus.'

'Dear God, so you take me for Donald Wolfit?'

And, giving no time for provincial motivation, he went on: 'Whenever I embark on one of these fucking monster roles I like to smell the audience first, so may I cross over to Derek Jacobi, listen to him for a moment, then cross back to my original beautiful position, from which I promise you I will not move until we go to the Senate.'

'But why do you want to know how the audience smell? It used to be called counting the house when I was in rep.'

'If I can smell them, I know what to give them.'

Behind him stood a long line of actor managers from Irving to Wolfit, with whom I had no intention of arguing.

The first reading has been more than adequately described by Ken Tynan, from the observer's point of view, but due to pressure of other work, he was never able to describe, or perhaps lacked the interest to describe, the process by which the texture of the play was built up. A half-man's eye view may be of interest. 'Dapper and Downright' was how Kenneth described me that first day. Sleepless and shaky would be more accurate to describe my frame of mind.

I was invited to join the National Theatre in 1963. In September of that year I directed *Saint Joan*. In 1964 I directed *Hobson's Choice*, *Othello*, and *The Royal Hunt of the Sun*. In 1965 I directed *Armstrong's Last Goodnight*, in 1966 *Black Comedy*, *A Bond Honoured*, and *The Storm*. In 1967 I was fired.

On 2 March 1967 I came back from New York, having opened *Black Comedy* on Broadway. In my diary for 3 March are written three things:

> 12 noon: Interview LO.
> Script S. Sondheim
> 1p.m.: Bill Gaskill

all written in red ink. The red is of no real significance except that it points out that different things were written at different times. In black ink, which was after the interview with Larry, is written:

> 10-minute interview with LO. Sacked thank you very much.
> Round to Royal Court.
> Phoned Bob Stephens, no answer.

In blue ink, later, I wrote:

> Merely confirming what I already knew. I was not trainee manager material. Chat to KT [Kenneth Tynan] who seemed stunned. Only then did I begin to feel like crying.

Under 'Royal Court':

> With a 'What can I do' to Bill. And what did I do. Think about that.

Under 'Bob Stephens, no answer':

> And no answer for ten years. I wonder if he remembers, or dare remember.

On 4 March Joan Plowright phoned. She was truly concerned and tried to minimise the damage. She asked me not to speak to the press, because it might cause a scandal. So I decided to go to Paris. I had an appointment with Peter Ustinov to discuss *The Unknown Soldier and His Wife*. At a later date I wrote on the 4 March page:

> Joan, bless her heart, tried to hear from me what had happened, asking me about the 'pictures on the wall' incident. I must have told her a lie as I said I took them down to change them all round and add others. I took them down in a bad temper as a result of LO's frosty reception on the phone: 'I hope to see you in my office at noon.' Not even 'did you have a good trip?' The frosting was on the cake all right, and just about to be willingly gobbled up. I wanted to be insulted so that I could let fly what I felt about the all-male *As You Like It*, the covert undermining of the production, and that betrayal of trust. He could not have feared, as someone has said, that I would be over budget. Over the top, yes. Budget *No*.

7 March. Saw Larry having lunch with John Gielgud. In my diary I have written: 'I walked by.' I was still very hurt.

9 March. Of Peter Ustinov: This was the visit to discuss *Soldier*. Actually to learn about Peter. What a gigantic collection of abilities. Too many for a man with no full sense of purpose beyond enjoying expressing himself.

After Paris I took the Blue Train to Nice.

16 March. And sitting on the terrace of the Negresco I read in the Telegraph that I had 'resigned', whereas I thought I had responded to 'sacking' with as much dignity as I could, and recalling how much better George did it when it needed to be done. The difference between LO and GD. One still has trust and no guilt and the other has no trust and is all guilt.

I never forgot that when Ken Tynan was asked who would replace me, his reply was 'No one can replace John Dexter.'

17 and 18 March: reflections.

So what of those years at the National and the Royal Court and the difference between my relationship with each: LO, GD, ME? And be as egotistical as I like but see how lives connect and interact.

If you love your work enough, any other kind of love is too demanding for too much of the time which love demands be given to work.

3
The Diverse Years

And thus began the travelling time: films, stage, television, New York, Paris, Hamburg, Singapore, and on and on in no direction at all – even the anchor of property in France could not hold me still. Just about the worst time for Riggs, I should think. Life did not seem to be peaches and cream for him.

In between lunches and dinners I was offered *The Lady of the Camellias* with Vivien Leigh. I had met her at the Court and was in awe, but believed because of my history with Joan Plowright I would be persona non grata with her. However, she asked for me and on 22 March 1967 I wrote:

> What a strange beautiful woman. Stretched tight, almost transparent, pink and white, she seemed ethereal – no other word. Room extraordinary, as though done by God's personal set dresser. And then that practical conversation about 'coming on the stomach'. (I wonder could I ever have got her to say it?)

9 August 1967, Diary Entry:
Simon Gray's play *Wise Child* arrives. Riggs decides to do it. So I did it, and quite profitably too and not many problems.

I spent 1968 directing the film *The Virgin Soldiers*.

Goodwood Park Hotel, Singapore
To Riggs O'Hara
As you will see, we have moved to another better hotel. Raffles is living on the reputation left it by Somerset Maugham and Noël Coward.

We've been away up country again to Malacca and Seremban. I've found a *filthy* swamp to drop you in, but as yet we haven't got anything like a barracks that will do. The beaches up by the jungle location are *great*, but unless we can find a barracks near at hand which has the right features we will have to do the whole film in Singapore and on one of the islands. But perhaps you'll get a day off to go up country, which I know you will enjoy. I am now longing to get started. Ned Sherrin and I have thrown out Ian la Fresnais' script, except for half a dozen jokes, and begun again. The result is *I* think very good. We've been working every evening until dinner time, when I pick up my chop sticks and go out to cover my new John Michael suit with sweet and sour sauce! However I am getting better at chop stickery and may even be good at it when I return.

Today we are off up the East Coast to Mersing, about five hours away, so I expect we will spend the night there and come back tomorrow. I'll cable you, probably this evening to let you know about Philadelphia and Sean [Connery]. Sean is our insurance if Tony is too pricey, as he (Connery) owes Columbia a film at a cheaper rate, and Max wants me to go with the new script which is being typed out here and is *much* stronger for Driscoll, then Ned and I are to chat him into it.

I'll have to play him and Tony against each other, which is something I swore I'd never do. Offering two actors the same part at the same time is very dangerous. There is always the possibility they will both say 'yes'. But if the film is going to be made and it *must* be, we have to have one more star to balance the cost of bringing the unit out here, and having seen Singapore, we *must* come out here.

At the moment Sean is in London but is on his way to Philadelphia and if he expresses even a vague interest, we'll see him there. It is in fact as quick to come back over the top as the other way, but as far as I can see we arrive two days before we leave! Anyway, you'll probably get a cable before this letter.

Do I have to say that I miss you and long to see you again and am more than anything looking forward to directing you, properly this time. I had a slight bout of fever the first week but it's all right now. I didn't mention it before in case you worried but as I am now fit as a fiddle it doesn't matter. It only held me up for a couple of days.

Evening:
The new script has just been sent back and I've read it and it's *good*. A bit wordy, but it moves very well.

I'll wrap up this letter otherwise I'll be back before you read it.
Love, love, love

12 May 1969, Stratford Connecticut
The Hamlet production – what do you think of it now? Didn't it
need J[ocelyn] H[erbert)?

27 June 1969, after opening Hamlet
Venice Lido – best place to be when notices come out.

In 1970, I directed my second film, *The Sidelong Glances of a Pigeon
Kicker*, and worked with Alec Guinness on a TV production of
Twelfth Night.

Cecil Clarke, the executive producer at ATV said to me 'What
would you like to do?' I said I wanted to do *Twelfth Night* if I
could have Alec Guinness and Joan Plowright and Tommy
Steele. So he said if I could get them I could do it.

I got my cast.

Alec and I had said after *Wise Child*, in the way one does when
things have gone well, 'We must work together again', but I was
very pleased when he agreed to do this. It is his only full-length
television play.

It's a play I've always wanted to do but no one would give me
the chance. I think what I like about it is this subtle interplay of
the relationships, of love at all levels. I had always visualised it in
the period of Carpaccio's paintings, very romantic, and partly
because the boys wore their hair quite long so that the business
of Viola becoming a boy works beautifully. That's how we did it.

I don't think I've done anything very much to the play, except
that we did as has been done before and switched the two
opening scenes to establish the characters more swiftly. And as
for directing – well, with a cast like that what do you have to do?
You don't tell them things. I just gave them their moves, maybe
made a few suggestions and watched it fall into place.

There is no point, is there, in worrying about the mass
audience? I mean what is a mass audience? You can't make the
verse easier by playing about with it. And when someone like
Joan works her way into a play like this, the meaning just
unfolds in front of you.

The Tempest
Svoboda
Laterna Magicka
Prague
Poss.

To Josef Svoboda

The problem with Laterna Magicka centres on Prospero's ability to control the magic of technology, therefore let us begin and end with a bare stage revealing all the technological projections, lights, and props. After a few moments of darkness an actor emerges from the depths of the half lit stage, he wears ordinary street clothes but carries in his hand a model of a galleon which he places on the stage floor. A magic cloak appears in the air, music begins, invisible hands attach the garment to his shoulders, place the magic staff in his hand, he makes a movement of his arms and the model ship begins to move, rising in the air as though pushing through waves, its sails bent in the wind, break and fall, and suddenly the projections come into action filling the stage with waves, sky, and lightning, and finally the full scale ship, sails shredded, ropes flying, bears down upon the audience and the play begins with the words of the Boatswain 'What cares these roarers for the name of King' and at the conclusion of the play when Prospero abandons magic in the final speech so do we, and as he speaks the final pedestrian words he takes the model ship apart, revealing the wheels and cogs. At the same time we reveal once again the bare stage and the technology with which Prospero created the magic (with considerable help from Josef Svoboda and yours sincerely, John Dexter).

4
Return to NT

The bare stage is almost all I want to work with: a contained space in the middle of an open space. There were complaints from the critics that *A Woman Killed with Kindness* was drab. They simply didn't know what they were watching. I think it's an extraordinary, very important and moving play. *A Woman Killed with Kindness* is also my favourite production of all those I've done with Jocelyn Herbert. The costumes were exquisite. It was the first time we worked with Andy Phillips, so the lighting was absolutely sympathetic with the scenery.

16 February 1970
To Kenneth Tynan
Thank you for your letter. I am finishing in Hamburg on 4 March 1971, so I would imagine the April/May rehearsal/open period would be best. Of course the whole thing depends on suitable casting being possible, and on the amount of rehearsal time allotted. I will have to go over the schedule very carefully with whoever is in charge. There will be a preliminary study period of at least two weeks of hawking, dancing, smoking, cooking, tatting, etc. After which general rehearsal would follow the normal routine.

17 February 1970
To Laurence Olivier
I see that our marriage has been announced before we have completed discussions on the dowry. I hope that the hasty announcement will not lead to a scandal in the divorce columns of *The Times*.

18 February 1970
To Joan Plowright
I have now re-read the Heywood several times, and am very enthusiastic, also I have had an idea which may remove one of

the major problems which we discussed. The play, it seems to me, is an enormously all-embracing view of Elizabethan domestic life. The title puts the emphasis on the Frankfords' situation and in effect makes this the central theme. A total revelation of the play would depend on our giving equal weight to the Mountfords (Susan and Charles). Susan's devotion to Charles, Charles' violence and passion are not a sub-plot but a direct counterpoint to the Mountfords' tragedy.

When we have made the audience understand the passions of the Elizabethans, who could kill over a hawking wager, Nan's despair at her infidelity, and Susan's submission to Charles will all become logical. The men go hawking with the same outburst of violence that we can see today at a football match. The women dance at a wedding with a sexual intensity which you find at a discotheque today. This must all be made apparent by the acting from the top to the bottom of the casting.

If you were to play Nan, and Billie Whitelaw Susan for example, the emotional balance could be sustained. Mountford and Frankford must be cast with the same weight. Only this way would the emotion of the play be properly sustained.

I think we agreed that the great problem is the swiftness of the seduction. I believe a carefully placed intermission and a strong scenic statement can go a long way to make this work for a contemporary audience. Let me explain:

In Act II, Scene 3, Wendoll's soliloquy beginning, 'I never bound him to be my desert', I would imagine taking place in the Spring, as would the whole of Act I and Act II. At the end of his soliloquy on the line 'Thus villains when they would, cannot repent', I would finish the first part, taking an interval. We would then begin Part Two at a January snowy christening, with Wendoll and Jenkin looking on. By this device, Wendoll would have been left on the rack and Nan much more aware of his presence over a long period. The audience would then be able to imagine the tensions of a not exactly specified gap of time and find the scene between the two of them much easier to accept.

Of course I would like to talk to you about this and letters are not my best way of communicating ideas, but I'm so anxious to do the play at the National, and to work with you again, that I feel it necessary to bring you up to date with my thoughts. At the moment, without casting on the level I have been discussing, the play becomes impossible. With it, we could achieve something as extraordinary and original as anything we have yet managed to do, both in the overall style and individual performance. One thing is certain: before we go into rehearsal, the amount of research I will have to do on Elizabethan domestic habits triples that required on sewage in Salford in the 1890s for *Hobson's Choice*.

Let us hope the results will be equally happy for us all.

Joan Plowright, in her reply wrote:
If you have a passion for the play I would most likely agree to do it with you, subject to everyone else's approval. Passion has a way of being infectious and is the main thing I personally require of a director.

13 March 1970
To Joan Plowright
I'm sorry I missed you in London. Time ran out on me and obviously I was not able to make your dress rehearsal, which is a pity. However, I shall be returning permanently to start preparing the next film in April and maybe by then we will know more about the play.

I had not received your letter when I left New York, and it was a great pleasure to find it here. It makes me very happy to know that you are considering the play. The more I read it, the more in love with it I become, and I am convinced that we can make of it something very special. Just imagine me directing you on the stage as a very glamorous young woman, gentle and fragile as opposed to the bossy frumps with which we have so far had most of our success together.

Did I guess that Larry was asking Tony Quayle to join the company? If so I presume he has a juicy lead to offer. Perhaps Mr Frankford might make an appetising second?

Remembering the horror of rehearsal planning in that little wooden hut, please keep an eye on the amount of time allotted to us, as next to casting, this is the matter of most concern to me, and one which in the hurly-burly of planning can sometimes become overlooked. The production will need as many specialised studies as did *The Royal Hunt* . . .

A Woman Killed with Kindness by Thomas Heywood, opened at the Old Vic on 7 April 1971.

27 July 1970
From Olivier
Might your remembrance of Bobbie Lang as the Reverend Hale in *The Crucible* place your impressions of him in a kindlier light?

28 July 1970
To Olivier
Darling Larry
No! No! and again No! Or if you prefer the words of King Lear, 'Never! Never!' Have I missed out one Never?
Fond love always

15 August 1970
To Kenneth Tynan
I know that Larry has been ill, but I have heard nothing about the casting of *A Woman Killed with Kindness*. Since we last spoke, I had a conversation with Larry and Joan in which we agreed that she could be replaced by Vanessa. Since then not a word from anyone. Without being difficult or temperamental, I must tell you that I do not intend to sign my contract until we have mutually agreed on the cast for principal parts.
    Congratulations on *Oh! Calcutta!*

7 April 1971 [opening – *Woman Killed*]
From Olivier
Dearest Johnnie-boy
Isn't it lovely that our erst Love-Hate should be changed to a lovely Love-Love? I think your work on this is glorious. And I am giddily proud of it.
It is with deliciously self-flattering pleasure that I like to think of you as my son.
Your devoted
Larry, always

Tyger, a celebration of William Blake by Adrian Mitchell, with music by Mike Westbrook, opened at the New Theatre. 20 July 1971.

It's great when you can get a modern play on and it does well. That's why *Tyger* is essential. Right or wrong it is essential to have the capacity for doing that sort of thing at least once a year,

otherwise the place gets musty. Of course, you're depressed when the thing doesn't work for everybody and it's not a total success, but without the ability to make that sort of experiment, to wander into that absolutely unknown land once a year, the actors get stale and there's no element of danger in the business. And you can't run a National Theatre on security; you can't spend your whole life watching *Lear* and *Hamlet*.
But to more serious matters.

From Kenneth Tynan
Adrian's poem *The Children of William Blake* is Adrian's property and Adrian's copyright. He conceived and wrote it long before you were involved with the show or indeed had even heard of it. I do not know by what right you dispose of it as if it were yours.

Next week Kathleen is going to have a baby. She has the show as close to her heart as it has been to mine. I promised her this song as a welcoming present for the child – she has not yet heard the score. It was to have been recorded outside rehearsal hours with a simple piano accompaniment. It would have been heard by nobody except Kathleen and myself. (And the baby.) The recording would have taken, at the most, five minutes. (You will be aware that the poem is all of nine lines long.)

I now hear that you have forbidden the taping to take place.
Forgive me if I am speechless.

2 June 1971
To Kenneth Tynan
You may be speechless, but you are obviously not wordless, nor am I. Yesterday afternoon I found one of my stage managers wasting time discussing a recording session whilst actors were waiting to rehearse. This is intolerable interference with an already over-burdened stage management. I am not concerned with you, Kathleen or your baby, only with doing justice to the show. What Adrian, Michael [Blakemore, co-director] and you do in your spare time is no concern of mine, what my actors and my stage management do is. Let me repeat, you may record anything you want with Hallé orchestra and choir any time you can get them together, but during rehearsal time I expect the stage management and the cast to be at the disposal of both the directors, as is the custom in any professional organisation. And really, should we be wasting energy and steam sending off

indignant letters to each other? If you want to discuss the matter, both Michael and I are available for conversation.

My next NT production, Oliver Goldsmith's *The Good-Natured Man* opened at the Old Vic on 9 December 1971. Then, after a season of three operas in Hamburg, I was scheduled to do Wesker's *The Old Ones* at the National Theatre but ended up directing it at the Royal Court.

9 March 1972
Dear Larry
I think the other day you were still slightly confused about dates of the Affair Wesker. If this is so, the enclosed might help you.

I keep a working diary from which I have pulled these extracts. Needless to say, I have eliminated all extraneous matter, i.e. rows with Liebermann, kisses from Kubelik, and various solitary encounters on the Reeperbahn.

If at any time you need me to elucidate, 'I will be happy to do so.' I will also be equally happy to forget the whole affair, with the exception of the events of January 19th and 20th which have given rise to a little injustice, but we will not talk of this for months, and then over a glass of wine.

Jan 2 LO [Laurence Olivier] phoned: 'Wesker cancellation'
Jan 3 Phone MA [Michael Anderson, JD's agent] 'Contact Arnold's agent. Arnold (Zurich)'
Jan 6 Paddy [Donnell – administrator of NT] phoned confirming decision Wesker
Jan 7 Try to phone MB [Michael Blakemore] No reply
        Bill Dudley [designer] phoned 'hysterics'
        Riggs phoned (1½ hours) 'Keep calm'
Jan 8 MA phoned. Copy Arnold's letter Zurich
Jan 13 Letter from Arnold
Jan 19 Riggs phoned 2 hours 'Wait'
        MA – what work around?
        Discuss – [Billy] Budd – [Rolf] Liebermann
Jan 20 Telegram from LO:
        Dear Johnny. Have tried to call you without success but know Michael got to you STOP This to assure you we shall continue to try everything imaginable to find

solution to our problems STOP I am sorry but I have to beg off all business and get right away for next four days as I am quite wrung out by recent strains STOP Shall be on the job again Monday STOP Please don't despair but hold on with trust in our good faith as I have in you and your lovely talent always love   Larry

Jan 22 R. Court interested date August
       Arnold phoned
Jan 24 Agree R. Court date
Jan 25 LO cable:

Dearest Johnny. Please meet after lunch if you can make it Monday STOP Suggest rehearse *Old Ones* 15th May open 4th/5th July STOP Am inviting Wesker meeting Tuesday afternoon with you love Larry
Reply to LO. Consideration of play's needs.

Jan 28 Wesker release telegram LO.

Dearest Johnnie. Thanks for cable STOP with personal regret at having to come to sudden decision feel I must do everything now to safeguard and expedite yours and Arnold's best interests STOP We will do whatever is appropriate to let him have his play back forthwith STOP Dearest wishes from Joanie and me for you tomorrow night [the opening of *House of the Dead* in Hamburg]
Love to see you Monday anyway as ever Larry

11 March 1972
Dear Larry
I would like just to go over the points I made in conversation this afternoon so that we may both have them in writing for reference should either of our memories give out totally. I know your memory is infallible, but I am worried about mine.

1. The Affair Wesker is absolutely closed. Completely forgiven, but not forgotten, as I believe we should always be able to learn from experience.

2. If we are to relieve you of some of the pressure of decisions which in my opinion cause you unnecessary strain, we must arrange a procedural mechanism which prevents your having to take decisions on your own and suffer the mental and physical consequences on your own. It is needful, I think, to establish exactly who is on the Artistic Committee and who is merely nominal. Should we in future be faced with difficult decisions

(such as the Wesker) the full Artistic Committee must be reconvened for a meeting to find a correct, untroublesome solution. For instance, had we done this last time I would have been able to persuade Arnold to take the play to the Court and there would have been no need to draw in the Chairman and Lord Goodman and put all that unnecessary strain upon you which I believe resulted in your extreme tiredness and loss of voice during *Long Day's Journey*.

I felt that [Wesker's] *Their Very Own and Golden City* and *The Four Seasons* were marvellously theatrical but hadn't been digested. With *The Old Ones* it was just 'I like it. I want to do it.' It's a much more complex play to handle than any of the others. It's like a collage. You have to lay one very gentle scene against another and make sure there's enough rhythmic balance between them. But there's no moment where you could confidently relax on an obvious piece of dramatic effect.

We had four weeks of rehearsal – it's standard but one always wants more – and four previews, which were helpful. You sit and watch and react – the director's the only litmus paper there is – not even the author can do that.

When you start rehearsing a play you have an idea in the gut or somewhere of what it's about for you, and you draw certain physical conclusions about the clearest way to do it. From then on, everything is a series of intuitive jumps. You play around with the actors and you say: 'Stop. Can I have another line here?'

Directing is offering possibilities to actors. You choose three or four or five and see which ones they go to, but you mustn't offer too many. Otherwise they get confused. My problem is always at the beginning of rehearsal to find out in a few sentences, in a telephone conversation if necessary, that my understanding of a play is emotionally correct. Having done that, the great difficulty is to avoid discussion completely. You have to find out how to screw the daughter for yourself. No one else can woo Cinderella into a glass slipper for you. That's why some directors don't like having authors around in rehearsal.

3 August 1972
Back trouble and Arnold trouble, which only really ended with *The Merchant* and that night in the flat in New York.

DEXTER   I suppose we see each other in working relations about as much as Morecambe and Wise, and out of it about as little.

WESKER   That's terrible. We'll become known as the Morecambe and Wise of theatre.

DEXTER   I don't mind being compared to the best.

I largely went into the National because of George Devine and the Court. If you were a director at that particular juncture in theatre history, and if you'd had some training and people wanted you to go there, then you'd better get on with it and do it, because that was the purpose of everything up to that moment. Which I think was difficult for Arnold to understand because we'd worked together in this smaller and more intimate situation at the Royal Court.

I was again in Hamburg, directing *Billy Budd*, when I heard the news of Larry's resignation as Director of the National. Peter Hall was to take over.

9 April 1973
Hall news.
Try to remember that day and Larry's call.

12 April 1973
LO phoned.
Hall news official.

13 April 1973
Ken Tynan phoned.

16 April 1973
Day off. Riggs phoned. Tynan lunch – wants to stay. Phone statement to Joan (supporting LO as I remember).

17 April 1973
Tynan phoned – not asked.

The Misanthrope by Molière, English version by Tony Harrison, opened at the Old Vic 22 February 1973.

24 August 1971
From Adrian Mitchell

Thanks for the talk yesterday, which lifted my morale higher than it's been for some time. Bless you for your generosity and everything.

Tony Harrison. I rang Tony because I didn't have his address, said you'd be getting in touch with him about *The Misanthrope*, highly recommended you and gave him some useful hints about the National.

He is very keen indeed. Knows French, most of his translation's been from Greek, including a black Aristophanes which he wrote for Africa with immense success, using the tribal warfare thing. And for my money he's the best man for couplets in England, can make them rough or smooth, but they sound like people really talking.

Because he is very very broke, truly living on porridge and fruit with his family, it would be wonderful if he could be commissioned as soon as possible – it would mean lifting the money worry he's had for years and years, at least for a few months. If you ask him to come to London, I mean, it would really be necessary to give him expenses.

Back to the Balzac. Time-shifts of a kind may be necessary in it but not to the extent that anachronisms were used in *Tyger*. But obviously I want it to connect to present-day experience totally, not a historical side-show. I think this can be done using the costume, furniture, settings of the time all right.

If there is any chance of some sort of job with the National/ Young Vic next year, it would be marvellous. Want to concentrate on theatre and poetry for the rest of my life. Novels are too lonely. And I'd rather turn farmer than go back to journalism. (Though I'd like to do Ronald Bryden's column for a month or two when he defects to the RSC).

It would be nice if we could have an ad for *Tyger* in the September Oz, but that's probably politically impossible. (They're going to print about 90,000 copies.) But maybe RCA would take an Oz ad when they do the LP.

I phoned Mike Westbrook last night. He's absolutely not at all upset about the song in the BCC, only thing is he wants it on the LP, and of course I agree it should be. Talked to him about Balzac and he's another keen good guy. Cautiously said that he really enjoyed working at the National. And several times to me and Celia he's said how much he admires your work and likes you very much. Honest you can say anything to Mike, and he'll listen gladly. Can't guarantee he'll do what you say, of course, but he'll do something good anyway. Am beginning to ramble. Have just travelled six hours in a car which turned out to have no brakes for the last five miles.

     Love
      Adrian

31 August 1971
To Tony Harrison
Mr Dexter received a letter from Adrian Mitchell suggesting that you might be of help with the translation of *The Misanthrope*. I have tried to reach you several times by telephone but to no avail. Mr Dexter wondered if it would be possible for you to come to the National to meet with him, we would of course pay your expenses. Please will you ring me collect and we can discuss the matter.

24 September 1971
To Paul Scofield
I am somewhat saddened that we shall not be working together as soon as I had hoped. I still would like us to meet and discuss general plans for the future, especially with regard to *The Misanthrope*. I still think this is the perfect play for you at this time if we can find a Célimène, and even more important a suitable version. I really believe it is necessary to have one done for us, and I have had what I think (naturally) is a brilliant idea about which I would like to talk with you. Of course this would depend on our doing *Misanthrope* after you have done a film, and this in turn depends very much on whether you really want to come back. It is for these reasons that I would still like us to meet quietly, away from the pressure of Waterloo Road, and St Martin's Lane.

May I say that both Michael Blakemore and I believe completely that on the question of *The Captain of Köpenick* rehearsals and your third play, you have your priorities in exactly the right order. I just hope that the general chaos is beginning to calm down. Certainly now that Larry has been persuaded to lose *Guys and Dolls*, the future seems much more hopeful.

29 February 1972
Cable from Olivier
Thank you for your long and trouble-taken letter STOP Please
don't think I am piling Pelleas on Melisande when I tell you that
Paul has turned down version STOP Could you advise me if
either you can think of somebody else you would find acceptable
or if there is some other subject you would like to get together
with Paul on STOP I slid toward conclusion that latter is
hopeless quest but will certainly try if you like STOP Feel bound
to repeat I think version excellent except for some obviously
incongruous modernisms and have written adaptor to tell him
this STOP Look forward seeing and talking
        Love
          Larry

Notebook:
What we've tried to do is to make the play available to a wider
audience by bringing it up to date with the 1950s, the France of
de Gaulle. We've taken a rough cue, I suppose, from the radical
newspaper Le Canard Enchainé, which used to run a regular
column called La Court, satirising the Gaullist regime. The idea
with *The Misanthrope* is to use satire to preserve the formality and
tone of Molière's play but also give it a contemporary edge,
which I hope will let people through to what Molière is really
about – and that's his characters and the relationships they form
through psychological conflict.

12 January 1973
The first [Anthony] Hopkins walkout. Discovered on the first
day of rehearsal that Oronte was not the lead. That'll teach him
not to read the play. Shifty, spineless, Welsh cunt. Has AA
helped him? I don't think so, once a cunt *always* a Welshman.
    And oh my God, the similarity to Burton. The self deceptions,
combined with ambition and cowardice. Sexually just as
catastrophic a failure.
    10 a.m. Hopkins wedding.
    At least I didn't offer him *Equus* as I had planned. Only New
York had that over-emotional indulgence forced upon them, but
by that time the play worked. But if we had gone with him first,
what then? Total disbelief from critics and public I think.

31 *December 1976*
To Tony Harrison [from NY, Met]

Perhaps it is because our working pattern has been largely conversational that I have enjoyed it so much – and now to have it out on paper intimidates me. Or is it the intimidation and distraction of other men's books which inhibit me. Anyway, why am I inhibited at my time of life? (If I have to tell you, you'll never know.)

I seem to think of the work in hand only in terms of the pleasure it gives me if I get it right at one dress rehearsal. I don't relate well to people outside a working situation. That is why I prefer to create and not to administrate. Through creativity, I have contact with other people and it is a contact which gives as much as it demands.

So in this sense, the work is for my sake and its sake. If there is any kind of race going on, and if I have ever taken part in it, I have failed; so why run? Do the work for its own sake, not for the sake of the empire we may build around it, and for the sake of the people who have the love of the work. I think I have always worked that way – certainly in our collaborations – but now I am at a point where I must recognise the pattern and turn it from an intuitive habit into a system. Maybe I will be able to make a lyric theatre function in the same way for the work's sake and for each other's sake, knowing that only in this manner can the whole become greater than any part, and each part and partner have as full a working life as I have. As full and as satisfying. There is, however, a large *but* . . . If the act of trying to systemise what has been personal and intuitive eats into creativity, I shall have to give up the Metropolitan, much as its possibilities excite me. In short, as always, I want to lay out the broad outlines of action and leave others to do the detailed work. I reserve the right to attend to all the details which delight me and to relegate those which do not.

Because I do not enjoy administration does not mean I don't respect the work and personality of administrators, but I don't altogether trust them, as the overwhelming complexity of administration makes them compromise far too easily. Yet, if I do not make the place administrate itself without the desperate need of a leader figure, it will not survive into the 21st century. That it should do so seems important.

These reasons may seem remote to you, but if you understand

them you will understand some of the undercurrents which have affected our past work and which will affect the future. What sort of person I am, I can only explain in terms of the working choices I have made over the years, and all of these choices have been affected by the people I care about who feel about work as I do. Work is the only worship I know and understand; for anyone who feels as I do, there is no further explanation needed. For instance, the web of relationships at the Royal Court has always seemed more important to me than the work we did. If you look at the upcoming *Man and Superman* production, you will see that it contains in its substructure a clearly articulated skeleton of the working life I have had so far and the relationships I have valued.

Shaw, Royal Court, George, Jocelyn, The Old National, both the Riggs, creativity as a Life Force, everything I have learned from you about language. All these elements come through me and flow back into the work, and the work can become better or gloriously worse because of this influence. All this preamble is to try to describe to you at the outset why my tendency will be to ramble and reflect on the work and leave the literature to you.

To begin at the beginning is, therefore, not quite enough. We are both what we were when we began to collaborate. I have changed and been changed by the work. Have you?

Where *did* we first meet? The place was Soho, the food Italian, and the wine Verdicchio. I cannot remember a single fragment of the conversation we had, and this seems to me to be a very dismal beginning to any memory of our collaboration. I can remember what I was thinking, but not what I was saying. I was wondering if I could ever penetrate through that 'northern gloom' in which Miss Rigg takes so much pleasure. You seemed to me aggressive, hostile. In fact, as I think of it now, you seemed to be a mirror of what I was at your age, although I didn't recognise that at the time. It is because I suppose I was trying to come to understand you that I remember so little of what happened.

I read the *Loiners*, absorbed it, thought I knew the sort of man I could expect to meet and found something so completely different that it took all my concentration to decide whether we could ever work together happily. In fact, at that time I was full of doubts of all kinds. The National Theatre was at a moment of extreme crisis and, of course, so was I. We had been forced into the West End by the Board who believed that we needed immediate experience of running two theatres. They, I think, were assuming that the South Bank building would be finished within a couple of years. How little they, we, or any of us knew of the wait that was ahead of us or, indeed, how few of us of that original group would be involved in the establishment of the National Theatre Company on the South Bank. However, if it hadn't been for that season in the West End, I would never have met Adrian Mitchell, and it was Adrian who first suggested that I get in touch with you.

I had asked him one day if he knew of any young poet in England who enjoyed the classical restraints of a rigid verse form, who had wit, humour, and above all whose language was dramatic and not literary. Adrian gave me a copy of the *Loiners* to read. I read it at one sitting and telephoned you the next day. Then I read the poems out loud to myself and I thought that perhaps I had found a voice for Molière and a stimulus for myself.

For a play really to interest me, catch my imagination, stimulate me into some sort of creative energy, I must know that I am going to learn from it; more than that, learn something new and discover something about myself. It is an egocentric way of working, but it is a pattern that I have come to recognise and in which I very happily indulge.

I have never seen a satisfactory Molière. I have never heard a satisfactory Molière any more, I think, than anyone else. Miles Malleson's versions were the most theatrically enjoyable. I appeared in one or two of them years previously and realise fully how skilfully he had brought the characters across the channel, but I was also aware that more had been lost in the sea change than I could ever have imagined.

Playing *The Miser* in rep in his version was a wonderful experience, but at the end of the play's run, I was aware that there was something else, something more savage, more intense, and above all, an incredible drive and resonance in the language of the original which were almost completely missing in the translation.

The Richard Wilbur version, on the other hand, seemed to me to fail completely. Graceful, elegant, witty – but it seemed to be striving for a curiously dead classical manner. Obviously, Wilbur was not working for this effect but for the sound of the 'period' and succeeded only in creating a museum piece, creating a distance between the character and the audience. On that score, Miles Malleson won hands down with a vitality and exuberance which seem to me truer to the spirit of Molière than the elegance and form of Wilbur.

For reasons I suppose I will have to go into at some point, I wanted very much to direct *Misanthrope*, not just because it was a great play but also because I recognised within it so much of Alceste in myself. And when we met at that luncheon there was the double stimulus of finding that I had begun to discuss the play with someone who also had more than a little of that character in himself.

I suppose it is possible to say that the universality of Molière renders this inevitable. But at that time, in that place, it was for me an extraordinary shock, surprise, and stimulus. I remember you talked about verse form, I remember you talked about discipline, I remember you talked about strength and toughness, but as I said, I really wasn't listening. I had a curious tingle of excitement which led me to believe that together we could explore ourselves through Molière. To find Molière in ourselves and ourselves in Molière seemed quite an original experience for me, original and unbearably exciting.

The Cherry Orchard

From Olivier

I am sorry we've both had a disappointment over *Cherry Orchard*. You know how much I wanted to do it with Joanie, and I know how much you wanted to do it with Joanie if I felt my association with it might not be to its advantage for reasons you by now know only too well.

Some weeks ago, early on in the run of *Long Day's*, [Constance] Cummings asked me – wouldn't I do it for her with Michael [Blakemore] directing it. I said immediately that I had plans for doing it with Joanie. Now Joanie is worried more than ever about clinging on to it in case it should get about that she had exercised as it were her Manager's wife's prerogative in doing it instead of Cummings.

This whole situation rather to my mind forces me out of it. I hope I am right in having thought that your interest in the play was chiefly on account of Joan. I am awfully sorry if I am mistaken about this, but even so, whereas it would be hard on Cummings to feel that I would be doing it with her wishing she were someone else, it would likewise be a little awkward for you to be doing it knowing that she had asked for somebody else.

I am very sorry that you and Joanie and me are – not for the first time – the losers out of all this scramble.

4 July 1972
To Olivier

Thank you for your letter which explains some things I had already imagined, but does leave unanswered the fundamental problem of lack of communication.

When I wrote to you on 24 March, in the second paragraph I touched on this point and asked that in future all major decisions should be taken in concert and all interested parties consulted. To find that in such a short space of time the same thing has happened again not only depresses me but makes me feel completely ignored and unwanted. Don't, I beg you, think that I am either sulking or losing my temper. The question of who directs what play is at this stage irrelevant. No one has indicated this decision to me and though I have spent some time in Michael's company he has never mentioned it. Nor did you mention it on Friday. I find it difficult to believe that you both had a lapse of memory.

As you know, I first suggested the play to Joan as a possibility for Chichester in February. A few days later I bowed out very happily to you with considerable pleasure at the thought of your completing a Chekhov triptych. I still believe that this should happen and you have allowed your scruples to manoeuvre you into an idiotic position. However, this is your concern. I am concerned with myself.

Paddy [Donnell, administrator], Michael [Hallifax, company manager], and indeed everybody knows that for the last four months I have been searching desperately for a play that I wanted to direct and which would suit the Company and the repertoire. In view of this fact also I think I might have been given the opportunity to refuse or accept the play.

I won't go on longer as it never makes me happy to give you more problems than necessary but I cannot let this matter rest without expressing my disappointment and disillusion.

5 July 1972
To Olivier
Thank you for your letter. We are obviously poles apart on everything except Joan. Of course you have the right to take all decisions. I think you cause yourself endless unnecessary worry by doing so, especially when you are away from the theatre as you are at the moment. But surely if you take such decisions it is also your job to pass them on to the interested parties, and if the title Associate Director means anything at all it must surely mean that I am an interested party in productions other than my own.

William [Gaskill] and I always regarded you as a wonderful Chairman, perhaps because George D[evine] taught us to do so, and perhaps having worked with George for so long, with his superb gifts as administrator, adviser and friend, it spoilt us for any other relationship. Perhaps we make mistakes in imagining you were thinking of us as George thought of us. That was obviously a mistake but a sad one.

Equus by Peter Shaffer, opened at the Old Vic on 26 July 1973

I agreed to direct Peter Shaffer's *Equus* because of the speech that says, 'You can't take someone's pain away from him. He's earned it. He lives with it. If you deprive him of his pain you deprive him of his passion and his life.' The central thing which attracted me – apart from the event, which is strange and disturbing and for which one saw no logical explanation – was the idea of personal pain as an essential part of life.

19 May 1972
Dinner Shaffer. What about. *Equus*? It could have been social. It never is, mean old bitch!

26 May 1972
Shaffer play arrives. EQUUS my God!

27 May 1972
Riggs enthusiastic. I saw scenes ill-felt in thinking and structure but immense possibilities if PS and I can work *together* without friends helping.

When the first draft came, the play was very much concerned with the event of blinding the horses and explaining it, and the character of the analyst had just started to emerge. I said to Peter, 'Yes, well, I think the event is marvellous, and the narrative is completely gripping and holds together, but you haven't even begun to dig into yourself to find the analyst yet.' He said, 'Now I start again. How?' At that time it was constructed much more naturalistically. I said, 'When you're reconstructing it, would you think more loosely in time? To make the chain of events clear, you've got to be able to cut across time illogically. And if it's horses and masks, you can't have three or four scenes of detective-like cross-examination and then suddenly produce an actor in a mask.' Which led to that first image of a boy caressing a horse.

He also worked at the characters of the mother and the father, who were both intensely religious. I said I thought that was a little too easy. In the final version the father is an atheist. I can usually tell when Peter's got near to a subject and flicked away from it because he doesn't want to go into it at that moment. You can usually persuade him back to it. Both our interests have moved away from the boy, who is fascinating, towards what his effect is on the analyst. What happens in Act One rips him wide open in Act Two, and the developing theme of Act Two now is the inadequacy of the tools with which he's working.

20 June 1972
Somewhere round here the Bill Dudley relationship crashed, with the assistance of Tony Richardson, and John Napier got his chance at *Equus*.

17 January 1973
To Paul Scofield
The new Peter Shaffer play has arrived on my desk. I have been working with Peter on it for some time and am very pleased with the results.

Peter and I have always thought that you would be ideal for the leading role but knowing your commitments I am writing to ask if there is any point in sending you the script?

It is not planned to do the production at the National Theatre but in some other agreeable situation. Hope to hear from you soon.

10 March 1973
This was the weekend when I tried to convince Shaffer of an idea I had only half formulated. However, a good wine, a lot of food, and an exhausting period of improvisation and all turned out well. Or at least the way I wanted it: No illusions, audience on the stage using *their* imagination.

I was very aware that one needs a different audience configuration for it, that we should all be observed to be observing. Everyone's in a witness box or an operating theatre during the two-hour span of the play. One was just looking for the shape that would indicate that. When the analyst is most exposed, he's not just exposed internally, privately, but totally and publicly to a whole audience. What's exciting is to watch the concentration, which is extraordinary. The on-stage audience is making the audience-audience listen harder. The situation Dysart, the psychiatrist, is trying to explain suddenly gets out of hand as he realises he no longer has any control over the events. A proscenium wouldn't give the right tension. One's got to be sure that the mental event dominates the physical. The man has to say, 'Until I accept the idea of God, until I have some way of knowing which recognises God, in the widest sense, I have no way of operating as an analyst. And because of my background, my life, my training, my beliefs, I can't accept the idea of God.'

26 March 1973
Noël C. died today. I ought to review all of those not many, but very happy meetings and that weekend at Les Avants, the apartment in New York, New Haven and all those times at the Savoy. The kindness, fun, wickedness and the privilege.

8 June 1973
To Stephen Sondheim
Just to let you know the developments in the search for 'Demon Barber of the Barbary Coast'. We have tracked down an original copy which cannot be taken out of the British Museum but can be copied and I am having this done but it will take about three weeks.

It was very good to see you as often as we did during this visit. I only wish it had gone on longer as there are many, many more things about which we have never talked and which would be not only instructive and amusing but necessary.

I wonder if I shall see you at the Princes' this summer. If not then we must wait for December and the Metropolitan. *Equus* is going very very slowly but is, I think, interesting and stands a good chance of working as Peter intended it. Success with the public is another matter. Anyway, as you have often said, who cares?

14 June 1973
To Tony Harrison

. . . You are a tempting bugger; the idea of *Phèdre* in the Raj is almost irresistible. She is a neurasthenic English lady; the trouble is she is also a queen and how you bring those two things together I don't know.

. . . *Equus* is bridling a little but might eventually take a few fences quite neatly. I shall be here when you come down and look forward to seeing you.

There is a possibility of New York for *The Misanthrope*, either under the National's wing or under private management depending on the way Peter Hall's wind blows. Diana Rigg and Alec McCowen are interested in going there, it is just a question of sorting out dates.

15 August 1973
To Stephen Sondheim

No doubt by now Hugh Wheeler will have handed you the British Museum photostat. I am sorry it took so long, but rushed orders are something of which the Reading Room seems to take no recognition.

I had a wonderful holiday with Hal and Judy [Prince], apart from the occasional intrusion of Ruth Ford and 'government inspected meat'. Judy will tell you all. We talked about you a great deal in an alarmingly complimentary fashion.

Equus is a sell out. The box office told me last night it is worse than the *Othello* days. I saw a bit of the performance last night which was unbearably sloppy and sentimental.

So rehearsals are to be called.

You may have heard, I am doing a double bill by Terence Rattigan [*In Praise of Love*] almost immediately. I can see the disapproving look on your face but I think they are very good and we have a wonderful cast with Joan Greenwood and Donald Sinden, and whilst Mr Shaffer and Mr Molière may be doing wonderful business, there is not a penny in it for me, and something has to pay the rent. So kindly spare me your expressions of moral disapproval.

9 October 1973
To Stephen Sondheim
Thanks for your letter. The Rattigan had a bombardment of bad press in the dailies, and a hysterical review from Harold Hobson and Frank Marcus in the two Sundays, which have made all the difference to the box office. So prostitution may not enter my life again this year.

I am now deep in *The Devils* and can find no way of making 51 nuns enter and not give the appearance of lesbians searching for Mary Martin. However, time may improve this matter.

14 November 1973
To Alec McCowen [who played Dysart in *Equus*]
Glad you have found your muscles. As soon as I have *The Party* on its feet I will come and see *Equus* – probably this weekend. And we will talk again.

19 November 1973
To Stephen Sondheim
A journalist named Peter Buckley has contacted me through the press office asking if I would give an interview on the subject of Sondheim to be reproduced in a book by someone called Craig Zadan. Do you know anything about the book? Have you approved it? There have been such horrors over here on a similar book about Olivier that I would hate to find myself repeating that pattern with you. I am not even sure that I know enough about you to say anything except in a private area which is of no interest to anyone but us. Please let me know your feelings.

In case you haven't heard, *The Devils* went very well. *In Praise of Love* is still on and doing well enough for me to be nearly out of debt. I am at the moment rehearsing a new play [by Trevor Griffiths] called *The Party*, with Laurence Olivier, Frank Finlay and other old chums. It's difficult but great fun. Also a little sad as one seems to be coming to the end of something nice.

3 December 1973
To Peter Shaffer

Either I did not make my motives clear to you on the phone, or a few days in America have served to make you lose sight of some values we always thought we shared.

Let me re-state my position for you and for anyone else who cares to read it. What I write now I believe with as much conviction as I had when I wrote to you from Hamburg concerning your doubts of the way I proposed to stage *Equus*, though I hope I express myself here a little more moderately.

Peter Firth's talent has been *used* by our play but not extended. If he leaves the National Theatre before he goes to New York he will simply do a long TV series which will place his voice and emotion in the area of dim charm in which we found it.

On a purely technical level, I ask you to remember how, after only six performances in London, his voice began to rasp. Since that time, he has *never done* more than four performances in a row and moreover has not continued his lessons with [Kate] Fleming. (His responsibility to his talent is something he has yet to learn and if I don't teach him no one else will.) That is my responsibility and is more important to me than loss of money in New York.

I tell you now that if he goes to play Alan in a normal eight performance run outside the protection of repertory, he will be off more often than he is on and the situation will deteriorate. Throat specialists in New York and London are a breed I know and distrust. They are repair artists with a drug-filled throat spray, or are sensible men who acknowledge that the voice is strained and must be rested for a week. The former give results, the evidence of which you have seen many many times and of which you have in the past expressed disapproval. The latter eventually cut down the run of the play.

I wish to bring Firth to New York as a trained professional, not an amateur, who will stay with the play and, I know, play it with more range and authority than someone who, through constant exercise of his craft, can develop into the *only* classical actor of his generation. There is nothing in this for me. I have neither a sexual nor financial interest in him. There is no ego trip involved nor money.

A Mobile production is not reviewed or seen in London. If I do this, and I *will* do it, it will be a gesture to the beliefs that I have always held and which I believed you shared. I am angry that I should have to make articulate that which you should already know. A talent like Firth's comes once in a lifetime; it needs watching, nursing. He needs to be shown just once how to climb mountains and he will never again be content with a stroll through TV studios. If I cannot do what I know must be done for him, I would rather give up New York, return Kermit [Bloomgarten, the producer of *Equus* in New York] his money and forget about profits for this year. It means you will have to wait for your £30 a little longer, but I don't suppose that will be a breach between us for ever.

As for Tony [Hopkins], I have known him since he was only three years older than Peter [Firth]. When I worked with him, the result is Frankford in *Woman Killed*. He is insecure but when loved his security eases his way to greatness. Arriving in New York to begin rehearsals cold under the critical and (he will feel) hostile eyes of American actors, his nerves will be in a most delicate state of balance. Arriving with his performance largely set and the relationship with the boy established, his confidence and emotion will give you a Dysart you have never even imagined. But I must have them both in England, together, secure, free from the pressures of New York, to teach them to know each other and the play before they expose themselves to strangers' eyes. Only in that way will they have the confidence to lead the company.

In short, all I suggest is for the good of the play. There can be no other consideration. Forgive my circulating this letter, but I would like everyone involved to know how strongly I feel and what I am prepared to sacrifice in order to achieve it.

cc: Doris Cole Abrahams, Peter Firth, Peter Froggatt, Kermit Bloomgarten

From Jocelyn Herbert
I still don't think Shaffer is a first class writer – but I think your production is really superb – and the treatment of the horses so beautiful – erotic and really moving – I do think it may be one of your very best works – many, many congratulations.

From Trevor Griffiths
I didn't get a chance to say, after *Equus*, what a perfectly blinding experience your production was for me. I stress *your production*,

not because I want to diminish the play, but to draw, between assembling and *realising*, a distinction the evening seemed more and more to insist on; for whereas Peter [Shaffer] seemed to have gathered extraordinarily rich materials together, the sense of *auteur*, the fundamental *creative* sense, lay in the tensions the production, in the large sense – shape, image, movement, rhythm – so superbly discovered.

The Party

To the cast
My contribution to this production is not going to be huge. I'll do the food and furniture. Trevor [Griffiths] can do the rest.

I think it's a totally optimistic play. You're all vocalisers, not visualisers. Let's get the bums on the seats!

It's awful what middle-age does to directors. I'm sick of all my best moves being pinched by Samuel French.

I hate the bloody word subtext.

These characters are all a part of Trevor, that's the important thing. There's no connection between the starting point and what Trevor has actually put on the stage. It's irrelevant. The rehearsal process is solving the problem of getting further away from that starting point. We must go right beyond this sort of social residue which starts with Ken Tynan and people like him, we must let the actor in so that he can take it further. This business of characters being based on real politicians is a dangerous red herring. I knew that in our work we'd get it out of the way. What I was banking on was people behaving responsibly enough not to spread these names around. I'm afraid we have to thank Tynan for that. These people whose only interest in theatre centres around gossip are dangerous. For Christ's sake, *Hamlet's* based on real people.

To Frank Finlay [playing Sloman]
You're clouding the speech. You're letting in feelings about your own father. Cancer wasn't it? Lead factory dust. My father went like that too. But arseholes to it. You can't carry it about like an old bus ticket in a crumpled suit. The subjective Francis! Cut it out forthwith!

To the cast
There's a technique to getting an exit round. It's a question of implying by the manner of your exit that you are forthwith carrying the scene, the play, the audience's interest and certainly any unfortunate actor left on stage off with you. Round! It's a narcissistic 'rep' device and rather easier to quash than the 'entrance round'. Olivier usually gets both and is equally embarrassed by either. What he's doing is stretching the exit out. He's hardly there by the time he isn't. He's confusing the audience's concentration on him and handing the responsibility for the scene over to you. Clever old bugger!

Hampton's *Savages* for example is just slop. There's no real thinking in it. It's just an opportunity for liberal non-doers to sit back and say how awful and shocking the plight of the South American Indians is/was. Christopher would have been better advised to write a play about how the English got rid of the Tasmanians in twenty years and no one's ever said a word. Larry saw it last night and he thought it was awful too. These parlour reformers may nick society's conscience, goad it into a sliver of guilt, perhaps even effect a few minor reforms. *Cathy Come Home* did that. But in no way do they viciously and uncompromisingly take on the society that causes the distress which continues to exist at every level and could I have a cup of tea with some lemon and aspirin, Boddington!

Thank you. Anyone that tells me you don't get good work from a company, rather than an ad hoc collection of performers, is an idiot.

The weekend. A full moon. Go away! Remove yourselves! Do whatever you do to relax. Take drugs. Walk your poodles. Fuck your unfortunate wives. Find a sailor. Banish me, cuddly me, to the back of your bereft subconsciousnesses. For God's sake, don't read the newspapers – we don't want you depressing yourselves. The run through was very good, quite good, not bad. Nothing that a little patience and a little bit of love can't put right and that's there in *ABUNDANCE!!*

9 December 1973
From Olivier
First thing this morning I must write you of my gratitude.

It is really noble what you are doing and I am, I hope you

know, aware of what it costs – swallowing all and generously seizing the bit between those gallant china jaws of yours.

'Good Johnnie, lovely Johnnie, a chap of character you can't say other' – was purring through my mind at every not unwelcome wakeful spell last night. Thank you Thank you dear boy for making me so thrilled and happy.

Looking madly forward to Thursday. Joanie thinks it's a fancy dress ball and going as Queen of the May, I think.

Notebook:
LO's performance in *The Party* was the greatest compliment he could have paid me. Not only the performance, the rehearsal and the first night. How to work and continue working 'til the last. They didn't like it much – fuck them.

And of course it was the performance which was the least appreciated or understood.

7 March 1974
To Olivier
I would also like to affirm in writing that my present ambition extends no further than helping you to complete the work we began together 10 years ago. I would wish my contract to conclude when yours concludes and not to last one day longer. I have no wish or hope for any further advancement from the Board, the Arts Council or any other of our lords and masters. My obligations are to you and only to you. When you think we have finished our work I would like us to leave together. As long as you don't think that is 'mucking up your exit'.

After *The Party* I left the NT to take up my position as Director of Productions at the Metropolitan Opera House in New York.

Diary:
Phaedra Britannica, by Tony Harrison after Racine, opened at the Old Vic 9 September 1975. The production had originally been planned during rehearsals for *The Misanthrope*, to open the new NT on the South Bank. But because of building delays, it was staged at the Old Vic.

26 September 1974
To Guy Vaesen [Literary Manager of the NT], from the Met
Thank you very much for the Harrison/Racine. I shall read it at length this weekend. I have so far dipped into it and the improvement on the first draft is tremendous. I begin to believe that the whole thing would work in a very extraordinary way. I still wish we could bring a French company into the other theatre for, at least, the opening week to do the original in the original, as I don't think anyone will appreciate what Tony has done without a direct cross-reference. Can you whisper this to him when you see him?

I am having a wonderful time here, hard work, but in the most luxurious conditions.

Notebook:
We decided that Racine's *Phèdre* was untranslatable. That is the reason for the new title, *Phaedra Britannica*. It will be set in a different time and in a different place. Diana [Rigg] plays the title role, and I am interested in having as many as possible of *The Misanthrope* team in it. Working with Diana reminds me of something Larry [Olivier] once said about Edith Evans. 'She absorbs all direction and makes it her own. A director's dream.' It will be my last National production for the moment, because I have other commitments in New York. I resigned from the National's group of associate directors because I did not believe I could make a reasonable contribution from a distance of over 3,000 miles.

8 October 1974
To Peter Hall [the NT's new director]
Thank you for your letter of 1 October 1974. I agree with you on all points about *Phaedra Britannica*.

I read in yesterday's newspaper that we are due for a postponement – not a total surprise. I shall do my best to make myself available for you whatever changes are forced upon you.

I will be in England for a few days during the week of 26 October.

To Gillian Diamond [NT Casting Director]
Not a very interesting list – Anthony Hopkins and Alec McCowen aren't available anyway, neither is Peter Firth.

Paul Rogers and Derek Godfrey are acceptable at the end of the list. Patience Collier is not acceptable for anything at any time.

We are having a reading of *Phaedra* next Sunday and I will give you my comments on Nicholas Clay then. Can you not find a coloured 'Indian' actress for Ayah, and if possible for Lilamani? I suggest you begin auditioning, and I will interview people in May. Robert Eddison is a possibility for Burleigh, and I will give you more information on that later.

What worries me most is your candidates for Sir Richard Metcalfe – Standing, Rogers, Finlay, Glover, Godfrey, Stride and Jayston are all very wide of the mark. I suggest you read the play again.

19 February 1975
To Guy Vaesen
We held a reading of *Phaedra* the other day with the *Misanthrope* company and it was very interesting. The first two acts a little sticky, but the last half very compelling. Tony is now in Washington or Leningrad working on the rewrites. Tanya Moiseiwitsch's set is more or less finished and Richard Bullimore [Production Manager] has seen it and seems to think it might work.

Misanthrope was a great hit in Washington but you know all this I expect.

I wish I could get some answer from the casting department about other roles. My last letter of 24 January remains unanswered. Most of the key suggestions were hopeless, they must have had something else to think about.

Notebook:
Phaedra Britannica opened in London. Somehow it didn't work for me. We should have adapted it from the original. The rigidity of Racinian verse combined with Victorian corsets made it very difficult for Diana and was ultimately unsatisfactory.

21 February 1975
To Joan Plowright
Thank you for your letter. It's all very confusing at the moment. My information about the National Theatre has completely dried up, and I do not feel in any way inclined to ask for news.

Misanthrope has opened to an enormous success in Washington and I think the production is actually better, or at least has more depth than the original. Diana, Alec, Riggs and all of them seem very happy in Washington (at the Watergate Hotel) eating and drinking, but no parties as apparently Washington goes to sleep at 11 o'clock at night. As usual the cultural attaché at the British Embassy has not made a move in their direction in two weeks. Considering it's the first visit of the National Theatre to the United States that seems a little odd.

As I told you, I shall return to Europe in April to rehearse in Paris and be in London in early May for a couple of weeks and want to see you then.

5 March 1975
To Joan Plowright
Thank you for the very informative letter. You must be in a state as it is almost the longest letter I have had from you. Let me know what happened with Blakemore. The business of the balconies in the Cottesloe is absurd. It always was. The place was intended as an open space and nothing else. It was John Bury with a grandiose idea who pushed that one through.

I have read of the successes of *Borkman* and *Heartbreak* but didn't know they were coming off so rapidly.

As for the news about the new host on the Aquarius programme [Peter Hall], what can I say? Except perhaps – who the hell is Michael Birkett [NT Deputy Director] and what has he ever done in the theatre.

All goes well here and *Misanthrope* is sold out in Washington and I am bracing myself for the New York opening on Wednesday. I altered something in the credits of the programme, which I found offensive. In a long list of Peter Hall, Peter Stevens [NT General Administrator], Birkett and others there was no mention of your husband. I have inserted a paragraph above this list of credits which says, in effect, *The Misanthrope* was first presented at the National Theatre on 22 February 1973. At that time the National Theatre Company was under the direction of Sir Laurence Olivier. If anyone in Aquinas Street [NT offices] notices it I expect repercussions. In fact I rather look forward to them.

27 October 1975
To Doris Lessing
I don't know why I never write to you, or for that matter why I never see you when I am in London. Of course I should do and then I forget, isn't that terrible. However, this weekend I haven't forgotten. I have had my first comparatively peaceful weekend for about eight months sitting in a nice new house that I have bought in New Jersey and looking at the sea which is fairly rough, thinking of you. Perhaps it was the roughness of the sea, or perhaps finally my sense of priorities caught up with me.

All I know of what is happening to you is what I read in the books and occasionally a word from Maria Tucci, but that's about all. As one survivor to another I think you make more out of survival than I do. However, I am really enjoying life and the complete change from England to America has been an incredible stimulus. I actually find I like New York. Perhaps I like it because it is the only place which has given me the kind of job I have always wanted, with the responsibilities I need and the challenge of doing something almost impossible. Now I have the house outside New York I also feel that I have a place to run away to away from the city, which is equally appealing.

I was in London in the summer working at the National and being very miserable. Whatever the faults of the previous establishment, at least it was run on fairly humane lines. Now it is a kind of laughter and tears factory with not much regard for the people working in it. I don't think the new director has yet learnt the names of the stage staff and in some cases not even bothered to learn the names of the company below the title. However, if I start off on that subject I will go on complaining for ever.

I do hope if you come to New York you will be more dedicated to searching me out than I was searching you out in London.

Love to you and your massive son.

5
Man and Superman

A chaste and sometimes severe beauty is what I look for.

Sometimes, if you articulate what you are searching for, you discover it.

11 May 1972
a.m. *Pygmalion* idea. Talk to Paddy Donnell at the NT.
p.m. NT didn't get that one – I did – so there.

Notebook:
The idea of reviving *Pygmalion* came to me a little over two years ago and it seemed a natural for the repertory. But for a number of reasons it could not be fitted in, so here we are in the West End instead. One of the attractions of the play to me is that I have never seen it done properly, although goodness knows I've watched it often enough and have acted in it three times myself in repertory. Quite a lot of people have made quite a lot of money out of doing it wrongly, but I've never seen it fairly treated.

It's a dry play, not a soft one. The theme, which was powerful enough just before the First World War, the time when *Pygmalion* was written, is the creation of a woman of independence: Liza learns to fend for herself. At the same time Shaw is saying just how unacceptable it is for a woman to go on being someone else's doormat.

All too often that is lost from view. To bring it back into focus I have gone back to one of Shaw's original endings. The source is a proof copy of *Pygmalion*, annotated by him, in the archives at Ayot St Lawrence, which is simply headed 'By a Fellow of the Royal Society'. Here after Higgins's closing shopping list speech, where he orders a ham and a Stilton cheese, a pair of reindeer gloves and a tie to match his new suit, Liza replies 'Buy them yourself'. It is a final and conclusive statement; it is Nora slamming the door at the end of *A Doll's House*. Of course we don't know what Shaw really wanted, any more than we know precisely what pressures Tree and Mrs Pat applied to make *Pygmalion* look as though it ended in a marriage. After all, the play is described as a Romance in Five Acts.

But I am trying to lay a few ghosts and ignore a few traditions: Doolittle must be taken seriously, for instance, not just as a figure of fun because he happens to be a dustman. And I want to show that *Pygmalion* is a much wirier, tougher play than most people think it to be. Earlier on I've replaced a line where Eliza says to Higgins: 'If I can't have kindness, I'll have independence.' That's the key.

With Shaw you've got a pretty good brief from the author, which Jocelyn [Herbert] responds to, as I did. *Pygmalion* and *Heartbreak House* were great fun to do and Jocelyn got them right both times. You know with Shaw that he's worked out the right place for everything and that it has been placed there for a good reason. If you even move a door upstage or downstage you can get into a lot of trouble. If Shaw wanted to protect his plays he had to do that. He also wanted to sell his plays as books so he had to make his directions as good as literature. It's as full a set of instructions as you'll get from any author.

26 May 1974
Write to Di [Rigg], Alec [McCowen], Viki [Brinton]. Shaw season idea.

22 July 1974
To Michael Anderson [JD's agent] from Viki Brinton, Knightsbridge Theatrical Productions
As you know, we have been having discussions with John since May about 1976 and 'Shaw at the Albery'. I thought it might be helpful to summarise plans and, if possible, settle all the details of John's contract before he leaves on 22 August.

Briefly, the plan is as follows:
Man and Superman in its entire version in repertoire with *Candida* and *Man of Destiny*. John wants Jocelyn to design the whole season as one unit (six sets) and plans to have one get-in and permanent lighting rig, which he wants Andy Phillips to do. We have discussed the whole question with Donald Albery who is very enthusiastic and is only waiting for us to give him a firm opening date.

John has already spoken to Di and Alec and sees the season including at least two more actors with names above the title, possibly in the area of Colin Blakely and Peter Firth. He estimates that the entire company, including understudies, will be of the same size as *Pygmalion* (nineteen) or smaller and the season will be planned for nine months.

20 August 1976
From Viki Brinton
Shaw at the Albery – 1976
I have pleasure in confirming that we have agreed the following in respect of your services as director for the above season in 1976.

You will direct *Man and Superman* and *Man of Destiny/ Candida*.

19 November 1976
To Julia Jones, The Shaw Society (as from Tozeur)
I hope you will please regard this letter as addressed to you personally and not to the Shaw Society, whose members I do not know. It seems odd to me, after some years of moderately successful work in the theatre in England that one's judgement is still much in question.

When, a few years ago, my ability to control Chichester was questioned, I gave up and took another job in America. This time, in the case of *Man and Superman*, I intend to put up a fight for my opinions and for my judgement. I have given Eddie Kulukundis the principle behind the production and how it came into being. I should have contacted you directly but work has been somewhat hectic and after all he is not the most blinding intelligence in the world and may not have represented me accurately.

In the year's gap between my first conception of the production and during the period in which I was working on it, before the disappointment (the fortunate disappointment as I now see it) in the refusal of Alec McCowen to play the role of Tanner, I thought very carefully of some of the observations Alec had made about the essential youth of Tanner's character. In discussing the designs with Jocelyn I asked her to look for and think of a clean, bright, spare and elegant physical design which would, through its lack of clutter, throw the emphasis on to the text in all its buoyancy and in all its wit. At the same time it became perfectly clear that if the concept were to work at all, I would have to reconsider the casting of the two major roles. After all, if you look at Shaw's description of Tanner, the comparison between Jupiter and Apollo, the height, the weight and the emphasis on youth. If you visualise his first entrance, violent as it is, in panic as it is, one must immediately see a totally different performance from that of the middle-aged star of whom one had been continually thinking. (After all, Eddie is throwing upon an unsuspecting world enough middle-aged productions of Shaw this year to last for the next 20, why not give youth a chance?)

More seriously, surely the biological drive between Ann and Jack, these two attractive animals, keeps the play as tense as a drumskin, totally eradicating the charge of intellectual chill which is always hurled at the author. Their wits cannot eradicate passion or prevent them from falling into each other's arms and when they fall into each other's arms, it is with an overwhelming physical impact, not in any way genteel or elegant. It is this animalism, this sexuality between the two which drives the play forward and gives it in a most extraordinary way its combination of tension and intellectual fervour.

This is all very well you might say, but where on earth is a young actor with sufficient vocal range, magnetism and experience to be found? I think I have found him. I have known him for a long time, worked with him at the National, know his capacity for sheer hard work, slog and sweat. His physical attractiveness is something of which you are obviously aware. What you are not aware of perhaps is his extraordinary vocal range. I think Sir Laurence would bear me out in this as he worked with him once intensively on the role of Dionysius and although Nicholas [Clay] was chosen finally to play the leading horse in *Equus* instead of Dionysius, I think Sir Laurence had enough impression of the boy's vocal range and, more important, teachability, to bear out what I am saying to you now.

In short, my dear Julia, please trust me. I know this talent, I can smell it like I can smell the camel shit around this oasis at the moment. It is just as intense, just as pungent and just as fertile if you will follow the image just an inch into the ground and beyond. You will not seriously imagine that I, of all people, would willingly undercast a play that I have wanted to direct all my life. Thank God I have not directed it before or I would have been stuck in a rehash of the excellent John Clements/Kay Hammond production which I remember so well. There is yet still something new to be found in the play. No, not new, it has been there all the time but the theatre, or at least the commercial theatre has always been afraid to take chances, perhaps because of the expense but perhaps because of an innate cowardice. That cowardice is best expressed in the casting at the National Theatre at the moment, by the way. Reliance on ageing stars and no young actors of any interest at all, developed or even seeming to be developed.

Please Julia, give the Royal Court its anniversary. Give the play its anniversary in its old home and let's give Shaw an opportunity to allow some new young people in the theatre a chance to let him explode like the old fire cracker that he is all over again.

PS: I am sorry for the length and if it seems somewhat over-emphatic. I'm dictating it on a tape recorder which I cannot fully manipulate, sitting under the palm trees by the swimming pool, with a temperature somewhere in the 70s. I say this in order that you should be impressed with my new found affluence and also realise that I am writing in a relaxed frame of mind, away from the Albery, Eddie and Colditz on the South Bank, or indeed my much loved Metropolitan. It is a time for thinking clearly but even so, if I think much more clearly and at much greater length, the post scriptum will exceed the letter, and that will never do.

19 November 1976
To Nicholas Wright, Royal Court Theatre
I am enclosing a copy of a letter to Julia Jones on the subject of *Man and Superman*. Keep it to yourself because on re-reading it I discover that I am not entirely complimentary about Eddie and I would prefer if it not be put on the Royal Court files or anywhere else. However, I do feel very strongly on this subject. It may be that my original intention of doing *Man and Superman* two years ago was not palatable to the Shaw Society and to Eddie, but the fact of doing it at the Royal Court Theatre at such an anniversary creates an entirely different situation, a situation which only clarified itself when I had looked at Jocelyn's models and discussed the play in more detail with her. I offer no apologies and excuses. After all, better to change one's approach now than

later. I realise also from your point of view as Manager of the Royal Court it would be more attractive to have two established stars calling and becking your box office. However, let's remember George [Devine] a little, it is not only the dramatist who should have the right to fail but also the actors (and if I may say so, the directors). There are actors who we know are not being stretched, pushed or pulled in any direction at all and it is about time we began to do something about that, otherwise the view of acting will be confined to that thin, grubby, microscopic televisual style which I find in almost every theatre I go to these days.

I want something bigger, better and more stimulating and I think the Royal Court is the place to initiate that attack.

If Eddie limits his contribution in that miserly way he has suggested, don't worry. I intend investing some of Riggs' and my money in the production in any case, and I am sure we can match the £3,000 that Eddie is offering. However, I can discuss with you in detail when Jocelyn's estimate is on hand.

20 November 1976
To Jocelyn Herbert

. . . Nor have I thanked you for the view of *Man and Superman* which, in 3 days, completely shook up my view of the play, made me realise how erotic, how sensual and energetic it was. Of course it has given us incredible problems with Eddie who wants a star, the Shaw Society who want a star, and our own differing preferences in the world of young actors and actresses, but as I always trust your visual judgement, trust my acting judgement. One makes visual mistakes, I make talent mistakes –that's what we are there to do.

I have just written a long letter to Julia Jones, at least it seemed like a long letter, giving her my reasons for casting Nicholas Clay (a few days in Paris with Nicholas, while we were thrashing through the latter stages of *Equus*, confirmed my view). If I can whip him and drive him, which I can because he is tough, we should have the most remarkable talent in the world. The question remains, what about Ann? I am going to track down Miss Mirren in Rome when I get back and try to understand her and see if I can trust her to do the same thing every night. After all, that is the most important thing in Shaw, to be precise, to be clear, to be like a draft of cold water. Unpredictability is not allowable.

I can work with a wild talent and an untrained talent as long as I felt that it were finally capable of subjecting to the discipline of the comma, the colon, the semi-colon which are so rigidly indicated in the text and without which a clear performance of the play is not possible.
So you trust me as I trust you.

22 November 1976
From Nicholas Wright re Eddie Kulukundis:
Gave him your Shaw speech. He received it well, in fact said the idea excited him 'personally'. He remembered Nicholas Clay from *Equus*, incidentally. He raised no objection at all to our doing the play with a non-star, young cast. However, as expected, he said that this would count Albery out, and that his own financial contribution to the production would be minimal. Patty Poke is over the moon about Mrs Whitefield, you will be glad to know.

25 November 1976
From Julia Jones
Further to my letter of the 22nd, this is just to say that I have now talked with the Shaw Estate's advisers and they are prepared to go along with your suggestion!
   So I hope you will feel that we have done our best for youth and your views! I have passed this on to Eddie and Nicholas Wright, so it is now up to them. I look forward to the rest of the casting, and even more to the opening night!

29 November 1976
To Mrs Donald Albery
I think I owe you and perhaps Donald an explanation. When you spoke to me at the Michael Jayston opening of *Equus* you were kind enough to express enthusiasm for the *Man and Superman* project. I think I ought to have told you at that time, and would have done so if we had not been too rushed, that my concept of the piece had changed radically in the past two years. It seems to me essentially a play about young people. Tanner is only 27, Octavius is 24 and Ann cannot be more than 23, and yet they are always played by 40-year-olds of immense experience (and star value). My point is that when this happens an

enormous and vital quality is removed from the play. Unless one believes in the inevitability of the sexual magnetism between Ann and Tanner, the tension of the play disappears and we are left with the long, brilliant but didactic discussion.

Therefore, I have decided with Jocelyn Herbert to make it what it has always been, a play about *young* revolutionaries caught in their own sexual awareness which, in turn, provides the motive force for most of their ideas. When I told Eddie Kulukundis about this, he was not particularly happy and told me that if I did it that way he would have to reduce his personal financial commitment. That doesn't bother me too much as I am intending to invest my own money in the production, but he did say that Donald would not be interested in doing it at all either for transfer or any other reason.

You and Donald have always been very kind and hospitable to me and, of course, I love the Albery Theatre as you know, and fully understand the necessities in the West End but I would not like you to think that I led you astray in the recent past as to the nature of the production I was intending.

Anyway, I hope this clears up any misunderstanding.

30 November 1976
To Professor Dan H. Laurence
As you may know, but probably may not know, I am embarking on a complete *Man and Superman* at the Royal Court Theatre in May of next year. The date of the first performance seems to be debatable and as the Royal Court wishes to make a Gala opening on the 71st (or is it the 72nd) anniversary, it is of some importance that we clear the matter up.

In the definitive text, the date of the performance is given as the 21st May 1905 and in the letters, the date is given as the 23rd May 1905. Can you give me any opinion that can throw some light on this subject? I have availed myself of all the available material at the British Museum and Ayot, but if you think there is anything you have which might be as helpful to me as the Doolittle note you kindly sent when I was rehearsing *Pygmalion*, I would be most grateful.

Also, can I ask your opinion on the misattributed speech in Act I? It does seem to make sense that the words . . . 'You know I am beginning to think that granny, etc., etc.', do belong to Ann, but with the intrusion of the stage direction, it looks as though it were intended for Octavius. Any advice and comments would be most welcome.

1 December 1976
To Nicholas Wright
Firstly, the number of bandits can be 8, which ought to be 10 but I think we can fudge it through with 8. They will all always understudy. The maid will understudy Violet and Ann and Miss Ramsden will understudy Mrs Whitefield. The male understudies coming out of the bandits should then be covered internally.

I suggest now that you go ahead and try and engage Helen Mirren to play Ann and Penelope Wilton to play Violet. David Yelland for Octavius and any others that we have previously discussed.

Riggs will shortly be returning from Paris and I would like you to assemble some possible Hectors for him to look at. Not that I don't trust your eye, but I think his ear, when it comes to American, is slightly more sharply tuned and as it is a rather tricky piece of casting, I would like to have it out of the way as soon as possible. Anyway, Riggs will be associated with me as he always is on my productions, so that it might be useful for him to spend a little time around the theatre.

14 December 1976
To Julia Jones
Thank you for your letter of 2 December and the information contained. Somewhat stunned by your last paragraph about cuts. I haven't proposed any cuts, nor do I intend to. When I say 'full length' I mean 'full length'! After all, with an evening of about 4½ hours duration, a few minutes more or less will make no difference.

For your information and for the Society's information, we propose to play Acts I and II without intermission, a long intermission before Act III and an average 10–15 minutes before Act IV.

16 December 1976
To Nicholas Clay
The battle to have you accepted as Tanner has surprised even me. However, that's all over, and now I can tell you about it. The

first resistance came from Eddie Kulukundis (this news may surprise you): You are not a Star! And no amount of verbiage from me could convince him that you might become one. In addition, the Shaw Society were reluctant to have the part played by someone so 'young and inexperienced'. I dashed off several letters in my most doctrinaire manner, made many phone calls, and now, if you can only twinkle, you can become a star.

However, all joking towards one side, as Bea Lillie used to say, I want to try and plant another idea about Tanner. You have the looks, the appearance, and the manner, and you certainly have the intellect for the part. But on the stage, as a rule, you tend to play your physical self and suggest a quite different, rather gentle, dreamy, mental self. Now, of course, that won't do for Tanner.

How you are going to develop an explosive, intellectual energy on stage, I don't know. I know your brain is sharp and retentive, but on stage it comes out soft and woolly. It isn't that you haven't got the ideas in your head, but you suggest that ideas take second place to a kind of dreamy detachment from the world's problems. Wrong for Tanner! The more Shaw letters you read out loud, act out loud, the more you will realise that ideas must explode from your mouth with almost erotic intensity. Put the energy you put into cricket and football into your mind and your voice. That's my Christmas wish to you. And God help Lorna for the next six months.

18 December 1976
To Kate Fleming [National Theatre voice coach]
I am sorry I didn't have longer time for a long conversation in London on the subject of Nick/Tanner, but you know what I want, which is the same thing that you will want, to get his voice out of the nose with more of an instinct for orchestration than was previously shown. I have had a tremendous battle with Eddie Kulukundis and the Shaw Society and, strangely enough, the Royal Court, about having someone they regard as an unknown cast in the role, but I know between us we can not only get him through it but also turn him into one of the more promising leading actors around. Keep driving him; 6 months isn't long. The thing to avoid is that slightly lethargic manner and his own innate gentleness. EST is all very well but it has nothing to do with John Tanner.

PS: Just discovered in the Shaw correspondence a reference to Robert Lorraine: 'He feels he is on the brink of a catastrophe, which is exactly what one wants of Tanner.'

11 January 1977
To Nicholas Clay
My last letter to you may have sounded somewhat negative but the only way I can begin to work with you on the part is to point my finger to all those areas which are not in your immediate reach. What is nearest to you will come through anyway, i.e. charm, warmth, sexuality, whatever other qualities you have in your personal rag bag. These will all come shining through. However, brain, and especially Shaw's brain, isn't easy to come by. If you can get those two volumes of his letters and read them out loud at the rate of one a day and realise what an extra-ordinarily energetic and intelligent life he led, you will realise that therein lie the areas in which you have to work.

I don't know how that man wrote all the criticism (incident-ally, have you read *Music in London*, his collected criticism or, for that matter, have you read the theatre criticism?) . . . as I was saying, I don't know how he did all the reviews he did, function as a vestryman of St Pancras, reorganise the Fabian Society, keep the peace between the Webbs and H. G. Wells and write all the plays.

It is all that fever and knowledge that you have to contain in your performance and I think the best way in the preliminary stage to grasp it is to read everything he wrote, *not*, repeat *not* too much of what people wrote about him.

For the Voice, I leave you in Kate's hands knowing she can do more for you than I can. I look forward to your letters and will reply with short bursts whenever I can.

13 January 1977
To Robert Stephens, from the Met.
I am thrilled to hear that you are going to play Mendosa in *Man and Superman*. I would write at greater length, but I am up to my neck in three operas at once.

It will be wonderful to see you again and to be working in Sloane Square after all these years.

18 January 1977
To Dan H. Laurence
Thank you very much for your letter and the trouble you have taken. It is, I am afraid, all to no avail. There's been an upheaval at the Royal Court. The Arts Council is refusing to increase their grant, and they may go into liquidation and the entire production has been cancelled, or, if we are lucky, just postponed until some future time.

21 January 1977
To Nicholas Clay
You will by now know the news which must, of course, distress you more than it does me but not *much* more.

I was thrilled at the thought of working with you on something that would stretch us both at the same time. I am a little confused to know how to pull the chestnuts out of the fire at the moment and will be in touch with you as soon as I have collected myself.

At the moment my feeling is that if England is an island sinking giggling into the sea, I can let it sink. One of the last concessions the Royal Court made was that it would consider going ahead with the production if I would cast Alan Bates. My answer to them is simple – there is a right and wrong way to do that play. Alan Bates is wrong as John Tanner and you are right. I am too old to involve myself in work which does not excite me.

Forgive the brevity of the letter, but I am off to rehearse *Carmelites*.

2 February 1977
To Nicholas Clay
Thank you very much for your letter. The only thing I have found upsetting in the whole affair is the fact that I have raised your hopes unnecessarily but at least there is the consolation that Shaw and the play seem to have had a marked and positive effect upon you. At least I don't feel you have been wasting your time entirely.

I am still hoping to get it together and will shortly be in correspondence with the new management at the Court to see if they have any hope of putting it on in the not-too-distant future before both of us will be too old for anything.

I wonder if you know how much I was looking forward to

working with you and regret this postponement, but I believe it is only a postponement so keep reading and sending out good thoughts.

4 March 1977
From Michael Anderson
. . . I do not know if Eddie Kulukundis has told you himself but I thought you should know that he is going ahead in partnership with the Royal Shakespeare Company with *Man and Superman* directed by Clifford Williams. According to Eddie, the RSC asked to do it when they heard the Royal Court were not proceeding. John Wood is playing the part of Tanner.

25 April 1977
To Dan H. Laurence
Thank you for all your assistance. I still hope one day to return to England and do the complete play. The present plan at the Royal Shakespeare is to do the abbreviated version. Don't the fools know what the play is really about?

I am beginning to doubt if I shall ever work in England again. Maybe something esoteric. Perhaps Mr Hall will invite me to revive 'Have With You To Saffron Walden'.

6

Opera File

My first venture into opera, *Benvenuto Cellini* at Covent Garden, was not altogether successful. There were some good things in it, with Gedda's performance at the top of the list. But in retrospect, I came to it green: I was naive about rehearsal schedules and misjudged just what could be done in the time we had. When it was all over I decided to be very careful before stepping into that strip of water again. Rolf Liebermann [Intendant of the Hamburg Opera House] eventually persuaded me back to do *I Vespri Siciliani* for Hamburg.

There we have the beginning of a life in opera. *Cellini* had been patchy and not very interesting to do. Because I chose to do it in their way and not mine. I arrived in Hamburg to meet [the designer, Josef] Svoboda, and that was a crucial turning point in that I at last had begun to think of finding my way into opera.

I began to tackle *Vespri* with only a general idea of the end I wanted and no idea how to get it. Would I still risk it?

I planned it with Josef as a Greek tragedy; I wanted a chain of violence through which the characters are destroyed one by one. It turned out to be a success.

24 February 1970
To Julia Trevelyan Oman [designer on *Falstaff*]
I am thrilled to hear that all may work out well, and am even more thrilled that you have an idea that pleases you for Act III Scene 2.

I have been doing fairly extensive work on the score and have some specific problems to discuss with regard to the first scene of the second act. The endless comings and goings require ruthless directorial logic, unless they are to look absurdly operatic. The question bouncing around in my head is: where do they go to? And from where do they return? Are they shopping, riding, or what are they? As I said, my first idea was to use a miniature Hampton Court maze, this would at least give reason to some dramatically unreasonable movements. I am now much in love with the idea of a Market Day in Windsor High Street. The bubbling of music would be enlarged by the jostling around; Alice and Meg, meeting whilst shopping; Nan and Fenton sneaking their meetings in an arcade to one side; Ford and Co. bursting out of the house into the pub.

I would have perfect control of the focus of attention using the crowd as a masking device. I would love to see two streets converge in front of Ford's house.

With this arrangement of the street, the crowd need never overwhelm, and it gives endless opportunities for fun and games: ladies can read Falstaff letters on a bench in front of Ford's house. Toward the end of the act everything falls, windows light up, people go home. Nan and Fenton could be placed in upper windows singing across the street above all the confusion at the end; he in the pub, she in the Fords' house. Don't dismiss this idea until we have met and acted it out a little. It solves so many problems for me, and I hope to convince you of its advantages visually.

29 September 1970
To Rolf Liebermann
You will no doubt recall that Julia and I came to Hamburg on 26 June specifically to present detailed ground plans to your production department. Herr Stahn was ill at that time, and Herr Sieglitz went through the ground plans with us in detail and foresaw no great problems. On that basis Julia and I have been working since July with the results you saw on Friday. If the sets were too big, we should have been informed of this in June, at the moment there is no time to re-draw and re-think the production.

Whilst I am willing to sacrifice one of the sets of Act I, the degree of compromise required on Windsor Forest and the exterior of the Fords' house seems to me to destroy the concept of the production. I repeat, we *should not* have gone ahead with our plans had we not received official approval.

We are asked for changes at this point, which cannot be made without considerable loss to the production. The mistake, if there has been a mistake, stems from your production department's approval of the *fully detailed* ground plans which were shown in June. I must confess to considerable annoyance that so much care and detailed work on our part should have been dismissed in the space of three hours, and I am extremely angry to find that I have been wasting my time.

When Julia returns, I will discuss with her the details and expect to see your staff during the 5th and 6th. Until both these meetings have taken place, the production's future must be regarded as being doubtful.

Diary:
This particular production was cancelled three times and finally not done.

13 September 1971
To Rolf Liebermann
I am quite interested in *Ballo* [*in Maschera*]. However, as you have already engaged a cast my ideas may not be possible as they depend a little on having a coloured Ulrica and a coloured Oscar. Perhaps I should explain. I would like to set the piece not in Boston in the 17th century, but in the Southern States of America, possibly New Orleans, at the time of the Civil War. Jefferson, Lee, Grant, and Lincoln up north, all move in an atmosphere of political assassination. Ulrica would certainly work best as an old negro mamma on a plantation, and indeed all the scenes would respond to the atmosphere of heat and war. I would think probably of asking Julia [Trevelyan Oman] to design it. Does the idea appeal to you at all?

I am having sessions with Kubelik and Svoboda in Munich during the next two weeks, and will report to you afterwards.

16 November 1971
To Rolf Liebermann
Can you see any musical objection to separating the two crowd scenes in the first act of *Boris* [*Godunov*] and playing Pimen's cell between them? In the first place I have always found the two crowd scenes following each other a little monotonous, and in the second place, if we are to establish Boris and Dmitri as the pivots of the opera, this would be a superb way to do it.

I know the idea once occurred to Diaghilev on the Paris production, but I know of no other precedent. In this arrangement we could show:
  1. The people of Russia duped into accepting Boris as the Czar.

2. Pimen in his cell commenting on the action we have just seen, and Dmitri establishing himself as a possible rival to Boris.
3. Coronation of Boris.
4. Inn scene. Dmitri's escape.
5. Boris etc. etc. etc. as you already know it.
   The interval would come after scene five.

Please let me have your thoughts.

26 October 1971
To Rafael Kubelik
I have just returned from Prague and a conference with Svoboda [on *From the House of the Dead*], and I am sure you will be pleased to hear that we have arranged that the scenery should at no point interrupt the action. I have an idea for a visual linking device in the moments of pause, which will sustain the action even further, and give the audience no release until you put down the baton.

It is difficult to describe in a letter, so perhaps I had better wait until we meet. But I think you will approve of it when you see it.

Hamburg Season 1972

Feb. *House of the Dead*
May *Boris Godunov*
     Billy Budd

24 February 1972
This working period [on *Billy Budd*] was good and wearisome. When and how did it start, did we just get it from the stage we saw? I remember getting up early in the morning and finding [William] Dudley staring at a model he had spent all night working on – and hating it.

11 April
Get lost in sea fight.

27 April
Finally get the battle right.

5 May
Hamburg notices good.

4 January 1973
To Schuyler G. Chapin, Acting General Manager, New York Metropolitan Opera
I have discussed the [Jan] Skalicky affair briefly on the telephone with your Technical Director. I would like to reiterate what I imagine might be the possible dangers of employing someone other than Jan on *Vespri*.

As Jan has finally defected to the West, not an easy decision for him, it seems to me churlish to say the least that the first gesture the West makes is to take away not only the financial rewards of employment, but the obvious prestige of working in one of the world's major opera houses. It also seems that for the Metropolitan to be dictated to in this fashion by the government in Prague could set up an unpleasant scandal; quite apart from the moral implications.

As you probably know, Josef [Svoboda], after the Russian invasion, signed a letter to the press aligning himself with the new government. As he had been a close associate of Dubček, and to all appearances one of the leading liberals in the arts, this gesture came as a great shock to many of his associates in Prague. I believe the gesture was forced upon him by his wife who is a simple woman, very anxious to retain the advantages that Josef's reputation had brought to them; and God knows, I appreciate the pressures and strains which force a man to this position.

Nevertheless, the fact remains that Josef is now regarded with suspicion by many old friends who will be looking for an opportunity to blacken his reputation. Many of these friends know Skalicky and have contact with him and would be only too delighted to prove that the present regime can exert its influence as far as New York. I would hate to see you and your associates caught in the middle of a political brawl but more than that I find the whole question of replacing Jan more than a little distasteful.

It is true that [Pat] Zipprodt is a better designer and I would like to work with her, but the point is surely that Jan has created, with Josef and myself, the production and has been Josef's closest associate over the last eight years. I do not think he should be robbed of this position in quite such a cavalier fashion.

Sorry to land you with more problems, but better face it now rather than have difficulties later.

27 March 1973
To Schuyler Chapin

Thank you for your letter containing the not unexpected news from Mme. [Montserrat] Caballé. It is not true to say that Mme. Caballé will only be required to sing when standing still, although naturally I do not expect anyone male or female to sing and move continuously.

To take a specific problem in Act I: at the end of 'mio fratello' she is required to move down 15 steps before embarking on 'in altro mare'. After 'Marina' (from figure 19) she moves further down 10 steps before singing: 'e Dio risponde'. Three measures after figure 20 she must move down two more steps to the French, leading the Sicilians who are behind her.

The finale of Act II bristles with movements, essential as she is leading Sicilians into the revolt which eventually destroys her own future. This begins from the first 'troppo gia' onwards. As for the duet I cannot see Nicki Gedda waltzing endlessly around the statue of liberty in order to compensate for that lady's congenital immobility.

Act IV presents the greatest problems of all as she must, during the finale of Act IV, mount the stairs having moved continuously during the ball-scene. As you know the 4th act will then segue into the Sicilian, infinitely the most complicated passage musically. This has never presented a problem to either lady who has sung it in this house [Hamburg Opera]. Should you or she doubt my word on this, you will, I am sure, consult Rolf [Liebermann].

I am not sure what the solution to this is, but if you remember when we first discussed my working at the Metropolitan on *Vespri*, I pointed out that the production was rigid and that I expected these problems with Mme. Caballé. I reiterated the problem to Maestro Levine and asked him to show her the model photographs. Whilst I would hate to turn into a prima-donna myself, or, God forbid, a tenor, there is not a movement in the piece which I am prepared to alter. Such success as it has had has sprung from the willingness of an ensemble of active and creative singers. Without these circumstances I can only gracefully withdraw 'for reasons of health' and leave Mme.

Caballé to recreate the Turin production of Mme. Callas. Naturally I shall make the financial adjustments as soon as I hear from you.

Sorry to give you one more problem amongst so many, but it is better to face it now than later as I am fully aware that the Metropolitan requires the presence of a star-soprano much more than a director.

21 April 1973
From Schuyler Chapin
Just to let you know that we had a very exciting and successful meeting with Mme. Caballé going over the models of the production and the stairs and climbing that she will be required to do.

She asked me to send you a special personal message – she is very sorry that she ever doubted the validity of the production concept, she hopes you are not insulted that she questioned whether or not it was something she felt up to doing and she is looking forward to working under your direction in what she regards now as being one of the most exciting productions that she has ever done.

I know that you will hear from Michael Bronson on various technical matters but I wanted you to know that the Caballé matter seems well in hand.

27 April 1973
To Montserrat Caballé
I am so sorry that any misunderstanding should have arisen before we have actually met. I raised various matters in connection with the staging to Mr Chapin well in advance because, in my short career in the world of opera, I have discovered that Intendants have a habit of leaving problems until the last moment, therefore ensuring that the director and singer face each other on the first day of rehearsal without either of them knowing or understanding the problems of the other.

It must go without saying that I am thrilled at the possibility of working with you and do not for a moment question your ability either as a singer or an actress but, as the production makes some special demands upon its performers, I wished the problems to be raised with you so that you might have time to consider them and decide if they in any way inhibited your singing.

The most important thing in directing an opera is to make the singers feel comfortable. This has always been my rule and always will be. I embarked on this production in Hamburg when I knew very little about opera and not very much about music; consequently it may be that some demands are excessive.

23 October 1973
Ring Schuyler – accept contract – and here begins the Met history!

6 September 1973
To Rolf Liebermann, [new Intendant of the Paris Opera]
This letter is to let you off the hook. I am saying 'no' to *Carmen*, *Don Giovanni* and *Otello*. *Carmen* because I have no wish to be guillotined in the Place de la Concorde at dawn; *Don Giovanni* because my idea really does centre round an older man, bored by fornication; *Otello* because I don't want to tackle this one with someone who has sung it a great deal before, and especially Vickers who is not exactly the most lovable tenor in the business. Thanks for offering them to me. Have you found Svoboda yet, I haven't.

17 September 1973
To Rolf Liebermann
I am so sorry that my nice letter to you came out nasty at the other end. I must look it up in the files and see if a mislaid comma or full-stop might have led to any misunderstanding. If not, I can only assume that my instinctive nastiness is coming to the surface and I no longer recognise it.

One of the problems about signing so far ahead for an opera is that, not being an opera director by profession, I can never fit these commitments in with my other plans. And indeed, in the case of *Forza*, has already caused the non-acceptance of a project with which I would very much like to have been involved.

If *Otello* requires an answer immediately, then I am afraid the answer is 'no' – though I take note of the cast change in the title role. I am in a perfectly angelic mood; why don't you go to hell!

26 February 1974
From Stephen Sondheim
You may be surprised shortly (and I hope delighted) to find

yourself receiving at your British address a weekly copy of New York Magazine. You won it in a competition, which I entered in your name: namely, the Christmas crossword puzzle. You won second prize, which was a copy of 'American Birds' or 'A History of the Peloponnesian Wars' or some such. I asked them to switch it to something more entertaining.

Your subscription should start with the issue containing Alan Rich's rave review of 'Sicilian Vespers'.

10 April 1974
To Stephen Sondheim
Sorry to have been so long answering your letter. I am now back in London having had a more than usually exciting and rewarding spell in Paris.

I have not yet received the New York Magazine and I wish to God you had never entered my name. You know how I despise public showing off of brains in any form. However, what can I do – return copies to you or to them? Or send you every new Agatha Christie book as soon as it comes out? Or better still, spread the rumour that you are collaborating with her on her next one.

Notebook:
I was asked to do the Paris *Forza del destino* long before the possibility of the present job [at the Met] came up. The demands there are quite different. Paris is a jewel of a house; the Met is a cave, although there's absolutely no reason why caves should not be filled with magic.

Forza: Paris or NY?
Decision to be taken after *Vespri*. NY decision rests on money and conviction. Paris on feelings after premiere on April 3. All future Paris decisions (Ravel, *Otello, Forza*) rest on *Vespri* technical problems and house attitudes.

Agree to *Forza*, cancel *L'Enfant* [*et les sortilèges*], use *Otello* as blackmail, all stated to Rolf by Riggs and self.

16 March 1974
To Schuyler Chapin
Peace be unto your house and all who labour therein. May the Lord increase your fertility and decrease your optimism. I have

been studying plans for the years ahead and think it is necessary that I begin to make myself unpopular now rather than later.

First things first, the season 1974/75:
I will be at all rehearsals in August of revivals and new productions unless otherwise ordered by your good selves. I begin to rehearse [the American premiere production of] *Equus* on 9 September, to open in Boston on 4 October and New York on 21 October. During that period I will conduct the rehearsals of *Vespri* specified in your schedule and attend all evening performances in whole or in part and deliver observations to you and Michael B[ronson] the following day. Unfortunately the *Equus* schedule means the revival of *Wozzeck* will lack my godlike attendance, and also to some extent [*Death in*] *Venice*. In view of the very limited technical time allotted to Colin Graham in his dealings with the lighting department, I am delighted to be out of the way. The optimism of your planning in relation to this production is on a par with the rest of the planning.

As to the matter of *Forza*: if you three optimists believe it is possible to deliver an *uncut Forza* in 8 piano rehearsals, and, God help us, 2 technical rehearsals, I must admire your optimism and question your sanity. The present arrangement would allow a director to stage three quarters of the music even in the unlikely event of *all* principles being available at every rehearsal. It would only be staged, it could be in no way directed. (There is a difference.)

Your safest bet is to settle for the Berman production you know rather than the Dexter you don't.

The planning of rehearsal time for Gus Everding is something which must make sense to him, but then he is much more experienced than I am. But I, along with Mussorgsky, am shaking with horror at the thought. But will do all I can to help with the accouchement.

To me the whole planning of 74/75 represents a triumph of optimism over common sense and need over standards. However there is nothing I can do about it and as my mother used to say 'what can't be borne must be endured'.

75/76 however is another matter and must be reconsidered. Not only in relation to what is done, but the time allotted for the doing. In short, you must make up your mind if you are really serious in hoping to improve the production standards.

My overall request would be to spend some of the vast amounts of money normally lavished on physical production and spend them upon rehearsal time. This is the basis of my belief that simplified productions make for higher standards. As long as your benefactors are prepared that some of the given money should be spent on time as well as materials.

As to the new repertoire of that season: why on earth are we considering another *Puritani*? Can you not persuade [Beverly] Sills to do *Thaïs* with me at that period instead of a year later?

As for the amorphous 'French' opera: if it is your desire to empty the box office by all means, go ahead with *Ariadne* or *Carmelites*. I would myself suggest a revival at that point as I think *Figaro*, *Trittico*, *Thaïs* etc. will make enough variety without adding a second and duller French opera for its own sake. The admirable idea of the triple bill should be handed over to Fabrizio [Melano, assistant director] now. Do not, I beg of you, divide Puccini between three directors, otherwise he will end like Gaul after Caesar, in three unrelated parts.

So finally in that season, there must be a minimum of 4 more piano rehearsals planned for every production and 4 technical rehearsals, unless your lighting department has changed its manners and work habits.

I use the specific productions named above as examples; realising that the season is littered with this kind of euphoric optimism. I understand the needs of the repertoire, but if we are to uphold the overall standard of production, the simple factors I have introduced should give us some food for discussion. Only one argument is unacceptable from your side of the table, namely that which insists 'it has always worked this way'. *It has*; and very badly, that is my point. Reform the rehearsal planning and retain the quantity of productions – there is a way, we find it or give up.

Now, where shall we discuss all this? London, Paris or New York?

PS: If this letter causes you to annul my contract, I shall not be at all surprised.

Diary:
Forza: NY or Paris
Basic stage shape
T-shaped raked platform divided by red half-curtains which

travel scenic elements in and out. No intervals between scenes and hopefully only *one* pause. This is for Paris only (May 74); design to be in hand by Nov.

London May 74
Chapin conversation and results: he presented the proposed plans – there isn't enough for me to do, **especially** in 75, 76.
However it is possible that the Mini Met may prove an outlet. He accepted that I ask L[aurence]O[livier] to direct *Macbeth*, but we move date to October 77. I also hope to persuade Larry to *Moses* in the year after. I try to persuade him to drop *L'Africaine* and substitute *Prophète* and/or *Huguenots*. Point out the similarities between *Rienzi* and *Prophète*, and question advisability of both. Think about *Thaïs* and directors for *Tannhäuser* (Jerome Robbins? Hal Prince?), *Fledermaus*. Can we accommodate J[ulius] R[udel]'s demands in time?

3 January 1974
To Lord Olivier
This note will be brought in by Riggs to cover the recording of *Moses and Aaron* that I am sending you. I am making one last attempt to interest you in the role. After all, why would Shylock be the only Jew to receive your attentions? Seriously, I have the idea that if you hear the score you will understand why I think it the kind of musical and dramatic challenge to which you might respond. It is to be done the same season as the already discussed *Macbeth*. The exact date depends a little on Solti who is to conduct.

If you are near to thinking about a designer for *Macbeth*, could I put in a word for Tanya [Moiseiwitsch]. (a) I know you like and respect her work. (b) She has already designed here most successfully (*Peter Grimes*) and, (c) Everyone from the workshop to the wardrobe is longing to have her back.

Notebook:
Moses and Aaron: The key note is ritual. To express the idea of God in physical terms is to run contra to the meaning of the work.

Camels and orgy in realistic terms are laughable today. Return to the image of the amphitheatre, the chorus masked watching, participating sometimes simply by being still, sometimes with gesture of the hands, sometimes moving on to the dance floor but always present as Chorus watching and waiting.

Schuyler Chapin conversations, 6 May 1974
Agreed on a rep thro' to 79! Think how old I'll be then. (Maybe old enough to do Mozart.) For me next year: Donkeywork on *Forza* and maybe a Brecht/Weill at the Mini Met. Then *Thaïs* at San Francisco prior to the Met. My work doesn't hot up until 76–78 with *Moses* and *Thaïs* coming in; *Huguenots* or *Prophète* plus in 78–9 *Rienzi* and *Lulu*, and then leave, I think, if not carried out in a plain pine box beforehand.

Engage LO to do *Macbeth* in the season 77–79. Merrill to do *Fledermaus*, a late peace offering. Get hold of Tanya [Moiseiwitsch] re *Moses* and *Huguenots*. *Dutchman, Tannhäuser*: possible directors: Robbins, Prince. Who for *Porgy*?

11 May 1974
The company situation at the Met is one of the many aspects of the job that appeals. Every opera house should be run by a triumvirate: a musical director, a theatre director and a general manager or Intendant. James Levine, who has taken over the musical side after Kubelik's resignation, and I will be spending a great deal of next season just sitting in the theatre, listening and observing. Then we'll be in a position to tell Schuyler Chapin precisely what we think we can achieve over the next few years. But it does mean that I'll have to give up my Associate Directorship of the National Theatre although I'll still be producing *Phèdre* with Diana Rigg.

As a matter of policy I am not taking over any of next season's new productions at the Met.

20 May 1974
To Schuyler Chapin
Not all the wild horses in Her Majesty's stables would drag me into directing *Rigoletto*. In addition, I don't think I would want to take on Meyerbeer and Schoenberg in the same season.
   I don't know how to sort out the Milnes/MacNeil problem. If they both have a new production, could they not go the other way round, or do age and seniority come into it? All I can do is

suggest that you give *Rigoletto* to Fabrizio and exile me to San Francisco again for that year.

Any letters after this one should be sent to the mill [in France] as I leave on Wednesday of this week.

Pygmalion, as you will no doubt have heard, is an enormous success [in London] which is a great relief to us all.

4 June 1974
To Schuyler Chapin, from France
Dear Boss
Well, here I am, trying to get my head into that bloody Berman *Forza* to see what he wanted and how much of what he wanted is permissible today (not the endless pauses, certainly). Obviously the lighting must be rethought and Rudy Kutner [Head of Lighting at the Met] should be warned. Oh God the thought of it! On that subject, how many *hours* has Michael [Bronson] allowed for relighting *Manon*? (And I can't see either [Leontyne] Price or Caballé in that idiotic costume.)

About the telephone: there was a violent storm last week, an elm fell over the wire and try as we will to use your name *and* Rolf's, the TelePoste take their own time. However, all the information you have is correct.

I do hope something can be done about *Thaïs* otherwise I'll go mad. I need figures on the Mini Met and I need those previous budgets in front of me as soon as possible – I want to do my homework!!!

Rigoletto never never never never never – Just like King Lear.

(PS: I ended up doing it.)

2 September 1974, New York
Talk to the chorus reps and Equity reps about 'open rehearsals' problems.
The problem is to 'open the house'.
The public (whoever they are) must be helped to an intelligent appreciation of the problems and of some solutions.
I must 'do' as many talks to visiting students as possible, but this is the equivalent of talking to the respectfully converted.
At the same time begin to examine use of rehearsal time and planning of technical rehearsals. If the standard of the basic rep is to be heightened, more time must be given to revivals, i.e. the

arrangements for *Forza* should be the required minimum for any revival.

Discuss possibilities of lunch time or evening talk-ins on new works – or old works in new form – i.e. *Boris*.

3 September 1974
To Tom Stoppard

Thank you for your letter, sorry for the delay in answering.

Am settling into my palatial office and an apartment which is palatial, but likely to become less so in view of the fact that your friend and mine, Riggs, has bought TWO Saint Bernards. Any questions?

PS: Do you realise that now I have crossed the Atlantic, I may never get to direct a play of yours. Shed a little tear please . . .

PPS: Couldn't say before, shouldn't say now, loved *Travesties*, hated the production. Love you.

4 September 1974
To Rolf Liebermann

Jocelyn [Herbert], Andrew [Sanders] and I have now completed the preliminary model for *Forza* and she will be asking your Technical Director to go to London to look at it before we bring in the detailed model in November. It is slightly more austere than *Vespri* and I am very thrilled by it. It is designed so that there should be no wait between scenes and only two intervals, one after the first monastery scene and one at the end of the Italian excursion. This brings me to the major problem on which I would like your assistance before we go into rehearsal.

I have spoken to Maestro [Julius] Rudel about the order of the Preziosilla scenes and he remembers in his youth in Vienna seeing the sequence in the order I have discussed. It was, I believe, initiated by Werfel in 1926 and has recently been used in Stuttgart. Is this of any help to your gentlemen archivists?

It is absolutely essential, in my view, to end the 2nd Act with the tenor/baritone duet and use the Preziosilla Melitone Trabuco section as an interlude, giving Alvaro time to recover from his wounds, (and catch his breath). This sequence of events tightens the dramatic impact and, as I have said, concludes the act on a high point of tension directly related to the main plot.

The problem that this raises springs from the temperament of the mezzo-soprano you have chosen. Whilst she is the best Preziosilla in the world, she is also the biggest bitch on two legs, always insisting on solo calls (check La Scala, *Don Carlos* and Franco). The whole concept and design of this piece, as with *Vespri* and *House of the Dead* and *Boris*, depend on the direct transition from scene to scene so that the musical and dramatic impact is continually building in the audience and is not dissipated by any outside force. You will appreciate that Ms Herbert and Mr Sanders and I have worked for some time to achieve this vital dramatic progression and whilst I am willing to tackle all the problems of rehearsing in Paris, I do think you or Joan should inform the Diva of the intention of the production and make it clear to her that you, as Intendant, support this view. With your tact and charm, you might be able to persuade her. But please, for the sake of old times and good work we have achieved in the past, take care of this subject now.

See you in November.

1 October 1974
To Joan Plowright
All goes well here and I am very happy. Tony Hopkins is on the way to being superb in *Equus*. He is calm, disciplined and every word is crystal clear. What has happened, God knows! All we can do is be thankful. On the whole it seems more interesting than in England, but I am still only half way through rehearsals.

Claude Chagrin [choreographer] has gone slightly mad and left New York saying that the play is immoral and Peter Shaffer is a wicked man. As it has taken *her* two years to discover this, how long will it be before the public finds out?

. . .

Alarming rumours of changing plans in the Waterloo Road reach me, but so far they are only rumours, and as you have no time to gossip I must wait for a·supper after the show for more details.

Do you think when I come back it would be a good time to talk to Larry seriously about *Macbeth*? I know it seems a long way ahead, but you know how far ahead we have to plan in order to find the right singers. So far I have instigated some rapid and radical changes in repertoire and rehearsal planning here. Two 20th-century operas in the first three-year plan and two nearly forgotten 19th-century operas. We are going to make a press

1. On the set of *The Kitchen.*

2. (*Above*) *The Kitchen*, Royal Court.
(*Below*) *Chicken Soup with Barley*. Frank Finlay and Kathleen Michael.

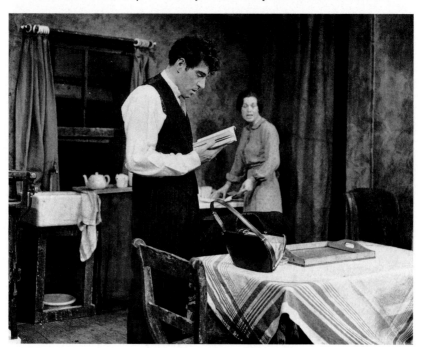

3. (*Above*) *Roots*. Joan Plowright, Alan Howard, Charles Kay, John Colin.
(*Below*) *Chips with Everything*. Royal Court.

4. (*Above*) Me, Maggie Smith and Laurence Olivier.
(*Below*) *Saint Joan.* Joan Plowright and Max Adrian.

5. (*Above*) *Black Comedy*. Derek Jacobi, Maggie Smith and Albert Finney.
(*Below*) *A Bond Honoured*. Robert Stephens, Maggie Smith and cast.

6. (*Above*) *A Woman Killed with Kindness*. Anthony Hopkins, Joan Plowright and cast.
(*Below*) *Phaedra Britannica*. Diana Rigg and David Yelland.

7. (*Above*) *Galileo*. Michael Gambon and Selina Cadell (*centre*).
(*Below*) *Heartbreak House*. Rex Harrison, Diana Rigg, Simon Ward, Rosemary
Harris and cast.

8. *The Misanthrope.* Diana Rigg and Alec McCowen.

announcement about all this shortly, which will either have us hounded from New York as lunatics, or hailed as visionaries! Who cares which as long as the work is done. The most important changes are in rehearsal planning, which will give everyone much more time.

23 October 1974
To Rolf Liebermann
Oh! Surely just a little love, a little particle of the love so generously lavished on late arriving tenors and sopranos.

Somewhere between Switzerland and New York English styles of humour change. It is, I suppose, all due to the Tower of Babel.

Fact No. 1. I am travelling from New York to London to check final details of the model with Ms Herbert and Mr Sanders before bringing it to you. I hope you will like it when you see it. It is less elaborate than Vienna, but I think has greater elegance. Now I go to an Executive Committee meeting to put the three-year plan in front of them. Let us hope that Mr Fisher and Mrs Belmont [members of the Executive Committee] do not share your opinion of me.

And one more word – do not please go to hell, come from it!

19 November 1974, University Hospital, New York
Discuss for the next few weeks the possibility of doing *The Seagull* next fall. Marian [Seldes], Tom [Hulce], Roberta [Maxwell], and possibly Tony H[opkins].

Why *The Seagull*? I've always wanted to do Chekhov and no one in England seems to consider my abilities in that direction. It seems possible *here* to make my own conditions (not financial) and to work with a group of people I love and respect on a play which is bigger than I am, and which requires a good deal more of me than a capacity for physical organisation.

The Seagull

Setting.
Wooden planking, gaps between. Lit from behind for exterior and from in front for interior. A permanent set. Branches. Back lit for garden and lawn. Interior: decorations on boards, pictures etc. NOW think of the play in that discipline.

19 November 1974, University Hospital
Now that *Equus* has become 'a hit' and it seems that a five-year plan for the Met can be accepted, the next few years in America seem interesting. If it is possible to combine activities at the Met with projects like *The Seagull*, a creative and interesting time could be ahead. The changing of a pattern of life and work seems good, so let's take care of health, teeth, body and all and *get on with it*. Approach your teeth and your body as you would an actor, with care, attention and respect! (Big deal, a bit late!)

The artistic life of the Metropolitan lies in the hands of the principal conductor and the director of productions. Rule by committee produces what already exists, leaderless chaos.

The Met is the only opera house built in the twentieth century which has always behaved as tho' it were in the nineteenth.

24 November 1974
Belated solutions and panic panaceas will produce nothing. If the executive committee (usually all people with some knowledge of world economic trends, at least as much as the average newspaper reporter, let us say) cannot act upon knowledge available to all ten years ago, it is no use flailing around looking for victims to expiate their own guilt. Nor can they now dictate an artistic policy. Economy is not a policy it is a fact. Imagination/ Simplicity is a policy.

It is an approach to opera for the twentieth century. When the theatre began to remove elaborate 'realistic' effects, it became free so that from Schiffbauerdam to Sloane Square, any physical and emotional demand a playwright could make was capable of fulfilment. Time and place could flow freely in the audience's imagination (which, according to Coleridge, is where the excitement lies).

Only at the Metropolitan has time stood still. The curtain can still rise on a performance and the audience can be transported back to the nineteenth century and sit and wallow in an imaginary world. Unfortunately drama is reality given meaning and form. Opera and drama are not a drug for the feeble minded, they are an essential enhancement of our lives from which we can enrich ourselves and from which we can learn.

Only when the operatic stage can share the freedom of the dramatic stage can the medium exist in the twentieth century and maybe help us understand the world and ourselves, instead of remaining the morphine of the over-privileged.

Economy as a watchword is meaningless. Imagination costs more in the mind but less in the purse. But the imagination must swing out from the stage to embrace the audience and the audience must be trained to join in an act of imagination.

To hell with economy, spend imagination.

26 November 1974
To Olivier
This letter should give you a lift. I was in hospital last week for five days trying to pass a kidney stone and for all the pain I went through I might have been passing the Rock of Gibraltar! However, it went and there is no pain now, mother dear, and I am back in my plush-lined office.

I hope you didn't disapprove too much of my shouting my mouth off about *Macbeth* at the Met, but Joan was under considerable harassment at the stage door and it seemed a good way of diverting their attention without actually committing you to anything. After the fact, however, and I do remember your dislike of publicity, it occurred to me you might be getting into a rage with me. I do hope not.

Everyone here is tremendously excited at the idea of your doing *Macbeth* and I am fighting off sopranos of all sizes (and colours) who are longing to throw themselves via me into your arms. Equally so, the line of Macbeths 'stretches out to the crack of. . .'. Perhaps I shouldn't finish the quotation.

Anyway, all my love to you and Joan. You have probably heard *Saturday, Sunday, Monday* was not tremendously received here. Eli [Wallach] was somewhat cross with Franco [Zeffirelli, the director] whom he said did not know the moves and it didn't seem my place to tell him that he never knew them in the first place!

Equus continues to sell out and Tony [Hopkins] is giving a performance which would I think impress you – clear, beautifully phrased, totally disciplined and deeply moving. It may be that all our trouble and care with him will be paid off.

Riggs and the two St Bernards send their love.

NB: Peter Hall eventually directed *Macbeth* with his usual Victorian approach to Shakespeare. He charmed his way into the inner circle at the Met until it opened and got booed. And then the inner circle came running back, cap in hand.

30 January 1975
To Rolf Liebermann

Do you think it would be possible for your staff to arrange for Svoboda and Skalicky to be in Paris during the *Forza* period? I have tried several times to contact him but failed and would rather avoid going to Prague at this time if it is at all possible. If anything is to happen with *Otello* we must meet this year.

All goes surprisingly well here. The NY revival of *Forza*, which is about the worst work I have done since *Cellini*, has been very well received even by the idiot Schonberg. I wish I could persuade you and Rudel to the revised second act ending. I realise the ending with the Rataplan is much more of a show piece for the conductor and chorus, but the tenor phrase 'L'oblio, la pace chiegga il guerrier' and the throwing away of the sword end the act, not only dramatically, but in a suspenseful manner. However, I realise that opera is not a logical medium and bow to your opinions and will do the best I can with the other version.

Notebook:

Jocelyn's work on the Paris *La Forza del Destino* was wonderful. That was the best nineteenth-century opera I did and the production worked as it was intended to.

30 April 1974

I arrived at the Met through Schuyler Chapin's invitation. He was somewhat foolishly dismissed within a few months of our beginning to make our first plans. Schuyler had wit, grace, knowledge, style and all one expects of a great intendant. His successor did not. However, the work went forward.

March 1975

Anthony Bliss, the Met's new executive director, has called for a 10% cut in all salaries.

By all means if it really means survival. But survival must be earned, it isn't given. How much more do the board give up? As usual the artists are being asked to subsidise the arts.

The NT made itself on the willingness of us all to work for less money, saying that it offered unprecedented opportunities – but *we* made the opportunities. And without us the NT could not have existed. We could, and would have. The same is true here. Whoever decided to build the biggest opera house in the world owes us all 10% of his money. In an age when any intelligent person in the arts knew that the age of the giants was over and that the biggest is not the best, what idiot made the decision and on what basis of fact?

Notebook:
The right to survive is not given. It has to be earned. The Met must begin to earn it.

I regard this opening period as a chance to get into the workshop and see how the machinery revolves and also a time to plan for the future. You cannot move into top gear right away, and we should be judged on how good (or otherwise) we are in the 1976–77 season. By that time I hope to be working on two new productions and two revivals a year. Part of my job here is discreetly to oversee from the stage point of view what is put on in the house; I also have to look at the operas we have in stock and decide which have a few more years' life.

I don't like the word 'spectaculars'. We've got to break the Victorian image of having whole streets on stage, which was totally false anyway because it was nothing but cloth and paint. There isn't the money to put slices of Egypt or Thebes in the theatre any more. So we've got to persuade audiences to accept a much freer and more imaginative approach to opera.

The Met is a big house and it requires large-scale works. There are constant demands for us to do 'small' operas, but it is much more difficult to scale a *Figaro* or a *Cosi* to fit in with the auditorium than is generally imagined. I feel that Verdi must predominate at the Met, although I'm very interested in moving into the French repertoire. I would like to do a *Juive* or a *Prophète* or even a *Huguenots* if we could meet the physical demands. Musically they are on a level with Bellini and Donizetti; dramatically they are far superior.

20 May 1975
To Teresa Stratas
I am writing to introduce myself and to say how thrilled I am that

we shall be working together on *Lulu*. I shall, of course, come and talk to you some time when we are on the same continent and discuss my plans.

At the moment there is a slight problem with the publishers as [Maestro] James Levine and I wish to incorporate more dialogue in the third act than they have so far been willing to permit. It is my opinion that two vital developments of Lulu's character are left out and can be played as dramatic scenes between sections of the Lulu suite. I mean particularly the scene Lulu has when about to be sold into a brothel. She makes that remarkable statement, 'I cannot sell the only thing I ever owned'. It is a question of inserting two short spoken scenes, and I hope the publishers will come to see it our way.

The designer I have been working with on this project is Jocelyn Herbert. I do not know if you are familiar with her work. She has recently designed *Forza* for me in Paris, with enormous success and, in fact, I have collaborated with her many times at the National Theatre in England and consider her to be the most subtle and atmospheric designer I know. You may have seen the production of *Othello* with Sir Laurence Olivier, which I directed and she designed, or perhaps the films of *Tom Jones* and *Isadora* on which she was production designer. The latter was quite interesting from your point of view as her work on Vanessa Redgrave's costumes is quite remarkable.

Once we have resolved outstanding difficulties with the publishers, and when Miss Herbert has freed herself from a film commitment, she will be in contact with you and arrange to meet somewhere at your convenience.

Once again, best wishes in hope of a happy and successful collaboration.

Notebook:
Accepting the widow Berg's contention that the third act does not exist, I must ask the question: do the first two acts make themselves a complete statement in comparison with, say, *Moses and Aaron*. They do not. In comparison with *Turandot*, they do. I do not believe the 'thought' of the work can be made clear without some attempt to state the events and emotions which lead to Geschwitz's last words: what are these events? In general all men take revenge on Lulu for the sins they believe she has committed against them. Without some text to convey her

innocence, Lulu must become the Demon, in which disguise most people recognise her.

Lulu, as a human, not superhuman force, needs the last act. Lulu as a human innocent, NOT a superhuman force of evil, needs the defence of the third act of Wedekind to explain her humanity. Her defence 'I cannot sell the only thing I ever owned' is essential. Alwa's 'in front of this painting' and Geschwitz's 'What do these people know of love' are hints, clues without which Lulu becomes the simplistic archetype of the female destructive force – which we know from the composer was not his intention.

24 June 1975
To Tanya Moiseiwitsch
It was nice to talk to you yesterday and to think that you will be available for *Boccanegra*. If I couldn't get you I would have gone to Giotto!

I have only one idea at the moment, but I would like to put it before you. It is necessary to find the unifying feature – the 25 year gap between the prologue and Act I, of which I spoke to you, is difficult. I have an idea at the moment that what I would like is to use from the beginning of the opera (the prelude) the figure of Boccanegra as an old man sitting in the Doge's chair with a globe of the world – he would (as it were) observe the events of his past and eventually the singer playing Boccanegra would take the place of a double in the last half of the piece. In feeling, there is a resemblance I think to the late Shakespeare plays, *Pericles* and *The Winter's Tale* etc., and the scene with the two old men realising that a life of hatred has been wasted has a lot in common with Lear and Gloucester. I think we need a permanent surround and a permanent central space dominated by the Doge's throne. Also in my head is an enormous map of the world or the Mediterranean as, probably, a permanent back cloth.

The piece is about politics/power, and, because it is set in Genoa, the feeling of the sea is never far away. Obviously I am leaning to a non-realistic interpretation in which the passage of time and place is fluid.

Notebook:
No way was I going to do *Aida*. It wasn't part of the bargain at all.

I picked it up because there was no one else around to do it and get it in for under half a million. The point about the production was that it went up quickly. We had to come in cheaper than the one originally considered, which would have swamped us – it would have been one more gargantuan dinosaur lying across the possibility of the future. So it was a fill-in job, an attempt to stem a tide that was getting out of hand.

Nowhere would you find me saying this is my statement about how it's going to be done in the future. You would find me saying only that I'm trying to find a way of presenting opera in the future in a more economic and dramatic manner. This is an experiment. Everything is an experiment.

Later . . .

Think about *Aida*. Intimate personal conflict against an immense political conflict. Only one scene is dependent on spectacle. *Also* the division between the archaeological accuracy and the nineteenth-century aura of the music – bring these elements together. Look at the La Scala original designs – see if they can be evoked not recreated (gauze not canvas, steel not wood).

Undated
To Arthur Mitchell, Dance Theatre of Harlem
I am sorry to trouble you again when I know you are so busy, but I wonder if I can pick your brains. I have (foolishly perhaps) agreed to do a production of *Aida* with [Leontyne] Price, [Marilyn] Horne and [Placido] Domingo. The most important problem to face is one of choreography. I view both the ballet sections with some alarm, but have an idea which might, in the right hands, be interesting. The ballet in the triumph scene I see as a two man gladiatorial combat – a re-enactment of the battle in Ethiopia with death for the Ethiopian at the end of it; like a bull fight – the ending is known at the beginning. The Amneris ballet is I think for a girl and erotic, not cute.

I don't want to waste any more of your time discussing theories, but if you can think of anyone that you would recommend I would be most grateful for your help.

11 November 1975
To Kenneth Tynan
My four day old copy of The Times shows me you are in print

again. Once we had stopped talking I did hope you would start writing and then we might establish a little communication.

However, it is nice to know you are well. Are you coming over here? I haven't been so happy in years as I am in New York. The work responsibilities are what I need and moreover, in about five years' time, Levine and I might have done something quite important. That is to say, dragged opera screaming somewhat into the 20th century. Anyway, do write if you can or get Kathleen to write, or better still come over.

20 November 1975
To Keith Jeffrey, Arts Council
I should have written long ago, but what with the opening of the season (95% capacity every week when we are only budgeted on 85% – tell that to Peter Hall) and the rehearsals and the opening of the National Company of *Equus* in Boston (a sell out and press slightly more hysterical even than before) I have been a little busy, gratified but busy. I am now about to depart for Acapulco for ten days to eat, rest, swim, fish and hopefully block *Aida*.

Sir Laurence is here at the moment and we spent an evening together drinking and moaning about Mr Sanderson Hall [Peter Hall had just done a 'Very Peter Hall Very Sanderson's' advertisement], ending up very drunk, totally bitchy and very happy. Little news reaches me from England. Riggs of course telephones to let me know how *Misanthrope* and *Phaedra* are going, but I haven't heard anything from the management itself, apart from a suggestion that I consider doing *All for Love* some time in the future (fat chance).

The house in New Jersey is now almost finished and furnished. The French Fine Arts Commission are holding on to some of our pictures in Bordeaux in the mistaken belief that they are French national treasures, but apart from this minor mishap, home is in New Jersey and I am very comfortable. So are the dogs.

At the moment I don't think I miss England at all and what with the threat of one bomb a week coming up, I can't see myself coming back for some time. So I doubt if we are going to meet unless you come over here. If you do, you can be assured of the usual welcome, quite apart from the fact that I would love to have a long gossip.

3 December 1975
To Joan Plowright

Thank you for your last letter and all the news. I am delighted to hear from Riggs that things are going so well and hope that the Ben Travers [*The Bed Before Yesterday*] is behaving itself.

I saw Larry very briefly when I was between Boston and Acapulco. We had a drink together and he seemed in very good form as far as I could see. He was off to dinner with Margalo Gilmore and God knows who else. He was assailed by various New York loonies as he left the hotel and whilst searching for a cab the doorman confided in me 'You have got to make him slow down.' I add this for your information and amusement, not in any way as mother's spy on father.

Everything goes well here. The Boston company of *Equus* opened to extraordinarily good notices and Dai Bradley's performance in his six months in South Africa has improved to an extraordinary degree. It is now not only as good as Peter Firth but better, stronger, and more interesting, though of course not as glamorous. Brian Bedford is the only actor, so far, to equal Alec in the dryness and pain expressed in the performance.

Life at the Met is becoming increasingly interesting. We have been playing to 95% capacity since the season opened, which is something that hasn't happened to them since 1950. Of course, Jimmy Levine and I don't really come into full swing until next year and I expect trouble to start flying about then. It is also possible that *Aida* which I am faced with in January, will be exceedingly unpopular as it is rather austere. However, press on regardless, as Tony Guthrie used to say.

Jocelyn [Herbert] is coming over next weekend to do some more work on *Lulu* and I am looking forward to seeing her very much.

I haven't seen Robert Stephens, who has been here for some time, but you will probably imagine that I haven't done much to search him out. There are so many problems one would have to go into that I really can't face at the moment. The enclosed section of the letter to Birkett more or less explains how I feel about the South Bank, Peter Hall, and working in England. I am sending it to you, not because it seems so very important, but because I thought you ought to know that I have at least put on paper my feelings. I don't imagine they will get circulated very far. Why should they? But I would like you to understand my attitude. I realise in re-reading it, I also said something not entirely pleasant about Larry, but you know this perfectly well and it is intended for your eyes, not his, anyway.

The house in New Jersey has been occupied for some time now. We have had the builders in downstairs doing a new super style kitchen and large bedroom and bathroom for Riggs. It has been a bit like living in Brighton when you were knocking down walls. However, it is a wonderful house, always available to guests, overlooking the water and very quiet.

Notebook:
13 December. Lulu
Work with JH [Jocelyn Herbert, on Alban Berg's *Lulu*] in progress. Revolve seems to be revolving out of sight, thrusting wedge. Sliding stages. Angled screens. Wide curtain. 3 different wedge shapes, moving in and out creating rooms, surrounded by screens (angled).

22 December 1975
To Jocelyn Herbert
It was so wonderful to see you again and to see the preliminary model in such an exciting state. I don't think I enthused nearly enough, but then you know me, taciturn and north country to the last.

Good news. Just after you left, the widow Berg from darkest Vienna has agreed to all the textual interpolations that we want to make, and anything else that we would like to do. This is wonderful news, and is a permission that has never been granted before. I do know, however, from Rolf Liebermann's experience when he was trying to produce the piece, she is quite capable of picking up the Ouija board tomorrow morning and consulting Alban to find that he doesn't want to do it.

Notebook:
Sunday 25 January 1976
Aida – the last week. What was the guiding principle – can it still work? And if so, how?

Probably I should have chosen a less convenient designer. Just how much the choice of designer was affected by my ego ('I can do it alone') and how much by practicality I shall probably not be able to analyse. Certainly a Herbert or a Svoboda, and probably only these two, could have added an enormous contribution but they could never have worked under pressure of time which David [Reppa] took in his stride.

In any case the decision is long since made and David's contribution is considerable. Certainly he has taken the directive 'simplify' and followed exactly my wishes at all points, perhaps that is the problem. What we have is less expensive and more durable than the Ponnelle production with which we were presented, but is it any good? Will it hold and convince an audience? Certainly the Triumph has possibilities and already an atmosphere of its own which supports the drama and squarely places the situation of Amneris, Aida, Amonasro, Radames in a dangerous context. Have I, however, considered that to the exclusion of everything else? And if I have, what is gained and can I recoup anything that has been lost in the one week (how many hours?) left? The notion that occurred this morning for Act II, Scene One, namely keeping the Amneris ladies still and simplifying the pattern of movement, has its possibilities through the work.

The first principle was to simplify. Have I over simplified at certain points? Could I have discussed this much sooner, could I not have imagined more and not waited for the decor, costume and lights? And if it is my regular pattern of work that makes me wait for the stimulus of decor, can I indulge this whilst working in opera? I could if I had some other way of working, but as I have not and at the moment can see no way of arriving at another process, I must make myself work more expertly within my own limitations. More important, I must try only 'to work where I am stimulated with minds that feed minds and not minds which I feed.'

The immediate problem of *Aida* and the few days left may be solved but for the future some decisions must be taken and others checked.

However: simplify.

Not having seen the whole performance I cannot judge how the starkness of the opening and trio compare with the Vulcan scene and the Triumph. Do they in fact counterpoint each other? Three figures placed in a triangle and a hundred and fifty packed around the same space – do they create the sense of private people in public situations? Is the balance between crowded and empty space clear, and if not what can I do now to make it clearer? Not, I think, elaborate but simplify. Make each duo and trio and solo as carefully placed as the mass scenes. Reduce the movements in small scenes and discipline the movements in large scenes. Aida's exits after *Ritorna* and *Numi, pieta* must lead from the isolation of one heroic figure to the onrush of the mass. One scene must lead to another more effectively than at the moment.

Examine each scene ending and beginning. Examine all unneeded moves and eliminate where it will not confuse. Simplify, simplify – it's always more difficult.

Saturday. [31 January 1976]
A good deal done, is it enough? The simplification of the Amneris scene led to an even simpler Aida Amneris duet which is very good now. I can't do anything about the Nile Scene now, maybe next season.

27 January 1976
To Lindsay Anderson
Thank you for your letter. On the contrary, I should have written to you a long time ago. Perhaps to explain and apologise why I thrust you and Joan in the Bridal Bed [LA directed *The Bed Before Yesterday* with Joan Plowright, in a season with *The Seagull*] but you both seemed to be at a loose end, and Joan was certainly talking about doing things, but not actually doing very much, and you are the only person I could think of who might have goaded her into activity. I also should have written to you both to congratulate you on the obvious success of the season and I didn't, so if anyone is at fault, I am.

Riggs has told me about both plays and I wish very much that I could come to see them but I doubt if I am going to be in England for a while. Which brings me to an immediate answer to your question. I don't actually know if I am available in terms of time at all, at the moment, and by the time I did know it would probably be too late for you, so I think the best thing is to say, with very many regrets, that you must count me out.

I have a feeling that if it is left to Joan the whole thing will probably fizzle out, which seems a great pity. However, I shouldn't say that as I am unprepared to do anything to help. I think really you will have to grit your teeth and try and keep it going and take charge of at least the next season yourself. After all, where else are you going to work? The South Bank or Sloane Square, or that place on the Avon?

I know how you hate being tied down, but I think His Majesty Hall deserves a disloyal opposition somewhere around London. And you are the only person who can be disloyal and imaginative enough to beat him, not only on his own ground, but on ground where he has never dared to walk.

Of course I would love to do a Shaw play at some time, but the two I want to do most nobody else likes. Namely – *Good King Charles's Golden Days* and *Getting Married*. However, if in a year or so we are all surviving and around I would like to talk about doing them.

You are quite right, I am having a wonderful time at the Met. I don't know if [James] Levine and I can do anything about dragging the place into the 20th century or even, for that matter, into the 19th. But the challenge it opens up and the occasions it provides for experiment are fascinating. Also, the Americans don't demand one spends a lot of time in administration, so that I am not tied to an office and spend most of my day either at other people's rehearsals or my own.

Just at the moment I am a little over-strained, due to the fact that *Aida* is one week away from opening and I suspect I have bitten off not only a good deal more than I can chew, but I am chewing it in the wrong way. It is a bit too austere, and its attempts at old style grandeur look to me rather paltry. Trouble is, I can't remember which of the two stools I wanted to jump on in the first place, and all I can see is an incoherent mess of bits and pieces. However, with the orchestra going for the next four days, I might have some chance to pull it together and if it hasn't got a style of its own, try and make it at least have a style of some kind and give it also a modicum of efficiency, which at the moment it doesn't possess. The cast is wonderful. They sing out full at rehearsal, which is a lovely change. And Miss Price and I, after an initial scream up at each other, are getting on very well. So much for women's lib, gay lib, and black power.

More than anything I am looking forward to doing *Lulu* with Jocelyn. Her short visits over here are always stimulating and make me get back to my routine functions within the house in a much happier frame of mind.

As if all my problems weren't enough, I am now rehearsing

Richard Burton into *Equus*. God knows what terrors lie in store for me. I wonder if he still can act as well as he used to?

27 January 1976
To Lucia T. Morison, The Guthrie Theatre, Minneapolis

Thank you for your letter. It is always pleasant to know that one's name has been suggested for any work, anywhere. Unfortunately, a detailed resumé of my past work and experience would take me an awfully long time, and as I am at the moment fully engaged at the Metropolitan, it would occupy more time than I can spare.

However, if you care to consult *Who's Who* or *Who's Who in the Theatre* you will find all the details enclosed there.

I am at the moment Director of Productions at the Metropolitan Opera House and am working on *Aida*, but I wouldn't advise you attending that. *Equus* has been on Broadway for one and a half years, maybe you might like to see that.

27 January 1976
To Jocelyn Herbert

So sorry not to have phoned. You are absolutely right. *Aida* is a pill and I am up to my neck in it.

I am sorry you have been having a bad time. I know how you feel about working on your own and I am so desperate to work with you again on something. I think you will have to move to America for a year. Why don't you emigrate? I could use a good designer permanently.

I am glad you are meeting Stratas and hope you get on well with her. I am told she's a bit crazy, but very intelligent. Do let me know what goes on.

I am now going into the piano dress rehearsal of *Aida* with no tenor, as he has flu, and without the understudy who has a temperature of 102. Two other minor roles are missing and I am not sure if I have all the 90 extras for the Triumph scene. However, the greater problem is that I think I have fallen badly between two stools stylistically and wish to God you were here all the time so that I could refer to you. However, I will try to imagine what you would prefer me to do under all given situations. So in some measure you are responsible for whatever you see when you get here. So there!

5 February 1976
To Keith Jeffrey, Arts Council
Aida opened last night and the notices this morning were very good indeed, to my intense surprise. So many people had been saying during the later rehearsals, 'It's going to be very controversial', and I was beginning to think I had lost my mind. However, it is not as controversial as all that, and it's certainly the best sung *Aida* I have ever heard. I wish I could see you, talk to you and get all the gossip about England, a country which seems to have become very remote from me at the moment. There is a possibility that I may be there for a week in the not too distant future as the National Theatre are now trying to put *Equus* on in the West End, having realised they are losing money by not doing so. How long does it take them to learn anything? I am also involved at the moment with rehearsing Richard Burton into the same play in New York. He is being extraordinarily good, totally disciplined, sober, and compulsive watching.

24 February 1976
To Alan Rich, New York Magazine opera critic
Thank you very much for the notice and for your consistent support. Obviously it is going to be a bumpy few years and any critical support one receives is not only welcome but invigorating. Naturally I expect to be clobbered like everybody else, but at the same time one's capacity for taking chances is greatly debilitated when incomprehension is the rule of the day. Informed hatred and dislike are one thing, wilful misunderstanding is another.

However, the object of this letter is not as entirely obsequious as it might sound. I must take exception to your observations at the beginning in which you discuss the reasons for a new *Aida*. Can we, once and for all, have the record clear? A new *Aida* was forced upon us by the burning of the entire wardrobe of the previous production and the fact that this production had toured and played so much that the canvas and woodwork were worn away, and not even the greatest lighting job in the world would have saved them. A new *Aida* had been planned by Gentele and Kubelik long before James [Levine] and I took up our positions. Indeed the design was completed by the time I arrived in the house, and on my suggestion was scrapped as being too expensive. I was extremely reluctant to take on the piece at such short notice. Ten months is no time to prepare oneself for a work like this, a work – along with *The Magic Flute* and *Carmen* – I swore I would never do. But, the most important point was, at no time was this production connected with James' and my incumbency at the Met, nor with the need to lure Miss Price to the house with a new production.

1 July 1976
To Franco Zeffirelli [who was directing *Jesus of Nazareth* for Lew Grade]
I hope you received my letter although I can quite imagine Sir Lew confiscating it if he discovered it as it might interfere with his possession of you, which is fine if you want to be possessed by Lew Grade, but I hardly imagine this to be the case.

Everyone is telling me that I shouldn't write to you on the subject of the production budget as you will be offended. However, I have to wear my Director of Productions' hat from time to time. It is a rather severe style and I would prefer a more frivolous chapeau, well decorated with flowers. However, here goes.

As you know, the financial crisis is intense, and I have now been given figures beyond which I cannot go for each individual season, so it is my responsibility to juggle and make sure that everyone has the best and most equal deal. What I would like to do, if you think it would be any help, is to send you some comparative figures of Met productions which you have probably seen, showing the cost when they were created and what that cost would be now, in both dollars and lire.

Janet Roberts has told me that you have the production design already. As one old director to another, may I say that if you can let us see *anything* earlier than the agreed date, it will be an enormous help in one area above all, namely materials. For instance, if we can buy lumber or canvas this year, we would save an estimated 50% rise in costs for next year.

I would propose to write all this in detail to you if it is not going to harass or disturb you in any way. I know well enough how easy it is to be deflected from a basic vision by material concerns, but you know how anxious I am that your return to the Metropolitan should be happy, creative and should reflect once again the success you have always had in this house. I feel that if I do not apprise you of these financial details I will be failing in my duty. Nevertheless, I must take advice from the people around who believe you might be in some way intimidated or insulted by such an approach.

Dear Franco, please tell me whether you want to be left alone or whether there is anything in this area I can do to help with the 'accouchement'. I need hardly say that there is no one in the house, from the Director of Productions upwards and downwards, who is not looking forward to your triumphant return.

15 July 1976
To Teresa Stratas

I am sorry to have been out of touch for so long but I have been in the middle of a monumental administrative blood bath for the last couple of months. The dust has now settled and I hope that in future things, at least in the technical area, will be run a little more economically. The results will not be visible on stage but hopefully in the accounting department, which is becoming increasingly important.

Tom Graham asked me to send you the text for the last act of *Lulu* as soon as it is finished. We have had large problems going from the Stephen Spender translation to the original of Wedekind's play. However, most of these difficulties are resolved, and I think the scene makes sense. I need, however, to work on it for a few days before sending it to you and please remember when you read it, it is an outline. Anything that you find difficult or unacceptable, please contact me and we will talk and correspond about it.

Don't worry about the wig colour. Nina has brought in more samples and nothing will be made up without your approval and Jocelyn's. The set designs are just about to go into the workshop and are absolutely stunning, creating a series of intimate rooms with enormous detail and atmosphere. The staff have been slightly shaken by the technique of scene change we are using (i.e. two motorised trucks operating from the left and right of the stage and thrusting the action down one foot over the orchestra pit). There were cries about fire department regulations and the most irritating of all, 'But we have never done that before', to which I was able to make the succinct but not particularly witty answer, 'But you are going to bloody well do it now.'

If it breaks down at rehearsal time I expect you to smile bravely, look confident and mop up my tears!

21 July 1976
To Teresa Stratas

Here, in rough form, is the dialogue for the third act of *Lulu*. It looks a little bald at the moment, without any explanation of how the projection screens work and of my intentions for the gambling scene. However, until I have written out a sophisticated version of the stage directions, which hopefully will give some of the intended visual aspect, I imagine the dialogue will put your mind at rest.

As you will see, the major point we retain is the great speech on the bottom of page 2 and the top of page 3, ending with the 'ich kann nicht' – the dramatic action following with Schigolch, Rodrigo, Alwa and Casti-Piani will I think be an extraordinarily effective way of suggesting that she is eventually destroyed by the men she unknowingly destroyed in the first act. If I go into a more elaborate discussion at this stage, it will be at least two weeks before I can send you the text, so maybe it is better to send you the text and hope that it doesn't seem too confusing.

27 August 1976
To the Earl of Harewood

To have, at last, become a footnote in Kobbé makes me feel that I have finally arrived on the operatic scene. To see the initial 'H' at the end of the article is a great pleasure. I hope I am not over-stepping the bounds of immodesty if I thank you.
Life is still hell here but exciting hell.

18 November 1976 [from Tunisia]
To Jocelyn Herbert

The temperature is somewhere in the 70s. I am slightly shaded by date palms. I have half a bottle of white wine called Thibar inside me, several chunks of ice diluting it, but I cannot avoid telling you how wonderful it is to begin blocking *Lulu*. Thanks to your precise observation of the composer's placings of furniture, doorway, window, etc., it is flowing like silk (does silk flow?). I am worried a little about the position of the ladder in scene 1 and have decided to put it downstage of the door if that is all right with you. I understand it mucks up Alwa's entrance, but I think I have a way of getting over that, but it is very important for Lulu, when she climbs the ladder and speaks of her world that the view of the world is as near to the audience as possible, and I think that after the scuffle with the painter, knocking over the screen etc., this is the best place. It also makes a marvellous holding point for the doctor, when he makes his entrance and frustrates him before and even to a final heart attack.

In short, darling, it all seems to work on paper, under the date palms, and even manipulating a tape recorder, stopping, starting, winding back does not intimidate me from saying what a thrill this is. Of course it has always been the same way but I haven't until this point noticed it and I have certainly never thanked you for it.

24 November 1976
To Robert Jacobson, Editor, Opera News
Is it necessary to be a bitch every day of your life? Miss Obraztsova did not 'eschew' my direction. On the contrary, she accepted beautifully.
You may discuss this with her at your leisure.
Direction in opera, as in every other form of theatre, adapts to the talent available at any given moment.

24 November 1976
To Olivier
Knowing what a scatterbrained old director you are, I am taking the liberty of putting the dates I am proposing on paper, as I don't imagine you had your handy note pad with you when I telephoned on Sunday. The rehearsal period for *Don Pasquale* would be between 6 November 1978 to the final dress on 5 December (the opera opens on 7 December). The cast would be Beverly Sills, Gabriel Bacquier and hopefully Alfredo Kraus. Not bad, I think you will admit.

I would also like to suggest that if you were to consider the work, you would use darling Tanya [Moiseiwitsch, as designer] because (1) she is perfect for it (2) you love her and (3) she knows this house backwards and will save you a lot of unnecessary hassles.

As to the work, I cannot think of anyone, with the possible exception of Eduardo de Filippo, who would bring the inventiveness, humour and humanity to the piece you would.

1 December 1976
To Teresa Stratas
Herewith a few documents which you might find interesting.

Probably someone has sent you the Met souvenir programme already, but it is the only way I can show you a couple of the set photographs, and in colour, without going to enormous expense. Apparently reproduction costs something in the nature of $150 and I don't feel that at a time of crisis, the total expense of all the set photographs in colour would be justified. The trouble is the black and white are not very inspiringly lit, but they will give you some sense of the space and where the doors and windows are. The costumes are also in black and white, but will give you some idea of the line Jocelyn has taken and, of course, nothing will be gone ahead with too far until you have arrived in New York.

I have been on holiday recently and blocked the entire play, move by move. And I must say for once I am pleased. Jocelyn's insistence on achieving complete fidelity to the composer's wishes paid off beautifully in that I was able to complete the blocking in five days and it all makes great sense and basically springs from the movements indicated by the composer and in some cases by Wedekind.

I, in fact, have only one worry which is that dreadful first week when you are involved with *La Perichole*. I screamed a great deal when Tom Graham informed us that he had made a mistake in your planning and that you would not be available for the week of the 14th, because it is of course in that week that I want to block out the play and try to solve all the simple, physical problems. It is going to be enormously difficult without your input. Obviously I must go ahead and attempt to put the opera on its feet and I have very little fear that you will find any of the moves uncomfortable. The danger is that an essential quality of ensemble might be missing, and it is also in those first few rehearsals that one can discuss, in a more relaxed situation, reason, motivation, movement, etc. However, I know we will be able to work something out. It is just a pity in terms of our personal contact that we do not have this time. As you probably know, immediately prior to your arrival I am involved in *Prophète* and then the *Carmelites* which makes any earlier contact a virtual impossibility.

About the character. What can I tell you that you don't intuitively know already? I have said to you and to everyone that I believe Lulu is as innocent of the destruction she causes as the flame is innocent of the moth's death. The former is as beautiful and burns because it is. The moth is beautiful and attracted to it, and there is nothing anyone in the world can do about it. What is most interesting to me is the manner in which each man makes *Lulu* in his own image, until all men drive her to prostitution. You, I am sure, have experienced as I have, that awful feeling which comes when someone who protests that they love you immediately tries to make you over in their image of what you should be. This happens to *Lulu* continually, while she continually is herself. In fact, she is the only person in the piece who does know her true nature and accepts it, and her nature is pure innocence. So innocent that she cannot even see the advisability of conforming to the world's demands in order to survive.

How do we arrive at this on stage? I think I have an idea but I can only really discuss that in conversation. As you will see, all the costumes tend to a very simple line, even the cabaret costumes have been made more like Isadora Duncan and much less than the customary Berlin tart which has been the habitual manner of presentation. The simple line and colour in contrast to all the others will, I am sure, help to generate the over-all atmosphere one wants to create around her. I suppose if I had any advice to give to you at this distance, it would be think simple, think still, eliminate gesture, rely on your extremely expressive face and its ability to project thoughts.

I hope in the first week of rehearsals to treat the opera as a play and not worry too much about the music, and I hope to have a little time when you arrive to adopt the same process, so that the patterns of thought are clearly established in your head without the stimulus or distraction of the music.

I am sorry if you have felt neglected over the past few months, but I really thought you would prefer to be left alone. However, feel free to write or call at any time and I will answer your queries.

22 December 1976
Memo to Bliss, Bronson, Volpe and Reppa
If we genuinely believe that our Chagall *Magic Flute* is a treasure, better care must be taken with the physical production before it can be revived. Specifically, the entire production needs to be repainted.

Due to an earlier misjudgement when the production was originally at the paint frame, the canvas was not correctly primed and as a result, all the colours have faded noticeably. To light the show with any semblance of the intended brilliance of the design is impossible.

Could I have your responses to this.

22 February 1977. Prophète.
After Wechsler lunch agreement to develop my basic idea of Sept. – emphasise Bruegel, maybe use figures as well as locations in projections – this opens up many more possibilities. The stage is a skeletal cathedral, wooden buttresses, perhaps a central cross, cart, buttress and window contain projection screens. The work becomes a mystery play exploring man's relationship with God and men. The work is 'acted' simply. The decor is (hopefully) a combination of the oldest and newest ways of dealing with the miraculous.

9 March. Wechsler breakfast.
Basic idea works – model too perfect. Cathedral should not be finished – scaffolding, rope etc. The people present a mystery in the shell of an unfinished cathedral. We will eliminate the central cross (too sophisticated a bit of machinery) and substitute 3 carts – maybe none. Flat stage agreed; possibility of big rear screen discussed. The whole theory of the projections to be discussed next time.

Notebook:
February/March 1977
Over a year since the last *Aida* entry. Why?
Better to do than write about doing.
However, there's a question I want to keep in mind. After the final dress rehearsal of *Prophète* there's been a great deal of sideline talk about a change in the working atmosphere at the Met. Is this a fact, or is it simply that everyone, given responsibility and reason, can see a direction, or is it that they feel *Prophète* is going to be a success?

(I am not in any way sure that it is. It needs three more days to simplify and consolidate itself.) Whatever the production's faults may be it is at least *itself*. It aims for a chaste and sometimes severe beauty and every now and then it achieves it.

But it will be interesting to see if the good feeling and will in the chorus, stage staff, and principals reflects overall changes, or is it only the smell in the nostrils of a little success?

7

Carmelites

Notebook:

I want to defend Poulenc against his detractors. Why can't a musical butterfly have religious feelings, even though he might have mixed the cult of the Virgin Mary with the cult of Venus?

In 1950 I first saw Poulenc's *Dialogues of the Carmelites* at Covent Garden. The evening never left my mind and I thought about it often, and what I felt it lacked.

It was the ending that most disappointed me. The procession of nuns up the stairs and to the guillotine always seemed awkward and extravagant. More than twenty years later, after my own production at the Metropolitan Opera House, I replied to one disgruntled patron's letter with this:

22 February 1977
To Mr Thurston Child
In the final scene, we did not work on two levels mostly for the reason of the enormous expense in building a structure but also because, having seen the production in London and Milan, I found it very unsatisfactory. All that happens in this production is that one by one the sisters disappear from the light into the darkness at the end of the cross.

As early as 1974, I was experimenting with the idea of a cross as the main focal point for an opera. In my diary in April 1974 my notes on *Prophète* included several drawings of crosses as floor plans and this note: 'Something to do with a cross and massive projections.'

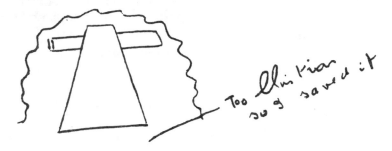

Later on in the same year as I was thinking of *La Juive*, I also sketched a cross but this time the notes read: 'Too Christian – so I saved it.' That same day: 'Why do I always impose the strongest physical discipline I can imagine on everything?'

When I first accepted the position of Director of Productions, my goal was to bring 20th-century opera to the Metropolitan but there was a great deal of work to be done both artistically and financially before an opera with the demands of *Carmelites* could be accepted.

When I arrived, there wasn't anyone who could give you a detailed reading of a working drawing with a cost on it. We had to find someone who could do that, so that we didn't continue to soar automatically over budget. We also tried to exercise a little more control over the kinds of sets designers put on the stage, which at that point were getting bigger and bigger until there was little room left for the singers or anything. Reorganising the workshops – that's what the first three years were about. Creating a working organism, making room to manoeuvre in, making room to experiment in, and at the same time developing an aesthetic slightly more practical in terms of 20th-century economy.

I wrote then: 'Two seasons are looking uninspired, lacking a flavour. A new work needed: *Carmelites* could be done *almost* out of stock! The work has not been seen for eight years and *never* with an international cast: Crespin, Blegen, Horne etc. I have a great response to the work. Conductor? French? Staging? Stark. Austere.'

Once I arrived at the point where the Met was capable of presenting an opera such as *Carmelites*, I set about dealing with the second problem: lack of interest in the piece. Without the help of generous and forward thinking patrons, it would never have been done. The nuns' costumes came from *Suor Angelica*, the peasants' costumes from *Andrea Chenier*, the raised floor was taken from *Boris Godunov*, and the copper tubing was donated by a patron. This kind of thinking and planning, new to the Met, made it possible to bring the entire production in for $65,000, which was $3,000 under budget.

4 January 1977
To Mr James Dolan
We are hoping to demonstrate with *Carmelites* that opera productions of a consistently high calibre can indeed be produced for less than six figures. A key element in that plan is the tremendous generosity of patrons like yourself shown to us through their special contributions.

Mr [Schuyler] Chapin was very concerned about the production style, which had got very grandiose, very heavy, on account of the size of the house. The thing about the Met is it has taken the grandiose beyond the limits of Cecil B. DeMille. And it seems because of all the gilt and grandeur inside that you expect what is on stage to top it. I think that's putting the cart before the horse. One of the first things I tried to do was to get a production of a modern opera into the repertoire with practically no bulk scenery – a production that said to the audience – 'Look, there is another way of doing things.'

It's amazing. If there is not too much on the stage you can see any detail, you can see every face and movement. If you concentrate and if you are shown where to look. It's a question of angle, of stage relationship with the audience, and volume. All those things were discovered very slowly.

The audience should be looking for faces, not windmills. The size of the Met creates a fight between the volume of the auditorium and the volume of the human figure, which has got to be made dominant to 4,000 people. So you try all sorts of tricks to thrust that figure into prominence. But with a 4,000 seat theatre that can be very, very difficult.

What we've been attempting all along is somehow in the

volume of that vast house to make the human being more important than the scenery. And that's one of the objects to work for – to create an audience that will listen in a different way and look in a different way. I want more acceptance for 20th-century work. In music, painting, and in the theatre. A lot more willingness to hear fresh and see fresh.

Taking certain decisions about how to do *Aida* enabled us to move forward to *Carmelites* and get the audience to accept modern works in a new style. But the work from *Carmelites* onward is all to create an audience for these commissioned American works that the Met must be responsible for, because nobody else will be.

Notebook:
Once the house was ready to handle *Carmelites*, I had to deal with the administration. The general consensus of opinion was that it would not be well received by the public, but the plans for keeping the costs down forced the powers that be to decide whether they were serious about the future of the house; if they were to continue to demand that costs were kept down, they could not refuse this project and still have their demands taken seriously. The battle was won but not without restrictions. The first being a Saturday matinée opening, hitherto unheard of, and of course they would not include the production in the next year's repertory.

Once the project was accepted, I could proceed with the casting. Top of the list was Maria Callas.

26 September 1975
To Maria Callas
As you probably know, I have taken on the job of Director of Productions at the Met. One of the operas I have wanted to put into the repertoire in the first season that I share with Maestro Levine is *Les Dialogues des Carmelites*. However, I made a very strict proviso that it could only work if the Met assembled the greatest cast of singing actresses available in the operatic world. When I suggested some weeks ago that you should be approached for the role of the Mother Superior I had very little hope that you would consider it. I need hardly tell you my reaction to the news I received this morning was more than joyful.

I have a particular commitment to the work, for reasons with which I will not bore you now. But on occasions when I have seen it in the past, however thrilling it has been musically, the sheer acting has left a great deal to be desired. In particular, the role of the Mother Superior has usually been subjected to a rather limited range of cliché histrionics. If you were to consent to play the role, I think the full power of the piece, its subtlety, atmosphere, and above all its deep concern with basic human fears, will at last stand a chance of full recognition.

I hardly dare write much more, for in a burst of enthusiasm one can very easily 'oversell'. I hope we may hear from you in the affirmative in the not too distant future. Until that time, to quote my national poet, 'Expectation whirls me round'.

With a certain amount of relief at her negative reply, I immediately got on to my real first choice, Régine Crespin. James' lack of faith in the piece meant that he didn't want to conduct it. Another bonus.

7 November 1975
To Régine Crespin
Can I tell you what a great pleasure it was to meet you, having admired you across the footlights for so long. It is even more exciting to think that, if Poulenc is smiling on us from above, you may be able to be in *The Carmelites*. I cannot tell you emphatically enough how this would thrill me and how immeasurably it would add to the production, which I hope will firmly obliterate any lingering sense of the work's inadequacies which may be left around.

22 December 1975
To Régine Crespin
I need hardly tell you how thrilled I am that we are going to be working together on *The Carmelites*. I am asking for a clause to be inserted (in small print) at the bottom of your contract, which requires that after the piano dress rehearsal you come in front of the curtain and, in the costume of Mother Superior, sing for me alone, 'Je ne suis pas ce que l'on pense.' Unless you comply with this request, I shall have to reconsider your contract completely.

30 December 1975
To Michel Plasson

First may I say how very happy I am that you have agreed to undertake the musical direction of *The Dialogues of the Carmelites*. It is an opera that I have loved for many years. As you probably know, I managed to slip it into the repertoire very late in the planning in place of a revival of *Vanessa*. I did this because I think the company needs this work in preparation for other modern operas which James Levine and I intend to stage here.

It seems to me, in a house of this size, where the production costs are so enormous, the only way to introduce modern works into the repertoire is to stage them as simply and economically as possible. If we make this experiment work with *The Carmelites* it opens up enormous possibilities in the twentieth-century repertoire.

The set is to be very simple. Basically, the floor, the shape of a cross at a not too steep angle, and a few elements of scenery flown in and out, to indicate the change of location. The visual interest should be sustained by a constant pattern of movement between scenes and during interludes, nuns either at prayer or going about the ordinary routines of work – scrubbing floors, preparing food, and so forth.

So far, the sketches I have made look interesting and I am now working more closely with the designer. I must confess to inventing one or two rituals, which I doubt if the Carmelites would approve. However, so far I have, as you will imagine, failed to gain entry to a convent and I am having to use my imagination and several reference books.

24 June 1976
To Régine Crespin

I hope you are well and having a good summer. I have just come back from L.A. which is, I think, the silliest city I have ever been in. The only thing sillier than the city is the people!

I have some good news, or at least I hope you will think it is good news. I remember when you first spoke to me about *Carmelites* and Poulenc, you were surprised that we were doing it in French and told us that you must be left alone to mull it over. When we had lunch at Sardi's you mentioned to me that it was the composer's wish that the work should be played in the language of the country in which it was being performed. The person who was concerned that it should be in French was Shirley Verrett. However, in the interim I have had a conversation with Allen Hughes of the *New York Times* and with Joseph Machlis who did the English translation. Allen Hughes points out that if it were done in French at the Metropolitan, when he does a long article for the NYT before the opening, he would have to draw attention to the fact that this was not the composer's wish.

I, when you first mentioned the fact that it should be in English, was very happy and hoped that we would be able to do that, but Shirley's opinion prevailed for a while. However, I have since talked to her and she has come around to the view that English would be better. I do hope that this will be agreeable to you. There is no problem with the language, as your English is more accurate than most of the Americans who sing in the house. I just hope that you have not begun learning in too much detail. The translator, Mr Machlis, is ready, willing and happy to work with us on the version and make any alterations we suggest. Therefore I am hoping to pick your brains once more about your part and indeed anything else that you feel is wrong in the version.

Well, now the summer is coming up and I am going to have a rest. The sets of *Carmelites* are in the model stage and very interesting, very sparse and bare, so that the whole responsibility will rest on the singing and the acting. That will give you something to think about until the Fall.

I don't think I have to tell you how thrilled I am that you are doing this work with us and how especially thrilled I am that your first suggestion (i.e. English) should become possible. Thank you so much for making it and planting it in my head so early.

Western Union Night Letter 29/30 June 1976
From Régine Crespin
Very astonished your letter because my opinion was always exactly the contrary. I even said I would not sing *Dialogues* if not in French. I do hope you will not translate Bernanos in English. I am definitely against it.

30 June 1976
Nightletter to Régine Crespin
I wonder if my astonishment equals yours. Please wait for my letter which follows immediately.

30 June 1976
To Régine Crespin
I feel a little like one of those characters in *Rashomon*, each of whom has a different version of the same event. My first concern is that I should not only have misunderstood you, but also I obviously caused you some offence. However, let me attempt to compound my sin by reiterating the problem.

Both Fabrizio Melano and I have a distinct memory of your saying that it was the composer's wish that the piece should be presented in the language of the country in which it was performed. This information struck me quite forcibly as it was altogether new to me. Now it is perfectly possible that in my excitement at the possibility of your even considering the Mother Superior, my enthusiasm obliterated an accurate memory. For this I can only apologise once again, and I beg you to believe that anything I have done in this area has been with the best interest of the composer at heart.

When, six weeks ago, I was faced with Allen Hughes of the *New York Times* pointing out to James Levine and myself (in the most friendly fashion) that were we to do the opera in French he would be forced to draw attention to the fact that it was against the composer's wish, and this in turn would affect Harold Schonberg, his colleague and immediate superior, I think I would have been foolish not to re-examine the situation once again. Having done so and listened to the arguments, I became convinced that Poulenc, Hughes and all the other parties were correct in feeling that the audience's understanding of the *Dialogues* was paramount. I was further convinced by my (obviously false) memory of your position.

So now what do we do? First let me beg you to do nothing until James [Levine] and I have spoken to you. You are, I believe, working with him at Ravinia on the 15th and 16th. Would you please discuss it with him at that time and I will make a point of coming out to see you if by chance you are not passing through New York.

Your appearance in this work is of paramount importance to

me and to the Metropolitan. Were you not coming to America I would come across to Paris to see you immediately, and I hope that we can arrive at a solution.

With much love and great regret for the worry I must have caused you.

Rehearsals for *Carmelites* – with Régine Crespin – started on 17 January, the day before the opening of *Le Prophète*.

Incidentally, once again I find that in spite of intense preparation (2 years) I still rely on the stimulus of light, decor and people to arrive at the final stop. Fault? Dare I ever risk walking into a rehearsal with only my instinct in my hand?

6 January 1977
To Leighton Kerner
Thank you very much for the article in the programme. For the first time in years the programme reflects accurately some of the production's intentions. It is going well but as everyone gets more confident, I get more nervous. You know the feeling. I expect, anyway, to see you on the battlefield.

6 January 1977
To Eileen Atkins
Thank you very much for your letter. Forgive me if I don't write in great length, but I am in the middle of rehearsals for three operas at once. When are we going to work together?

18 January 1977
To Arnold Wesker
. . . I have learned that to direct plays is not enough. One must, in order to achieve anything approaching perfection, control all of the elements: promotion, building, budget, even the choice of carpenter and costume workshop, and become, in effect, producer as well as director. The results of this have always been, if not perfection, at least on-budget and efficient and sometimes original.

25 January 1977
Memo to Patrick Veitch [Head of Publicity]
With ears half-tuned in to the car radio this morning, I heard the

most appalling piece of bad taste I have ever heard in any advertising campaign. The actual words were something like: 'What did Poulenc say before he died? Civilisation!' Either my car radio may be faulty or my hearing defective, but will you, in the future, send all publicity to me before it is presented to the public so that we may avoid this sort of unfortunate thing in the future?

27 January 1977
Memo to Patrick Veitch
I think the *Carmelites* poster is enormously successful. Congratulations! Also, the figures for the sales report for the week of the 17th: There is one column I would like more details on in the complimentary area. Can you give me some sort of break-down on Complimentary 'other'. It seems a very large figure and I know it is justified, but I would like to know how it is made up.

31 January 1977
To Carl Edwards
. . . Thank you very much for your very kind congratulations on *Prophète*. I apologise for taking so long to answer your letter. However, we began rehearsals for *Dialogues of the Carmelites* even before *Prophète* had opened. All of the reviews have been most appreciative of our efforts, but I especially want to thank you for your keen and perceptive congratulations. You have indeed caught one of my deepest concerns here in the house. With such a vast stage and even larger house, the acoustical problems are enormous as well as variable. I believe those few feet helped us tremendously, and I hope that with the other new productions – of *Carmelites* and *Lulu* – we will be able to achieve similar musical standards.

Notebook:
I made one of my rare visits to a cocktail party the other night and a grand lady with a loud voice came up and said: 'Mr Dexter, I trust you will not make *Carmelites* as austere as *Le Prophète*?' I replied, 'Madame, the production of *Carmelites* will make Bert Brecht look like a Renaissance voluptuary.'

1 February 1977
To Jocelyn Herbert
The inevitable has happened. Teresa Stratas has cancelled [*Lulu*]. The details are too boring to go into at the moment, and I am too busy killing nuns to have had time to be angry. I'll give you all the details when I see you in New York.

3 February 1977
To Sister Michael Ann
I would like to take this opportunity to express my gratitude to you for your help to all of us in the forthcoming production of *Carmelites*. Whilst I am sure many small details will be wrong, that fault will rest on my shoulders and not on yours.

It was most kind of you to give your time. I am not sure if your order permits you to attend theatrical performances but if you can and would wish to see a performance of the opera, I would be very glad to make arrangements to send you whatever seats you require.

Diary:
Think through the working process again. How much preparation is too much – or too little.

Diary:
Carmelites worked! Two years later it returns as part of the rep. How and why did that happen? And why did *Rigoletto* not? Obviously, do those things which you want to do. You are a rotten repertoire director. Consider your position vis à vis the Met.

John J. O'Connor in The New York Times:
John Dexter has mounted a theatrical event in which there appear to be no seams between the music and the text. There are no pauses for scenery changes or applause. The conception flows as inevitably as the tragedy itself.

Diary:
Remember the miscalculation at the end of *Carmelites*. **Never** re-block anything without checking it from the front. No matter how many musicians are waiting in the pit.

Byron Belt on the revival at the Met:
From the opening tableau of prostrate nuns through the hideous impact of the scene at the guillotine, the Met's *Dialogues* is a shattering emotional and artistic experience.

7 February 1977
To Tony Harrison
. . . The success of *Carmelites* has raised many interesting questions about opera in English. It's been very successful, which surprises me as I thought the work was too quiet to appeal to a Met audience. Apparently not to judge from the reaction.

Prophète also seems to be successful so the batting average is two out of three balls hit over the boundary. And the googly is about to be bowled at me by Alban Berg. I pray for a straight bat, 'Bumping pitch' *and* a blinding light.
All may yet be well.

Diary:
But the funny thing is that *Carmelites* will now do better business than *Madame Butterfly*, unless *Butterfly* has a superstar. Quite a few of the standard bread and butter works are not as bread and butter as they used to be. The public wants to see some difficult works.

Leighton Kerner in The Voice, 1987
I hope no Metropolitan Opera administrators have missed the irony that, in the 1986–87 season, which ended April 18 and included no less than three Zeffirelli-Puccini extravaganzas and a couple of expensive-looking new bombs from other hands, the finest production by far was the revival of John Dexter's decade-old staging of Poulenc's *Dialogues of the Carmelites*. . . . It was an oasis of theatrical sanity and poetry in a desert of antidramatic indulgence.

Diary:
Now that the *Carmelites* is over I think that the struggle to achieve a tolerance in the public and critics is over. Not exactly the right to fail, we have not yet earned that, but perhaps the right to make our own mistakes.

8

Opera in America

14 August 1978
Billy Budd: Begin Tech. week. If we have shaped a new instrument, we are this season testing it. It's good to know that it *can* be tested to the maximum with *Budd*. Then the responsibility and the blame is mine for pushing too hard too soon.

And now that all I have to do is work, it should be possible to work more thoroughly in, on and for each production. Don't cut corners or compromise. Talk, explain, *communicate*. You can't do it on your own.

Re-commit for another three years, one production a year. Once or twice in the office, talk to James Levine about repertoire. Now. Control of administration. If the administration does not work for *us*, we change the administration.

21 August 1978
Budd begins.
Act I, Scene 1
Ghastly day. Think about why, and get the work pattern and tempo right. I could kick myself for not thinking of this method of work as pleasure before – why waste agony when you can use enjoyment.

22 August 1978
Continue Act I, Scene 1. Act I, Scene 3 (fight), Act II, Scene 3, Act II, Scene 4
Always begin with 15–30 minutes of the music. If the music has not been learnt, the acting can never happen. You must be able to sing and think at the same time. Can a singer think thoughtfully *and* get the music right? Too often the direction is blamed, when lack of musical knowledge is actually guilty.
Indicated acting is no substitute for thought.

Note to JL: Use your homosexuality, don't flaunt it. It does not matter if we all end up in bed as long as the work improves. Don't worry, we WON'T.

24 August 1978
Billy Budd Cabin scenes.
James Morris: your arms are part of your body but you don't sing with them or *think* with them, they are used for physical labour.

25 August 1978
If I can keep to this work pattern I may get better.
Don't forget to explain the relationship between *Billy Budd* and *Bartered Bride*, beyond the initial one!

25 August 1978
To Anthony Bliss
. . . *Budd* is going very well, having been almost completely blocked in 3 or 4 days. Peter [Pears] is in marvellous voice, if a bit spotty on the text, and everyone seems to be impressed with the look of the show.

28 August 1978
Comedy is about good living.
Tragedy is about good dying.
Everything is old fashioned when it has been seen, so don't worry about being fashionable.

29 August 1978
Should we ask them to stand for Ben after the perf. or is it too sentimental and would Peter be upset?

30 August 1978
Act II, Scene 1. Battle completed!!
Early finish.

1 September 1978
Home early. Three days off!!

6 September 1978
Talk about the directions.
Job to make connections for Forster/Melville/Britten.

16 September 1978
First Dress rehearsal *Budd.*

19 September 1978
However *Budd* turns out, I must have a clear visual picture of the movement so that there is time for development, repeats, and character establishment for the chorus.
BUDD OPEN.

20 September 1978
It worked. Does this make the future easier or harder?

Notebook:
Opera has borrowed many things from theatre but not, I think, a sense of purpose or social responsibility.

Only in a permanent house with all the resources available can I experiment with teaching. If singing, music and dancing are part of life, they can, if taught properly, be part of *everyone's* life. Find the unconverted and convert them. When I refer to total theatre I take it as understood that in any view a theatre is only total when its involvement with the community is total.

Schools. A pre-season note prior to an end of term report. I can, quite literally, claim to be a true representative of the unrepresented – those uneducated by the state. Leaving school at thirteen or fourteen, education began. I had learned to read, I had not learned arithmetic. I could speculate for some time on the interior reason for my acceptance of – and greed for – words, and my rejection of figures, but this note is to discuss why I feel so passionately about teaching and being taught, and why also I feel that it is the only step to survival and the future that can be made by the Met. Everything else is window dressing. Only teaching is for the future. Each night's performance is for that incredible night only. I talk about teaching because I have so much to learn that I could have learnt years ago. All art teaches by direction; it teaches even when the artist does not want it to. It teaches because, after looking, a man or woman must think. All art has the mindless side alleys which are supposedly the province of opera. Idiocies and illogicalities only last in a work of art when they have something to teach. Learning and teaching interact upon each other. The artist must always most want to teach us how to see, how to hear, and many, many of us do not want to learn for fear of disturbing our instinct, facing a reality or a new vision.

However, if the artist is forceful or original or obsessed enough, we will be forced sooner or later to learn from him. It appears to me odd that opera, surely the most available of the arts, should have become such an élitist area, and not just the money élite and the intellectual élite, but that vast screaming horde, packed with facts and arrogance, who presume that the way in which people see and hear must be their way, who never hear or see anything for the first time without a film of preconception across the eyes. They are unteachable. Begin at the beginning, forget trying to train an audience to see our work, we must train people to see the work done by those who follow us. See the work and hear it fresh each time should be the aim of any audience, the major part of our work lies in that direction.

Do we all know how to communicate to children? How can you teach without influencing choices which properly belong to the individual later in life? Try to offer up the choice and leave it to them.

'Let them see through a window,' said Tony Bliss at dinner. 'Yes,' I added, 'and let's open a door.'

Somehow we must take them to the threshold but not push them through. Let them walk on their own and in their own time, but they will have seen and heard enough to propel them, if they have any guts, to be moved by what their eyes and ears can do to enhance every moment. That is the objective. How to reach it?

Firstly, set a target, call it *Parade*; you have three years to take your aim. Keeping that target in sight, consider the muscle that will be needed to hit the bull. Consider also the stillness and concentration. Keep a Gradgrind eye out for facts. Facts of money, material and time. Make these facts our servants not our masters. Use the economic pressures to build, not a mini Met but a mobile Met.

Discuss the stepping stones. Student discussion and TV, *The Bride*, intermission features, ballet, mobile met, *Parade*, opera for students, not slapped on performances of *Butterfly*, etc. Student discussion in general (and *Rigoletto* in particular).

The 'Mini Met' in my view began in a far too grandiose manner which bore no relation to the economic situation or to the needs of the future. It was bound to collapse in the face of the first fiscal wind which blew against it. It is my proposal that we begin modestly with one small project directed towards the smallest audience (8–12 year olds), a group of dancers and singers *totally* mobile and instantly available. During the upcoming tour to perform in schools prior to a full-scale attack in the NY area in the following season. This in turn will develop into the group which will tour in the following season first in tour cities then in NY a special performance for students of Carl Orff's *Der Mond* and finally in the Milhaud operas in the 80/81 (or *Parade*) season.

I can find no evidence that wisdom is a natural property of age and obesity. It should belong to the young and beautiful.

Whatever the final results are from our production of *The Bartered Bride*, and however much public approbation or disapprobation it receives, it must be said at the outset that our old friend, serendipity, played a great part in its inception. At one of the earliest meetings I had the confusing pleasure of attending, *Die Fledermaus* was under discussion, in spite of the fact that a new production was being presented across the way [at the New York City Opera]. After the meeting, Maestro Levine and I were walking in silence down the corridor – and silence, I can assure you, is an unusual quality between us. This silence was slightly more tense than usual. I remember breaking it with a phrase which, without stopping the conversation, sprung it into another channel: 'Jimmy, wouldn't you rather do a less played-out comic opera – *Bartered Bride*, for instance?'

By the time we had sat down to supper the opera was cast and both its translator, Tony Harrison, and its designer, Josef Svoboda, chosen.

As to the style for which we were aiming, it was to be an impression of a village, an attempt to render Southern Bohemia in imaginative rather than realistic terms, and to allow the audience to grasp the theatricality of the design rather than its realism. As is usual with Prof. Svoboda's scenery, one has the infinite pleasure of seeing it on the stage for the first time half lit, badly hung and not working, or not seeming to work, in any coherent way at all. And yet, after a few hours, suddenly new ideas appear. In this case, a complicated idea which in its final analysis should be simplicity itself. It is fortunate that the preparation we have all done into character, background and village life has been fairly deeply prepared, for the greatest part of the stylistic experiment lies ahead of us.

14 February 1978
To Teresa Stratas
My friend, Tony Harrison, who is doing the English version for *The Bartered Bride*, is in town through Thursday, February 23rd. It might be instructive and, I think, fairly interesting if you and he could find an hour to go over each other's ideas.

15 September 1978
Bartered Bride. Begin to concentrate on Theory and Practice of Shadow Play; including how to tell Svoboda about the horse and cart. Settle work plan.

18 September 1978
At this stage my visual picture of *Bride* is packed with autumn qualities. Need shadow light to rehearse to see if the silhouette idea is valid.
SEASON OPENS with *Budd*!

29 September 1978
To Teresa Stratas
You were talking yesterday about doing some more reading, so get your gorgeous Greek eyes into this [*The Golden Bough*, James Frazer], you clever bitch, and you will know, when I stage the last act fully, why, in the final moments, you and Jenek are the consummation of a fertility rite. Get well soon!

Notebook:
This year, for the first time, it is planned that the director, designer and their associate artists will make preliminary visits to the schools rather than the schools coming to us as strangers. These contacts would be made through the *Bartered Bride* Intermission Features.

The initial contacts with a variety of schools in the New York Metropolitan Area would be through the new Production Director's rehearsals. These are a series of 4 or 5 rehearsals, open to 50 students with a question and answer period conducted by various production staff members and the director, after each rehearsal. They would eventually lead selected school children to participate in a new production (*Tirésias*, *Parade* and *L'Enfant*) in the 1980–81 season.

19 June 1978
Memo to Bliss, Levine, Ingpen, Riecker, Volpe, Coughlin, Berkowitz, Sarsen, Bronson, Reuben, Browning, Hoestetter [all staff at the Met]
Bartered Bride Intermission Features
As I am committed to the *Bartered Bride* telecast, I feel that its format must be re-examined. It appears to me that we are preaching our message to the already-committed in the most stiff and formal manner. For that reason I would like both of the *Bartered Bride* intermission features to follow a different format, entirely based on questions and answers and the reactions of 30 to 50 students to the process of creating an opera. This format can be worked in with the Student Director's Rehearsals and the New Production's Previews, and would follow the production through discussions and its first rehearsals, through the problems of text with Tony Harrison and David Stivender, through the problems of interpretation and integration of dance with Pavel Smok, design with Josef Svoboda and Jan Skalicky, then finally music with Maestro Levine. It should be aimed primarily at a group of uninformed, unprompted students. In short, a format aimed at the uncommitted. These discussions can be punctuated with short extracts of rehearsal tapes to illustrate various points or certain shots of the production staff discussing models and plans.

With careful editing and frequent taping sessions, I believe we can achieve three things – actually teach 50 students to look, think and listen to a piece of music; present an intermission feature to the committed that will be informative, interesting and may contain some things they would not already know; and perhaps reach out with an approach not just aimed at the opera buff.

28 September 1978
To Anthony Bliss
Yesterday I received a message that I was to find time to discuss with Michael Bronson education, schools, and the tour cities. This I cannot do.

Michael was ignored in the preliminary plans of the school

programme because I know that his influence would have robbed those of us who were giving our time to launch a new and risky enterprise of any energy, drive, and good humour we may have been able to bring to the experiment. I must tell you that if he should initiate the schools programme with the tour cities or in New York, I feel I will have no alternative other than to withdraw from the programme. I feel that strongly about it. I must ask you to assist my work in the development of the educational and touring programmes by allowing me to select the staff who are to develop it. The decision is of course yours as Executive Director, and I will accept it whatever it is.

The last time I tried to raise this subject with you in the presence of Joe Volpe [technical director] and Jane Hermann, I was accused of creating a cabal. I feel that the accusation was entirely unjust. I had merely intended to bring an intolerable situation before you in the company of two people whom you respect, but who admittedly were finding it impossible to function in the face of Michael's perpetual interference. Your accusation that day negated any further serious discussion and, furthermore, made me withdraw from any further attempt to disperse the fog which continually surrounds all discussions concerning Michael. (Incidentally, this fog is made all the more dense by his staff, who are as out of touch with the present reality of the Met's goals as he is himself.)

Now, please do not regard this memo as an ultimatum. I am deeply distressed. I also believe I have my limitations. In order to develop and extend this programme with all its attendant extra work and headaches, I need people of intelligence and imagination around me. Without this it simply becomes a treadmill. If I have expressed myself in language stronger than you find acceptable, I am sorry. However, I have put a great deal of thought and effort into the education and mobile planning because I believe in it. I believe it to be the path to a living future of public service for the house, without which it will become a museum, unconnected to the city or to the world around it; and not least importantly, with little justification for any claim on federal or even local aid. I think you share this opinion. If so, please allow me to select with you the staff most suited to the on-going needs of this administration.

I would not like to be faced with an educational department

chosen without my consultation as has been the case with the television department.

2 October 1978
Bartered Bride starts.
Get all principals blocked *and* run thro' this week *or else*.

3 October 1978
So many actors, in the search for inner truth, lose interior clarity.

10 October 1978
If everyone *knew* it was going to be like this with a new text then why the fuck did they let me attempt it in five piano days?

17 October 1978
STAY IN FRONT!

18 October 1978
STAY IN FRONT! *Very* calm.

19 October 1978
WORK ON YOUR FEET!

20 October 1978
WORK ON YOUR FEET!
NO Keep calm. Concentrate on diction. Make-up. Lights. Costume.

21 October 1978
FEET UP.

25 October 1978
BRIDE OPEN.

25 October 1978
To Anthony Bliss
In the past two years I have studied a variety of educational approaches to children between the ages of 9 and 18, and it has become increasingly evident that to present a programme with any effectiveness, it must have a clear, and more importantly,

continuous presentation. We must likewise be able to present a consistent programme to funding sources as 'The Metropolitan Opera's Educational Programme'. The following is therefore my latest thinking on Education. Any school wishing to participate in opera education would follow the four phases I will outline.

Although the position of the Metropolitan as the only real national theatre in America is, I am sure, a big selling point with funding sources, I believe that, given the obvious time restrictions on most of our staff, our interest must primarily be a local one (that is to say New York City, the five boroughs and local New Jersey and Connecticut). There are certain national spin-off possibilities through touring and broadcasting that will become apparent, but the concentration of my approach is strictly within a local context.

Phase I (9 and 10-year-olds)
American children today are wrapped in an atmosphere of visual excitement created by discos, planetariums, movies, television and the 'New York experience'. Subsequently they are often bored by the simple elements of theatrical imagination which caught my eye at the same age. Children get their first glimpse of a TV set sometimes before they can even walk and are often taken to movies soon after they can talk. A child of nine or ten has already been exposed to the most sophisticated visual assault imaginable. We can never hope to beat these other media in our presentation. However, I believe the way we can interest young children today in the true magic of opera, is to present to them the operatic stage peopled by human beings rather than by electronic images on a screen. Then we must show them the tools of the theatre and through these tools they will learn to appreciate the sophisticated and truly magical art of the opera stage. We must do what we do best, and let them delight in *knowing* and *seeing* **how** it is done. Our advantage over these other media is being able to show the trick and still retain the magic; to show them the singers and the scenery and still to delight them. We must develop a continuous programme, beginning with the last two years of elementary school at a time when their imaginations are not yet troubled by the stigma of opera as a foreign, incomprehensible and boring art.

After watching the phenomenal success of various children's TV shows such as *Sesame Street* and *The Muppets*, it seems to me that a *puppet theatre* would be an ideal way to capture the imaginations of this youngest group of children. Combining all the various puppet techniques of Bunraku, glove puppets, marionettes and Balinese shadow puppets, we could construct a stage approximately 15 ft across and 12 ft high. It would combine the most sophisticated types of scenic diversions available. Using rear projections, film, flown scenery, and silhouettes, the stage would be constructed and lit in such a way that all, part, or none of the mechanics of the puppets and their operators would become visible to the audience as required. With the option of two pianos and singers seated in front of the stage, or with taped sound coming from speakers built into the stage, we would have an easily portable and, I believe, novel presentation. The repertory for this puppet theatre would include abbreviated versions of the major fairytale operas (*Hansel, L'Enfant, Rossignol* and *Hoffmann*).

In addition this first phase would include preliminary visits by singers and production staff. I believe it is essential that the first exposure children have to the world of opera is direct contact with people. These visits would be along the lines of the *Abduction* and *Mahagonny* school visits made this season. They should, however, be geared to the repertoire the students would first see in the puppet theatre. With some careful planning, I think we could enlist the commitment of staging and musical staff as well as our 'apprentice singers' to those visits.

The funding for this phase might most easily come from PBS TV or one of its sources. The easily televised nature of the puppet theatre would give them in return a highly marketable project.

Phase II (11–13-year-olds)
The puppet theatre project would be carried into this second age group, anticipating repertoire these students would be exposed to in the last two phases of our programme.
The main project here, however, would be the presentation of our Mobile Touring Projects (*Babar, Renard* etc.).

It is essential that personal visits by staff and artists be continued throughout all four phases of our educational programme. These contacts would then carry over into familiar faces in the opera house, which I hope will be one of the keys to capturing these children's attention.

In addition, the 12 and 13 year olds would be given a complete tour of the opera house. This would be followed by one dress rehearsal, most likely *Hansel and Gretel*.

At this age, children need to develop an awareness of particularly different forms of theatre and, for that reason, the Mobile Touring unit and a visit to the opera house should be introduced.

I believe that this phase of the educational project might best be funded through either private foundation support or the New York State grants, as the individual production nature of the Mobile Touring Projects is highly tangible and, therefore, most acceptable to these groups.

Phase III (14 & 15-year-olds)
By this age group the puppet theatre will have been fully explored and will in any case be considered 'kid stuff' by high school students.

The Mobile Touring Unit will continue its programme with an expanded repertoire.

Open dress rehearsals will be expanded to 2 or 3 per student.

The main addition for this age group will be the in-depth director's rehearsal meetings held on new productions or important revivals.

Finally, in these last two phases the beginnings of a junior subscription will begin with Opera News and other 'promotional' contacts with the students directly as opposed to all previous contact which was through their school system.

Phase IV (16–18-year-olds)
All aspects of this programme are the same as Phase III with a heavier concentration on director's rehearsals and perhaps some participation in the Mobile Touring Unit's presentations.

28 October 1979
From Bernard S. Miller, Hunter College, City University of New York

If there is a special spot in heaven – if there is a heaven – for people on earth who help lift horizons, then surely the John Dexter chair is already in place. Our students have been exposed to the finest minds at the Met as you prepared them for your production of *The Bartered Bride*. What's more, you and all your colleagues, treated them as adults. And they responded accordingly.

You would have done much if by this special exposure a select group of students learned both to appreciate and understand the beauty and the tremendously difficult work in staging opera performances. But you did more. Virtually our entire school has now become aware that opera exists, that history and literature, and art and technology and psychology as well as music are involved.

Some time in the future it may prove beneficial to discuss alternatives in the format used to acquaint teenagers with opera. Your initiative in seeking out students in the way you did can only mean that your heart is as noble as your mind. Thank you again.

22 November 1978
[Rehearsing *Don Pasquale* and *Don Carlo*]
I am not working as hard on these two, or at least not putting as much of myself into them. Maybe they will be better received.

Don Carlo

Now, admitting all the administrative bungling and total dishonesty of the original director in taking on more work than he could honestly execute, combined with the gigantic strain the decor (as indicated in the eight-months-late preliminary sketches) would have imposed upon the house, in addition to the lack of thought given to chorus disposition – or indeed any thought at all as to time, bulk, or money – the decision was forced, resisted and finally accepted that I would have to take on the production with Reppa and Diffen, and from that moment on the story is only of mild and somewhat gossipy interest!

The next problem was to convert James Levine to a full version (Fontainebleau and the Peasants' Chorus at the opening) and to find a way of keeping the projection costs below the estimated half a million. A little unsolicited hate mail was of enormous assistance in this area although James Levine and Anthony Bliss insist that this has not affected their judgement and that the only concern was a dramatic version which pleased *me!*

NOW THEN
How to give the impact of *Vespri* and avoid the mistakes of *Rigoletto* and *Aida* (can these be connected?) and think about them. Shakespeare for some reason seems a key. History for Schiller and Verdi was a starting point only. The theme is still the idea dominating *Aida*, *Ballo*, and so many other works, the collision of small, infinitely complex human beings with the gigantic political, religious disputes which seem only to destroy humanity. The sets must be as monumental in feeling as *Aida*, but more specific, less self consciously commenting on the overall, implacable granitic force of a crumbling empire, without losing the scale which dwarfs but does not finally overwhelm the people.

12 December 1978
Memo: **Turandot** 1980–81
The reason for attempting a new production and an *exxtra* production in this season is that it seems no longer to be possible to present our present *Turandot*; not perhaps the best of a very distinguished artist's work in the past (certainly now shabby beyond the standard admissible by the Metropolitan) and also lacking in certain dramatic values which might be easily, and not too expensively, reconstituted.

We will use as our basic design unit the steps from *Vespri*, covered in black velour, and arranged into configurations in which they have not so far been seen. In every act the steps are dominated by harsh, glittering, floating steel pylons, reaching into the sky, bearing in the first act the skulls and tattered remnants of the previous would-be lovers of Turandot. The elements which supply the feeling of barbaric China will be flown or tumbled silk cloths, painted either representationally in Chinese manner as landscapes, or in simple dramatic devices: i.e., a scarlet cloth that drops away, as Turandot enters, to reveal a white cloth behind it. Most of this will be impossible to describe without reference to a model. It is very important that these are interchangeable into different positions and that we are always aware of them, because, at the end of the opera (where Puccini finished Liu's procession of death), the stage picture will be her body being carried across the background up against the sky. A drape will slowly fall between us and that sight, and in front of it, Turandot and Calaf will be divested of their robes by invisible (Chinese) stage hands, and revealed in simple black costume. They will sing the final completed duet in these costumes with the chorus behind the drape or scrim, so that the emotional impact of the performance is sustained throughout. But the difference between the point at which 'the master laid down his pen' and the final conclusion is emphasised without destroying the overall atmosphere which will go from the riddle scene. (Furthermore, I believe we can handle this without blowing our economy skyways.) It will also enable us to say to Luciano [Pavarotti] and Montserrat [Caballé], 'Look, we cannot do our old production for you. We are devising a new one.' But it is also very important to stress to them at that time that the director has a particular theory of how to handle the end of the opera, after the death of Liu, and their consent to this must be obtained beforehand, preferably in the course of a meeting rather than in a letter.

The budget should be in the proportions of *Carmelites*. I am aware that this is asking for a great deal when one considers the exoticism of the background, but I am sure that, by taking the peasants' and as much of the supers' costumes as possible from the original Beaton costumes (only dyed down) and adding new principal costumes, we shall be able to arrive at a magnificent spectacle which also contains within it the rather sinister background of the piece.

Diary:
How to persuade 'Northern Gloom' [Tony Harrison] to tackle *Mahagonny* in one year? Tease him with the chance of outstripping Auden's version.

17 January 1979
To Tony Harrison
Your letters arrived, the first one last and the last one first, and I must say they depressed me more than anything in a long time.

Your statement that the March date is a non-starter has put the issue squarely on the table. If the translation [of *Mahagonny*] cannot be concluded by that March date, it would be unfair to expect the singers to have to learn it in the time remaining to them. You will know how very much I am distressed by having to say this, but I have no alternative.

As to the matter of Andrew Porter and Dale Harris, the *Bride*, and your reference to *Don Pasquale* at the end of your letter, Porter and Harris will write what they will write but you must not become paranoid on my part. There will always be envy, jealousy and plain stupidity. I am glad you have written a cool letter to *The Guardian*; however, as for myself, I do not have time to enter into a correspondence with newspapers and critics.

2 February 1979
To Tony Harrison
. . . It is neither sane nor artistically advisable to go ahead with the translation of *Mahagonny* under these conditions . . . We have decided to present *Mahagonny* in German for the first season and then reverse the process in the third season or in whichever season the television transmission is to happen.

5 February 1979
To Teresa Stratas
God knows you are having problems of your own at the moment but life here isn't much fun. How would you fancy doing *Don Carlo* and not having your principals TOGETHER until four days before the opening? So don't tell me about Paris, *Lulu* and strikes. Looking forward to seeing you on that date, by which time you will be too up or down to create any problems for me.

No doubt you are fully aware of the problems we are having with the Brecht estate which has now pushed us into an impossible and dangerous position, namely Tony working too fast and under too much pressure and needing a completion date of June instead of March. Of course you will realise how impossibly late this will be for most of the singers, though I have no doubt that you could accomplish it in that time. However, having worked with Tony as often as I have, I know that rushed work will be finally detrimental to him and to you. And so, in conjunction with Jimmy Levine and Joan Ingpen, we have decided to present the first run of *Mahagonny* in German, giving Tony another year to work and produce the definitive version he is capable of doing.

I tell you all this in advance of the others not to add to your problems at the moment but, hopefully, to relieve any pressures.

8 February 1979
To Eric Bruhn, Royal Danish Ballet
I was very surprised to read your letter to Joan Ingpen expressing your rejection of the Pasha Selim [in Mozart's *Abduction*]. I wish you were here and I could grab hold of your beautiful head and bang it into the wall. You must have seen a terrible production in which the dialogue was cut to ribbons and where the effectiveness of the Pasha seems to have been completely destroyed.

I am not such a fool as to offer you a small part (although in the words of Sir Laurence Olivier, or somebody or other, 'there are no small parts, only small actors').

Dear Eric, the part is superbly placed. Not only in its dialogue but in its dramatic force within the action. Consider the music of the entrance and in the scene that follows it. Consider what you and I can do with those 50 odd bars before 'Martern aller Arten'. Think of the ending of the piece.

Think, in fact, Eric, think, think, think! Please don't say no yet without us having met. My idea to cast you was not to cast a leading dancer in a small role, but to cast a leading actor in a leading role which is usually rendered insignificant by the miniscule mind of the performer wearing the costume. I look for something much bigger; as big as the cultural shock Vienna received when it realised the Turks were not barbarian, but also more cultured, more civilised and more humane than those treacherous coffee drinkers in Sacher.

About *Traviata*. Simply, my idea was this. That three or a maximum of four dancers are invited to Flora's party to entertain. That a small troupe have hitchhiked their way up through the Basque into Paris and are working in an 'amusing' proletarian café on the Left Bank. Flora, in a fit of enthusiasm, brings them into the house. They are far from being the exotics we normally expect but rather more have the slightly shabby aspect of Teresa and Lusillo (or have you forgotten?). As the dance proceeds various members of the ballet who are dressed as party guests, crinolines and all, grab an occasional shawl or a fan and proceed to imitate the 'genuine article' in the middle of the room. The genuine article, I think, should be rather shabbily dressed in black, but with brilliant shawls, fans, mantilla, etc. and the rest of the party guests, later in the scene, put on a kind of Parisian Spanish fancy dress made out of Spanish shawls and hair pins and bits of tortoiseshell comb. So don't worry about the look of it and don't worry about it not making any sense. I think that idea will make sense of it and turn it into much more of a party piece and also take the curse of the interpolated ballet number away from it.

Please, think about the other matter once again and let me talk to you about the part if it is at all humanly possible. I will be in Paris and London in a couple of weeks – where will you be?

17 February 1979
James Levine: I cannot any longer make the compromises needed to run the Met with you, and I am not developing.

19 February 1979
If the work is not creative and gives no pleasure, then stop boring people with complaints and MOVE ON. The only creative work I have done this year was on the *Bride*, and the full development of that work was hampered by a lack of collaboration with James Levine, who attended only three staging rehearsals prior to the orchestrals. Plasson may be a second rate conductor, but he at least collaborates. JL – either conduct less and administrate more, or don't make life more difficult by interfering in areas where you cannot comprehend the problems – i.e. *Manon, Bohème, Carlo.*

Week beginning 16 April 1979
The object of a revival: not necessarily to please those who did not like the original conception, but fully to realise that conception and make it more clear, and reveal its style more purely. The key is *Carmelites* – continue to develop the work you believe in and do *nothing else.*

23 April 1979
The administrative slog has a deadening effect on my own real work.

25 April 1979
Carmelites/Budd – all cast and conductors present at every rehearsal. Results good. *Bride/Carlo* – cast and conductor not present. Results bad. Any comments before I give mine?

23 May 1979
To Tony Harrison

I have put off writing this letter several times for perfectly obvious reasons, the last of them being that I had expected to be in London at this hour, rehearsing *As You Like It*. However, I expect you know all those complications.

The bad news is that the Board has decided that we must do *Mahagonny* in English as they do not believe the piece stands any chance in German. There is nothing I can do at this late date but accept their decision. And so, I am writing to tell you that the fall performances could take place in the English version by David Drew, and that I will talk to you of future possibilities when I see you in a week or two. I will be in London on 15 June and Jimmy at the National stage door will have my address. Please get in touch as soon as you can.

10 August 1979

The Met is a feasability study but in no way a passion. Therefore – leave.

5 September 1979
To James Levine

I am out here in New Jersey and I am putting my penny's worth into the Lenya textual problem [Lotte Lenya, widow of Kurt Weill]. (Incidentally, I am assuming that like me, you agree with 60% of the points she is making.) However, we both know that there is very little time for people to study the alterations we make, and the more alterations we make, the more rehearsal time will be eaten away.

I think Lenya might ease up on some of the 'to us' less important points if we could concede some major ones. To explain: it seems to me after the last few days of trying to pound the words into my head, I have been forced back to the Auden version time and time again. For instance, in No. 11, 'The Night of the Hurricane', Auden's 'dreams have all one ending' seems to me, both musically and poetically, so many light years ahead of anything else. If it were possible to reach an accommodation with the estates involved, we might be conceding various of the major points and affecting the principals only. We may also save ourselves a great deal of fiddling work which will finally produce no major effect on the quality of the evening, whereas the use of Auden's first stanza would be worth so much to the poetry of the evening that I think any hard work would be rewarding 100%. I don't think we should tamper with the translation of 'as you make your bed' as Drew/Geliot seems to me to be superior.

I am going to continue for the next couple of days to pursue this line. I wonder if you and David Stivender could find the time to pursue the same exercise whilst Charlie Riecker handles the contractual problem, and then possibly we could all meet on Monday or Tuesday to see if there is any hope of bringing the real *Mahagonny* to fruition on the stage of the Met. A production at the Met is too important to have a second best text. I would suggest that we consider the Dream and the Crane duet in the Auden version. Perhaps you might be able to come up with one other major, clean alteration we could make. I would then suggest Lenya pleads with Kalman [heir to the Auden estate] and we plead with Cassilly and Stratas. (There will be no problem with Stratas as she has already expressed detestation of the Drew/Geliot version.)

If we can bring this off, however much it costs, I think we will all be much happier. The snobbery implicit in the Auden will appeal to Jasper William Fisher [board member], and the poetry of the Auden will appeal to Drew. The former will pay the cost if appealed to on a personal level by one of us, and the other will agree, I think, to share the credit for the sake of the work. Regarding Mr Geliot, I am not so sure – he is a director and you know what that means!

13 September 1979
There is no one highly placed enough to interfere with what I want to do and if there is, I'll save my energy to deal with him or her. I will get on with my work at either the Met or the NT, but it will be my work and done as well as I can without compromise.

13 September 1979
Memo to Tony Bliss re Mahagonny Fight Director
With reference to the attached memo, may I ask you to reconsider? Whilst an ex-boxer may be able to stage a 'slogging match', without a professional fight director's guidance this will, I know, lead to serious accidents, and whilst Alaska Wolf Joe [Richard Cassilly] is supposed to be killed at the end of the fight, I would hate to see Plishka laid out on our stage.

I would not like to accept responsibility for a fight staged by an amateur.

9 October 1979
Memo to Werner Klemperer re *Abduction – Die Entführung aus dem Serail*
The Pasha chooses *another* rose (Werner dear), a white or a red it's up to you, but it's the climax of the opera dramatically, for you, NOT freeing Carthage. Consider the classic position of Islam in its attitude to women: one woman being much like another but every rose is different. Then at the water's edge give her the white one and return to your people and to your roses. (Don't just stand there – tell me!)

10 October 1979
Persuade them to act the scene as though the music were there. This wins an acting diploma if they can pull it off. Rehearse it as a play full out so that you are eventually ready for the music.

27 November 1979
VACATION
Don't think or write about work for three weeks. If you must write then write about yourself but best is to read and teach. WALK a great deal, anything else is peripheral.

29 November 1979
The Alps still work. Lufthansa lost luggage and was rude about it.

4 December 1979
Good evening walk. Koestler gets easier. Kanin sillier (the gossip good, the writing poor and the narrative hell).

7 December 1979
I don't remember a dream so vividly since after *The Merchant*.
   The Merchant dream a pleasure to be aroused from because it was so awful. Last night, for the first time since arriving here in Tunis, my ears popped and I relaxed. More than that I felt a strong recognition that the dream linked the snob dreams of my twenties ('Hello Larry, Viv. Hi Noël' etc.) with today and the years between. With the reality of those I came to know a little

and the dream of knowing them. But somewhere a vague memory that it began with a discussion of JH and AP's [Jocelyn Herbert and Andy Phillips] lighting rig and the Bury/Bund School ('Burybund' all one word meaning theatrically moribund); but I can't remember who I was talking to or where, until the Princess fell over ('Oh Ma'am' I called out, very correct). From picking up from the asphalt of Berkeley Square a drunk and plump Princess Margaret, who was never in my snob dreams, to discarding her for Vivien, Larry and a baroque nightmare palace, including waterfall, where a drunken Joan and Larry gave a party for Tracy and Hepburn, where I tried to persuade Noël to allow me to do *Tonight at 8.30* with Viv, *Red Peppers* especially, whilst Tracy and Hepburn met Riggs who had emerged crying from Joan's bedroom and greeted us both with 'and how long have you two been together?' and at that point I woke up more relaxed than for years – well two years at least. But why was Dorothy Welford assisting Riggs from Joan's room?

Now, getting from dream to dream. From twenty-one to fifty-three. For the first time I have a sense of belonging with Noël and Larry and all, or at least being up there with them. So from now on RELAX. 'You made it, Avis.' Now enjoy it.

End of Year
Best work or at least the work I have liked most best since Sloane Square – see why I think so.

Repeat once a month after me! At the Met I do my best in an impossible situation and relax, and at the NT I continue to grow and relax.

9

Parade

Parade is, incidentally, a very personal philosophy about opera, or better still, the thing performed, its past and how it has survived, its future and how it may survive. Beginning originally as a defence against the very *unmerry Widow*, the work is better than that, and I will not involve myself in making the second-rate first-rate. It is a task beyond my powers and interest. However, once the idea took root of a French-related triple bill involving the hopefully reconstituted ballet, it developed into an absolutely unrepeatable opportunity to put into practice my theories of community involvement, teaching, and all the richer side of life. With the blessing of hindsight I think I can see that I came to the Metropolitan because I wanted to play with some theories, which had hardly been formulated, about lyric theatre and why its totality had not been fully explored.

In all the forces to be deployed in an opera, there is a community to be observed. Let the community outside observe and, by an example, so conduct itself. But WE will have to lead in teaching, and begin now. We must keep the old doors open but open new doors as well; come into our tent for a while, it may be risky but it's never dull, or at least we'll make sure it isn't by all the means in our power.

During the whole of my time in New York I've been trying to overcome the prejudice which claims that the Met is a house for grand opera and grand opera alone. But of course you can play the so-called intimate works if you stage them in the right manner. I think we proved that with *Billy Budd*, and later *Lulu*. *Parade* is a step in the same direction and something more than that. I wanted an evening that would stretch everyone: the new ballet company, the children's chorus, the stage crew. *Parade* is meant to be an entertainment, indeed I actually enjoyed directing it, which is rare for me. The three pieces are all concerned with survival and that particularly French aid to survival, wit. But I hope, too, that its success will prove to be an open invitation to 20th-century works in the future. I remember when we did *Carmelites* here, I insisted on opening it at a Saturday matinée because I did not want the normal first night crowd in. It went down well, and the bookings, which were very poor before that opening, suddenly took off. In the middle of the run, a member of the board came up to me and said, with a critical tone to his voice: 'You're not really attracting a Met audience.' To his surprise, I agreed, and added that we hadn't really *changed* the audience, we'd just brought a new one in.

You can have a satisfactory evening in the opera house without going to *Madame Butterfly*. We have her anyway. The usual works don't fill a house any more, not even *Cav* and *Pag*. My God, we're three-quarters through the 20th century. It's time to get into it. Experimental work doesn't still have to happen in the closet. I want to open the door wider on the 20th century. I want to keep an eye on something more than survival into the future. I want to make a gesture for the future. The sweetening on the pill is to give audiences modern music while doing a *presentation*. In each case you must be visually simple while having a theatrical concept. I want to go steadily year by year and lead people into the repertoire, so that they will feel a season that hasn't a modern work is an empty season. I feel a great sense of the challenge of these works. At my stage of life I'm no longer afraid, but can I make my experience rise to the challenge? Then later, can the audience rise to that challenge?

Ravel pavanned into my life long before I came to the Met, via Sargent and the London Philharmonic Orchestra in the forties, and has glided in my head ever since. In Paris, Liebermann, Ingpen, and Rosenthal had discussed with me the possibility of a Ravel evening. While I was doing *Carmelites*, I had the idea for a triple bill, though triple bills are supposed to be death in an opera house. This would be of three early 20th-century French works which to me had always seemed related: Satie's *Parade*, Poulenc's *Les Mamelles de Tirésias* and Ravel's *L'Enfant et les Sortilèges*. One of the relationships, apart from the purely nationalistic one, was that they were all conceived during the First World War when the Germans were about 30 miles from Paris. They all sprang out of French culture at a time when it was under the greatest possible threat. The three composers and Apollinaire were made deeply aware by the First World War of the mentality of war, the waste of it, the mindlessness of it, and they attacked it with irony and tenderness.

5 July 1984
Parade as an essay in gratitude to a culture which, by its survival between two wars, gave me when young a first sight of a world civilisation whose wit and grace had a profundity and sanity which my own puritanism lacked.

26 September 1978
To David Hockney
It was very good to see you, finally, at the Metropolitan the other night. Ever since I saw the possibility of helping to jerk the place into the 20th century, I have been trying one way or the other to seduce you into the house.

Many possible subjects have crossed my mind, and, as the only acquaintance we have in common is John Cox, I took the liberty of discussing them with him. My first thought was to ask you to think of the classic Mozart *Idomeneo* and see if you had any response to it. He countered with the fact that you both were thinking of the *Barber* and would we mind sharing one with Glyndebourne. The truth of the matter is, as I told John, I very much doubt if any designer would want to design the same production for both houses. One or the other would suffer. But in the meantime I had a thought of a production which I have embedded into the season of 1980/81. At the moment it is still waiting for a few contractual releases. This project ties in quite pivotally to that programme and it sprang out of my thoughts and theories on musical education in schools, colleges and, most important of all, with the public.

At the moment I am engaged in a three year mobile opera plan for the Metropolitan and am now more than hopeful of arranging foundation grants to cover the costs, which I expect will be far from minimal. In the 1980/81 season I hope to celebrate this jump into another area of the opera house with a parade of all the things which have never normally been permitted in that august establishment. I sent to James Levine and Tony Bliss my thoughts on the triple bill, which I hope will not seem too cut and dried a concept for you to join. Let me promise you that it is only six months old, fraught with dangers and can change in any direction, subject to an exciting battle of tastes and theatrical instincts between ourselves. Such a collision I look forward to with an excitement which I hope Fokine felt on meeting Bakst, or, better than that, Ravel on meeting Satie.

To cut the cackle and into the flesh market, I propose a triple bill of French music of the 1930s: *Les Mamelles de Tirésias* by Poulenc to open the programme, *Parade* by Satie (choreographed by Nureyev), and *L'Enfant et les Sortilèges* by Ravel, directed by myself as would be *Tirésias*. I have already spoken to Nureyev on the overall concepts and the egotism which lies behind it, but if you remember the first two lines of Ben Britten's setting of *Les Illuminations* you will know precisely what I mean. That is not the enigma at the heart of the charade but probably the charade at the heart of the enigma.

The evening will begin with the audience coming into the theatre, and very few expectations will be disturbed. The great gold (and impossibly heavy and noisy) curtain will be down, the orchestra in place in the pit, the chandeliers moving up with astonishing regularity and occasional rounds of applause, the conductor will come out, and we shall continue with all the normal flummery of an opera performance. The conductor raises his baton to take us into *Les Mamelles de Tirésias*. I have thought here that the setting should be cloths, and cut cloths only, and that they should not take up more than three quarters of the stage space, that is to say leaving air around them for stage hands, lights, property boxes and bare walls. This still gives you a height of something like 30 feet and more than 35 feet across. From this point everything follows logically. At the end of the performance of *Tirésias*, which I now believe will include the delicious spectacle of Richard Stilwell in drag with one blue bosom and one red. The audience pitch can be set towards the central part of the evening – to parade our wares in public and to display the fact with as much mystery as possible, so that the preparation for the painting, dancing, music and staging is, I believe, made more fascinating.

What I would like to make of the evening is a full-scale display of the kind of totally theatrical illusionist theatre to which I believe opera belongs.

At the end of *Tirésias*, the cast come out to take their curtain calls. When they are all in front of the gold curtain it swings away to reveal the set. Soloists leave the stage and working lights come on and the crew begins. During the first intermission the audience may leave the theatre completely, take a leak, or watch the scene change. When they come back, and before the conductor steps into the pit, the set is changed for *Parade*. The whole ballet would be choreographed by Rudolf Nureyev, and takes place in front of cloths. It is important that these cloths should not be full size but should float in space, surrounded by lights and the bare theatre walls. The roughest indication of their size is that they should seem to fill three quarters of the proscenium arch, leaving space around clear for lights.

At the end of *Parade*, when the dancers have taken their last bows, without use of the gold curtain, they divide at the middle and turn to the Hockney backdrop, which flies away to reveal the stage crew who proceed to make the second intermission feature, the scene change for *L'Enfant*.

This may not be quite as striking as the first scene change and will require raising the orchestra pit, striking the stands and instruments up-stage to the first three stage elevators and resetting them there. The elevators rise. The orchestra takes its place, the soloists and children take their places in front of the orchestra and the chorus behind them. The soloists sit on chairs in a semi-circle reaching from stage centre over the orchestra pit (which you will remember is up). The conductor comes out, takes his bow and we begin the performance of *L'Enfant et les Sortilèges*.

During the next two years I propose to be working in various junior high schools around New York with children between the ages of 10 and 12. Indeed, the programme is beginning now by introducing *The Bartered Bride*, with us going out to the schools rather than their coming in to the opera house. These children would form the cast of *L'Enfant*, acting out a play on a space normally reserved for the orchestra pit.

I don't know how often you have attended performances at the Metropolitan, but you will realise that they have become somewhat tradition-bound over the years and the audience almost totally bound, hand, mind and foot. Therefore, one of the objects of my life, now that during the last three years I have restored the technical area to some degree of order, is to throw the audience out of that tradition.

During the week beginning now with *The Bartered Bride* in the schools, I shall begin to choose children without a painting, singing, moving background and out of them make a nucleus of a company for *L'Enfant*, although I shall not begin working with them for a year or so. This will include working with their teachers for at least six or eight months on 'how does milk look, how does arithmetic walk', what they look like in terms of costume. It would be wonderful if your timetable worked out so that when these classes, of which the end result will be unknown, are in operation, you can begin to absorb some of the atmosphere the children are bound to create. At the end of this period, my idea was to then hand you the schoolchildren's sketches of themselves and the characters and see if you can make them theatrical. Personally, I have a feeling they will all end up wearing perfectly ordinary plain street clothes and acting out the play very simply with only minimal gesture and as much truth as Colette, Ravel, you and I can put into their heads. The imaginative impulse I want to try to lead from them, hence the bare stage and the mechanics of soloists and orchestra and lights being totally exposed. A variant of my usual 'look, there's nothing up my sleeve' trick.

The forces we will require on the stage are roughly as follows: full orchestra, 15 soloists, full chorus, full ballet, and, I suspect, all props and electric stage crew visible in working clothes.

The cast of *L'Enfant*, apart from those singers engaged by us on account of our interest in their stylistic education and public appeal, will be chosen from those artists available to the house, i.e. Stilwell, Farley, Ewing. It looks as though I am asking for a very simple show with cloths and costumes and a working surround exposed, and I may be doing this, when you might be becoming fascinated with the technical department of the Met. Think of *Parade* as only the first venture and then in the future come again and play all the technical games your heart desires.

Sorry for the long-winded letter which has probably only succeeded in making matters more complicated. It would be easier over a bottle of wine somewhere. Think of somewhere nice.

29 September 1978
To Rudolf Nureyev
This is a difficult letter as I have at least three subjects on which to concentrate. I think I'll deal with *Parade* first as it is the one I

believe will most strongly attract you to the Metropolitan as a choreographer as well as an actor, performer, and friend.

However, to the point. I see *Parade* as the end of three years, work at the Metropolitan in training an audience to realise that the magic of the stage is different from the magic of cinema and television and that the tonnage of scenery is not necessarily the only way of evoking atmosphere and revealing truth. 'Revealing what truth?', you might ask. If the world is mad and the theatre is sane (which seems too true and always has), the mystery is that the theatre seems to behave with more madness in the creation of its truth than the world does. At least our madness is life-loving and not destroying.

You will read in all the books of squabbles between Cocteau, Picasso, and Satie that the original theme of the circus performance, its preparation and the behind-the-scenes activity, remained a constant theme, however much squabbling may have gone on. Certainly the myth of the circus is a tempting one, but what about the myth of the opera stage in rehearsal? What about the myth of the ballet rehearsal room? All these places are ones in which the sweat and desperation lead to the creation of an illusion with very minimal means (as I believe we said in our conversation at dinner). There are run-throughs without costume, scenery, and lights which are infinitely more moving than any final performance. I would like the ballet in *Parade* to reflect that sadness and mystery.

Now as to the narrative form we should use, whether we use the circus as a background or the ballet rehearsal room is another matter, and for discussion at a later date when you are a little closer to the Cocteau-Satie background material. I ask you as a choreographer to consider the basic concept most seriously, bearing in mind all the limitations of working in our opera house, because I believe you are the only one who might see how to render the distinctly poetic idea of Cocteau into modern terms and into terms that will relate to the rest of the evening.

As I told you, the rest of the evening consists of *Les Mamelles de Tirésias* (Poulenc) directed by myself, and *L'Enfant et les Sortilèges* (Ravel) also directed by myself. The designer will be David Hockney, I hope, whose work I'm sure you know, if you do not actually know him, which seems unlikely. I shall try to arrange for us to meet soon to discuss all the possibilities.

When David came to look over the Met space, we agreed that something had to be done to relate the vast stage to the audience. I've always had strong feelings about how the Met space could be used to intensify the dramatic and visual qualities of our productions. When I first arrived there, I found they were only really using three quarters of their proscenium height. Those great gold drapes were always chopping it off and the further back in the house you went, the more it was like looking into a letterbox opening. The proscenium size you actually saw in no way related to the volume of the house itself. You couldn't let the audience feel you were shutting them off from the vital action on the stage. So, beginning with *Carmelites* and carrying on through *Billy Budd*, I removed the gold valance and used the proscenium's full height. Now, you could sit at the very back of the family circle and feel you were seeing the whole space of the stage.

Once David had mastered the geography of the Met, we began collaborating on the production designs in earnest.

22 December 1978

To Rudolf Nureyev

I've got a suspicion the enclosed synopsis is for a one-man ballet but anyway, here goes – at least it's a basis for discussion when we all meet in New York in February.

As you know, Cocteau was elbowed out of the creative nest by Picasso and from then on his contribution was minimised very unfairly even by Apollinaire. I think we could find a way of bringing him back to the centre of what was, after all, his idea.

The theme of the ballet, Cocteau as Fregoli. If the Steegmuller biography of Cocteau has arrived by now, you will have noticed on the title page, 'The Poet as Fregoli', and a little further on a description of Fregoli. I quote:

> FREGOLI (Leopoldo), Italian quick-change artist, born in Rome in 1867. Apprentice watchmaker, soldier, prisoner of war in Abyssinia. He was so successful at entertaining his fellow-prisoners and the Negus himself that the latter granted him his freedom. He was endowed with an uncommon talent for assuming different roles – in turn singer, dancer, imitator, mime, conjuror. He wrote scenarios in which he enacted up to sixty different parts,

both male and female. Fregoli travelled with 370 trunks, 800 costumes, 1200 wigs and 300 tons of stage properties. His engagements took him several times around the world. . . . After more than thirty years of unbroken success he retired to Italy.

In the Parisian world of the arts, Jean Cocteau was a Fregoli, and more than a Fregoli, for over half a century. Poet, novelist, dramatist, portraitist, designer of posters, pottery, tapestries, mosaics, glass, pipe cleaners and other media – the list of his transformations could go on indefinitely.

And so this is the theme as I see it in dramatic terms:

The stage is a clutter of torn cloths (in the manner of Picasso à la Hockney). Prop baskets, step ladders, lights on stands, practice barres, costume racks, in no apparent order. In the midst of them stands Fregoli/Cocteau (dressed as an Academician, or in the raincoat which conceals the harlequin costume just as Cocteau once wore for Picasso). He wanders around amongst the 370 trunks, 1200 wigs, 300 tons of stage properties, and puts on first one mask or another, one costume or another, and recreates his personal parade – maybe if we can find the original texts he might pick up the megaphone and recite at least some of these cut texts (in memory of a past from which he was unkindly excluded), trying to make his parade live from fragments of the past and in the end vanishing into the depths of the littered stage.

I believe that in this manner we will be able to catch not only the wistful side of the music but stay close to Cocteau's belief (and mine) that magic in the theatre must come from a stimulation of the collective imagination of the audience, not with the clutter of timber and canvas but from the magic of the simplest tricks performed in the Empty Space itself.

2 January 1979
To Manuel Rosenthal [the conductor]
In trying to define the scenario for us all, I had worked at the opening very extensively with the music but, of course, had left the ending unclear, as my excitement at the discovery of Cocteau as Fregoli caught me up. However, the ending is there, perfectly visible (or audible, I should say, in the music).

Quite simply, dear Manuel, the climax is the best anyone has had since the ending of John Osborne's *The Entertainer*. At the climax of the music – I'll give bar numbers later – all the props and masks are invisibly (by Chinese-type stage hands) wheeled away or flown away from him, and he stands alone on an entirely empty stage which, incidentally, should include the rear stage. If necessary, to make him seem lonely enough, it should include half of Amsterdam Avenue.

Fregoli/Cocteau is then left alone without his props and masks, with nothing, perhaps, save his body in the middle of that vast empty space at the Metropolitan, and on the cut-off of the music, or maybe just before it, the working lights snap on and the stage lights snap off, and all the illusions created in the Parade have disappeared.

Oh, dear, this is very difficult in a letter. I do wish we could meet very, very soon. *Parade* is, in fact, the central portion of the evening and we all need to go over the details together rather than thinking silent thoughts on our own.

Above everything, I need contact with you all. Can't wait. Because of this gap in time, you must forgive me if I communicate at steady intervals. I'll try and render the whole scenario of *Parade* as clearly as I can once the television of *Don Pasquale* is out of the way and before *Don Carlo* gets too much of a grip on me.

12 January 1979
Manuel [Rosenthal] saw Fregoli in 1925 – the year I was born and the year of *L'Enfant*, and the year Satie died.
Think about Cocteau/Fregoli shot from auditorium (as in score) then, like Petrushka, gets up and puts on another mask.

16 January 1979
Red Curtain.
Prelude just that.
A torn but brilliant red curtain, which rises to reveal a vast, almost empty stage. After Fregoli enters, another cloth descends behind him. Include a man shooting Fregoli from the orchestra and, like *Petrushka*, keep a 'war' thread through all the works – for instance *Mamelles* Act One 1918, Act Two 1945. In each act the war has killed, so more bodies are needed. Only with the children in *L'Enfant* comes peace.

David and I met again in another couple of months in Los

Angeles to talk about the structure of the triple bill and to discuss specifics. He had produced half a dozen different versions of the Norman house and garden for the Ravel. That was also when he came up with the idea of using huge alphabet blocks as a visual theme to help relate the three French operas. We agreed that the scenery, in addition to its colour, feel and intensity, must have a dynamic of movement about it, otherwise you're lost. That's why I responded to the blocks he left around. We decided on how many we would need to spell Maurice Ravel, then decided to carry the motif through the whole evening, also spelling Satie's and Poulenc's names. Thus the blocks became a device that would begin the evening and that people would still find acceptable by the time we got to L'Enfant. I then suggested it might be interesting to use the other sides of the blocks to make up the furniture – the armchair, fireplace and other objects in the room – and he said, well, it would take a bit of working out. So we sat down and worked it out. Serendipity, is that the word? That's the way we work together.

We arrived at a working method. Realising the difficulties of arriving at a design from sketches, I said you must work from a model. You can have a quarter-inch model. He said, I can't work quarter-inch, it's too small. So I had a big one made. It's really the only way I can think of that will get him to specifics. Sometimes he can be exasperating. I've worked with Laurence Olivier for 15 or 20 years; for two weeks during rehearsals of Othello, Larry disappeared from the world; you couldn't contact him at all. And he was working out his own problems, which he had to do. But when you don't know that it's happening, it's very difficult. I learned that he would eventually come back, to give him time, and what I learned on Olivier I used on Hockney! Whenever he goes off into an area which is absolutely irrelevant or repeats himself for the 199th time and goes on with the same point, you just say, 'Yes, David, yes.' I also just sort of say Othello! Othello! Othello! and let him go on until he's talked himself out. And I wait for a moment till I'm sure, and say yes, that's what we agreed on two days ago. Now we can get back to work. He would show me a model of a set; I'd say, 'Can you cut a bit off that or take a bit off this?' He allows me to do that and, anyway, I regard that as part of my job. If he didn't I don't know how we'd work together. But he did, and we do, and that's that.

7 February 1980
Cocteau in the Arlequin costume and Fregoli as Cocteau. Half masks for Picasso etc. Explain the binding element of Arlequin in the trenches, if 'Commedia in the Trenches' is the subtitle of the evening, for the benefit of those who like to know where they are.

Originally the idea was to have *Parade* in the middle, not as a prelude. But after about six months it seemed to me that the best thing would be to treat it exactly as the French would have: not as Cocteau's ballet with its complicated little episodes, but as a simple parade before a performance introducing all the elements that were going to appear throughout the evening – not only the characters of the child and harlequin, but also the visual elements that would help tie the production together – the alphabet blocks, the ladder, and the circus ball. Our idea was that this motley group of acrobats, magicians, dancers, and other circus types would perform in front of a painted curtain, behind which the audience would be led to believe a major theatrical event would occur.

Though *Parade* was the last of the three to be designed, we decided to open the evening with it.

8 February 1980
To David Hockney and Rudolf Nureyev
Please forgive the collective address, but a sudden unexpected excess of early waking hours, to which I am finally becoming accustomed, has given me time to note down a few observations on the development of the French Bill, or *Parade* as I would like to call it. (I feel the use of a single word spells out precisely the intent of the evening, which is to some degree a personal philosophy of possible alternatives in musical theatre.) Maybe this is a *Parade* which offers up other possibilities to those who want 'a parade', or perhaps I am trying to lure a new audience into a different tent, to discover whether there are not still ways of making evenings of theatrical excitement in an opera house which are restricted neither by the disappearing breed of star international singers nor by the weight and expensiveness of the decor. I am hopeful that we will be able to develop other evenings along these lines which will ease the strain on the Metropolitan Opera resources, creating a changing repertoire for a changing economy.

I would like to define my thoughts on the development of *Parade* as it now stands after the last few sessions with David, before we all meet to go into the final details. You remember, I hope, we discussed how the overall pervasive atmosphere of the First World War would be established by a periphery of barbed wire surrounding the stage on three sides and in front of which the scenery and characters would ebb and flow. But during the last few weeks some new characters, who have been lurking in the wings, have stepped forward, calling to be seen. For example, at the beginning of the evening the stage is empty except for the barbed wire. On the opening chords of the introduction, the figure of Pierrot begins to pick his way through the barbed wire down to the front of the stage. At the appropriate moment, he throws off his Pierrot costume, revealing his Stage Director's white tie and tails. I suggest we repeat this at the beginning of *Parade*: this time another figure in the costume of Arlecchino emerges from the same barbed wire, but this time instead of becoming a stage manager, he becomes Cocteau/Fregoli/Nureyev. (Do you remember the passage in the Steegmuller book in which Cocteau, in order to impress Picasso, flung off his raincoat to reveal the harlequin tights underneath?) And I would hope that at the beginning of *L'Enfant* this same Cocteau/Harlequin figure would lead the children through the barbed wire to the downstage play space. Remember this space is dominated by a number of children's play blocks which, when facing the audience, spell out Maurice Ravel and which, through the assistance of the children in turning them, become all the *sortilèges* for the evening. In other words, I want us to consider, in costuming all three operas, the use (especially for the chorus in *L'Enfant*) of variants on the Scaramouche/Arlecchino, Pierrot/Pierrette costumes. The theme of the evening hopefully has a gentle reminder throughout of how wildly and weirdly the arts survived in a time of world chaos.

With particular reference to *Parade*, as I said to you Rudi about the synopsis, I think we made a mistake in expecting too much historical information to permeate our audience's first performances, and I would like to suggest that you disembarrass yourself of the load of narrative implied in 'the story of making *Parade*' and concentrate rather on the series of brilliant divertissements arising from and out of the Romances, Advances and Disappointments of creative artists in full turmoil of creation, still of course using the ideas of the *pas de trois* for Satie, Picasso, Cocteau, umbrellas and all the other devices we have so far discussed.

Also, David, I would ask if we can't reconsider the bleachers in Ravel as if they could not have more the look of an open-air orchestra stall, red, white and blue, if you like, on which will stand, sit and move the chorus and principals, dressed in the Commedia costumes, particularly in reference to the Tiepolo catalogue I mentioned to you. I will see that you all get a copy. It is the Scaramouche figures in this exhibition which seem particularly interesting in connection to the whole enterprise. At any rate, the exhibition will still be showing when we are all together in New York.

Apollinaire had arrived wounded from the front to attend the première of *Parade*, so for our production it seemed there was a poetic point to be made by using barbed wire on the stage to suggest that war is always imminent. Don't forget the theme he presents in the scenario of *Les Mamelles*: 'We need more babies, make more babies.' It doesn't come through in performance unless you are French, and, for people who are not, the barbed wire serves to remind them of when, how and why the French government was ordering people to have larger families. The possibility of war surrounds us all the time and particularly threatens the lives of our children. But using a child and a harlequin at the beginning of *Parade* and at the end of *L'Enfant*, I hoped to make the point that the only sanity for our children is in the arts – music, painting, literature. The only thing that any civilisation is remembered by is its art, and we'd better, I think, consider that when we come to educating our children.

15 February 1980
Memo to Met staff: Ashenden, Callegari, Cappiello, Clark, Diaz, Graham, Hacker, Hall, Hauser, Lawson, Reppa, Volpe
cc: Miss Malfitano
Parade
Concerning our meeting, which I enjoyed as I always do, there is one unresolved question upon which I would like your most determined endeavours!

Question: Who is responsible for Miss Malfitano's red and blue breasts? Is it carpenter, wardrobe, props? I do not think it is electrics!

Awaiting your reactions with some interest.

From David Reppa
I would say it belongs to Props.

From Stan Cappiello
Subject: Jurisdiction of Miss Malfitano's red and blue breasts
Please excuse the delay in replying as I am surrounded by mounds of work. I notice the scenic department was not mentioned as a possible *department* responsible for the points in question. However, when points of jurisdiction are not clearly defined, logically they should fall to the department best trained or prepared to meet the challenge.

I therefore offer the services of the Scenic Department at least for the preparation or construction phase, (on-stage fondling, I mean handling, we are less prepared for). We have cumulatively many years of training in figure drawing, painting and sculpture, plus years of practical experience. If producing an exact colour match is of primary importance, what department would be better equipped?

Not to belabour the point, a number of members of the department are at present attending classes and seminars in an effort to keep abreast of new materials and techniques.

If further argument is necessary to support this position, I will be happy to supply examples of our work.

In conclusion may I quote a remark uttered yesterday by one of the more effusive tour guides, referring to a group of scenic artists at work on a current production: 'These men can do anything.'

From Peter J. Hall
Concerning your question regarding *Parade*
Of what is Miss Malfi's poitrine to be made,
Of rubber and glue in red and in blue
Or some other fabric in some other shade

Mamelles de Mam'selle as portrayed in *Parade*
Smack, as it were, of the Marquis de Sade.

Of metal they'd rust and a bust of sawdust
Might very well sag in the heat of charade.

Such objects of art are not made on a bench
Or twisted awry by a spanner or wrench
So this is the shop for breasts that don't flop
We're used to supporting the needs of a wench.

29 April 1980
To Manuel Rosenthal
I am terribly sorry not to have been in contact before now, but I have been suffering for the last five months with the most boring case of shingles imaginable and have spent the vast majority of that time flat on my back in bed. I plan to be in London beginning May 17 through the middle of August and I would gladly come to Paris during a break in my rehearsals so that we might be able to discuss this all further before you come to New York for *Parade*. In the meantime, please make what sense you can of these notes which are an attempt to unscramble the various strands of *Parade* and recent developments in my work with David [Hockney] as it seems to be ready to go into the workshops.

I ought to construct a first sentence of such length and complexity as would itself explain the many strands and shapes out of the past which govern my thinking about the French trio. Throughout my whole life, and indeed through the life of most of us, there has been a war going on somewhere in the world. The arts have survived and we have survived working in the arts. *Parade* was and still is, as I believe Richard Buckle has said, 'the doorway to the 20th-century theatre', and that opened out of the First World War. Its importance was recognised by Apollinaire, not only in his eulogy of Satie and Picasso written for the programme, but in the prologue to the original play of *Mamelles* which I quite happily quote here. I trust you will forgive the translation as I do not have the original to hand:

> One tries here to infuse a new spirit to the theatre
> A joy, a delight, a virtue,
> To replace this pessimism, old by more than a century
> Which is quite ancient for such a boring thing.
> The play was written for an ancient stage,

> Because one wouldn't have built a new theatre for us,
> A round theatre with two stages;
> One in the centre, the other one creating a ring
> Round the audience and which would permit to express
> The big display of our modern art.
> Putting together Often Without Any Visible Link, as in life,
> The sounds, the gestures, the colours, the cries, the noises,
> The music, the dance, the acrobatism, the poetry, the painting,
> The chorus, the actions, and the multiple decors.

This seems to sum up everything the evening of *Parade* ought to be. It serves as a fitting acknowledgement to Satie who died in the year in which *L'Enfant* received its first performance, although of course as you told me, Ravel and Colette were writing the poem and some of the music at the opening of that war that has been going on all my lifetime . . . So to begin at the beginning, as always there is –

A stage surrounded by barbed wire waiting for the audience . . .

From the darkness behind the barbed wire, a figure appears wearing a very smart uniform (designed by Poiret). He climbs the barbed wire to the first bars of *Parade*. Oddly, and very suddenly, a bright blue ball (designed by Picasso!) rolls toward him from the prompt box. He stops it like a soldier, with his foot, and looks around him. What to do with it? He balances it. He balances *on* it. Then throws it into the wings. It is thrown back to him! Taking the hint, he takes off his trench coat to reveal to the audience the Arlequin costume Picasso designed for *Parade*, just as Cocteau did in order to explain his kind of astonishment to Picasso. But at this time Cocteau has become Fregoli for the rest of the evening. (c.f. Page 117 *Diaghilev* by Kochno). He has an audience of Punchinelle/Soldiers and to entertain them, he tells the story which ends at the Châtelet on 18 May 1917 and which begins when he calls up the scenery as he needs it to tell his story.

The first cloth he commands rises from the ground behind the barbed wire and represents a vast panoramic view of Paris 1917 (Eiffel tower and all). He follows this by calling down from the flies Satie's studio and Picasso's studio and when he needs it, the Châtelet Theatre on the afternoon of 18 May, etc., etc. The

Punchinelle/Soldiers assist him to tell the story of an act of survival which, drawn from the classic French theatre, also opened the doors to 20th-century theatre. He tells it with the aid of a cast in which Satie plays Scapino, Misia plays Colombine, and Diaghilev plays Brighella, etc. By using the traditional figures and masks of French pantomime, we simplify all our references and the 'Cocteau/Fregoli/Arlequin' confusion vanishes. In each individual variation in *Parade*, and in all three works, we may want to use handwritten placards carried by Punchinelle bearing a simple title such as *Les Mamelles de Tirésias by Francis Poulenc* or the number or name of a variation in *Parade*, for instance *Seduction Trio danced by Messrs Satie, Cocteau and Picasso* or *Inspiration Pas Seul danced by Mme Misia Sert*.

Using the oldest devices of theatre, we can tell the complicated story of Picasso, Cocteau and Satie and in addition allow Cocteau to have the last word at the end of *Parade*. He will be sitting on the floor of the Châtelet Theatre, where Diaghilev, Picasso and all the others have left him alone after his triumph. However, our Fregoli is still in command of the evening and with the same sleight-of-hand as that with which he summoned up the city of Paris from the floor, and the whole decor of *Parade* from the flies, he calls down the blue fleur-de-lys front curtain of *Mamelles* and thereby obliterates Diaghilev, Misia and Picasso, who are agonising in the Châtelet or the Dome about who really did what. Then, reaching down in to the prompt box, he pulls up the white figure of Pierrot and hands over the stage, in the name of Fregoli, to Apollinaire and Poulenc.

The Pierrot figure (on the lines 'Vous trouverez ici des actions qui s'ajoutent au drame principal et l'ornent', page 6, first stanza, third bar) throws his Pierrot costume away and assumes the garb of the stage manager, whilst the scenery of *Mamelles* descends behind him. In this manner *Mamelles* grows out of the music and scenic background of *Parade*, just as it did in what we are pleased to call 'real life'. As E. M. Forster never stopped saying, 'Only connect'. Even the children, who are created in *Mamelles* to replace those lost in the 1914 war, are the children who, with wooden playing blocks and masks, will try to create the world of theatrical imagination called up by Ravel, working with the simplest and oldest techniques.

You can be sure that the evening has taken on a life of its own, which seems to be leaving me for the first time in a long while and for which I am very grateful. Finally, what is best of all for you, your principals will be immediately to your left and right on the *forestage* and in **front** of the proscenium!!

I wanted the evening to make several points, not only about the salvation of humanity through art, but also about a new kind of theatre that could change the relationship of the audience to the actor. Consequently, that statement by Apollinaire was important to the conception of the French triple bill and, later, to the Stravinsky evening. Indeed, it remains important to all my work because, by bringing together opera, ballet, drama, and painting, I hoped to produce a strong, unified statement. Opera audiences no longer go to ballet; ballet audiences no longer go to opera; a few of each go to the theatre. They need to be reunited rather forcefully and that's really what I wanted to initiate at the Metropolitan Opera over the next few years.

10 March 1980
The problem is to prevent the Russian cuckoo [Nureyev] throwing the English golden eggs out of the nest!

David and I collaborated very quickly. We locked into gear at our first meeting and we really didn't have any problems. It was just a question of the right order or technical problems. By the time Rudolf Nureyev was suggested by the management and by the time we got hold of him, David and I were forging ahead. Because we were unable to have much contact with Nureyev, we found ourselves on divergent paths. It was a very unfortunate and time-wasting procedure. But really the important part of the collaboration was David, myself and most important, Manuel Rosenthal. Manuel brought all the experience of the past, including the original *Parade*, to bear on the musical interpretation and on the physical and visual interpretation. So, in that sense, the collaboration was really David, myself and Manuel.

21 June 1980
David Hockney from 1–4 p.m. Rudi 1 hour late, walks out after 15 minutes, dresses for 20 and finally walks out. Let us hope for good. Work recommences on *Parade*. Outline finished 8.30.

29 June 1980
Parade meeting AT LAST. Rudi walked away reasonably quietly if all people say is true. But on the evidence of my eyes and ears, he is a stupid cunt.

30 June 1980
RN note afterwards.
There was nothing in it he could not have done if only he had done as he was told. Unfortunately, however, he may have been the grit in the Margarita. I suppose Anthony Bliss would have preferred the pearl. Well he will have to make do with the healthy oyster.

24 July 1980
Sensational night – begin to make *Parade* function. Key jammed at the flat. Locked IN and OUT!

26 July 1980
Work on *Parade*. I am beginning to enjoy learning how to work after all this time instead of feeling inadequate.
A really mixed week taken day by day but on the whole good.

1 January 1981
I never had the slightest curiosity about my grandparents until *now*. My parents were middle-aged in the twenties – they were young in 1914.

24 March 1981
To Peter Shaffer
Thank you for your most exhilarating letter. As Stella said to Joey, 'If I could write letters like you I would write letters to God.' However, we all know where that correspondence ended up.

The actual rehearsing of *Parade* was more hair-raising than anything I have experienced in years. Having intended to begin with the children in September and work through gently ('No DEAR, you do not put your block down on Miss Harris's foot, that's not stylish DEAR'), unfortunately the reasoned approach had to be abandoned as we only had four weeks in which to put the piece on the stage. So one was reduced to the usual screaming, storming and, in one case, bodily throwing a child out of the rehearsal room. Plus ça change, etc.

I have had a letter from Beverly [Sills], or do we call her Bubbles, telling me how much more exciting it is to work in her theatre and asking me about *Alceste* in 1982. Fortunately the period she wants is already gone and I am just about to disappear to the National Theatre.

Notebook:
I feel the time has come to pull the chair away from the desk and float a little. In any opera house it is administration that is the killer. I've had more than enough of that, to say nothing of being subject to the vagaries of singers' sore throats and imminent babies.

The strike at the start of the season had a crippling effect. No one ever gains from strikes, but there are usually losers. On this occasion, they were Jimmy, Tony, and myself. It annihilated the shape of the programme we had constructed, so that *Parade* became the first true new production, instead of the divertissement in the middle of the season we had planned.

19 May 1981
To Manuel Rosenthal
Do, please, excuse the brevity of this note and the delay in writing it. *Parade* was also for me one of the most stimulating working periods I have had. I also wish that we could work together in the future, and shall be missing your knowledge and experience of Stravinsky later this year. I look forward to seeing you some time during the period I am working at the National Theatre, so do not be surprised if you receive a phone call.

Parade was the most personal statement I was able to make at the Met. I was able to pull my own memories into the fantasy, I quoted Apollinaire, who made the poem which most reflects my kind of theatre, in language which I cannot emulate, only quote. To use this kind of theatre to present as egotistically as possible the influences which have shaped my view, from Guthrie to Strehler, from Picasso to Hockney, Van Appent to Herbert, Ravel to Weill, and who opened the door to all the rest of the twentieth century. To use this new theatre to revitalise the old.

Our original idea for *L'Enfant* was that at the end of the garden scene, the animals would begin to fight viciously among themselves and slowly the garden would disappear. You would be left with blackness and barbed wire. In the revival, I still hope to get the final image I wanted: a return to the barbed wire so the child's cry of 'Maman', when all this happens in the garden, is more a warning to the audience.

Parade said (and will say more clearly when we do it again) something of the horror of children left to the mercilessness of grown-ups, who have left the world of instinct and imagination for the world of fact.

20 February 1981
French Triple Bill opens – and AB cancels Stravinsky. And has second thoughts on reading the notices – and so do a few others.

10

Murder at the Met

1 January 1980
Any year that begins as badly as this one can only get better, I
hope.

And now, in order to make known what I have done I shall have
to make known who I am. Is it worth the sacrifice of privacy and
silence – well hardly. But I *am* proud *and* aware of hubris. But *if* I
can make these next seasons show what I mean in revivals as
much as in new productions, then I shall have made a
contribution to the survival of a Mastodon (I like elephants).

15 January 1980
My needs if I am to stay: input in planning, e.g. *Tristan*,
Idomeneo, *Lulu* rehearsals – 2 years since I was included.
[Anthony] Bliss – will he listen to my complaints about them if I
list them starting with JL [James Levine] and himself. Gossip can
only thrive where it is nourished especially in AB's respect for it.

16 January 1980
SHINGLES!

28 January 1980
Discuss with JL the commitment to the new production. More
discussion less pissing outside the tent. That is what I *thought* we
were trying to create but you don't work with your director as I
work with my conductors.

Week beginning 4 February 1980
Divisiveness is built into the system as long as the Rule of Three
lacks a philosophic core as well as a productive one. I repeat:
why should the Met go on? The people I need at the Met will tell
me what is wrong, not use fear as an excuse for creating
dissension. There has not been a criticism which, when

examined, would not have come better to my face from the party concerned.

Week beginning 11 February 1980
Define the problem. Get rid of the disease. My weakest moment, and the moment when I was most likely to resist infection least, was during the week of *Mahagonny* when I realised I was on my own with *no* real honest critical back-up apart from JH [Jocelyn Herbert] and no real technical control except JH – tell that to JH.

Talk to JL as if I were older than he, which I am, *and* theatrically wiser than he, which I am. Try to explain without offending.

Get the Met problem in the open and out of my body.
Last night I felt *how* getting excited affects the nerve ends! Watch it and learn.

22 February 1980
AB Summation
NO MORE *Aida Rigoletto* NO MORE *Vespri Abduction* NO MORE *Don Carlo Don Pasquale*. Therefore do not do *Figaro* or *Traviata*. And I do *not* audition for anyone. JL must decide and tell *me* his decision on the above and then I will tell him mine. A difficult decision will be good for him.

Hume Cronyn phoned re artistic directorship of Stratford, Ontario.

23 February 1980
If work is the only religion I practise then I'd better get into a real place of worship. Think about '81–2–3. Do more Shakespeare. The Met. Stratford Ontario, 81–82. Drop Mozart for Buxton. Finish at Met with *Corigliano* and the SHAPE is complete. Everything connects.
Change yourself and the circumstances may change.

28 February 1980
Maybe the shingles are 'destiny' as we go into week nine, so, as they are *still* painful, let us hope the doctor's estimate is correct – two more weeks.

3 March 1980
To John Osborne

I suppose it is a sign of advancing middle-age when the diary becomes a place in which to record observations and not just appointments, or perhaps it is merely that the untangling of this Metropolitan plate of spaghetti requires a daily entry to maintain some sense of order. But certainly it is a sign of middle-age when I, who have never enjoyed correspondence, have a desire to communicate with the old folks at home.

Over the last few years, for instance, I thought about Derby a good deal – even Derby in the pre-Osborne period, Boy Scouts, buggery and all. I have even made attempts to renew some old acquaintances, some of which should have been forgot, but one or two of them have reminded me of things I should not have forgotten. I suppose it is something of the same feeling which moves you to the land of memoirs and perhaps the need to create a little order in one's life, so that we can see where we are and choose where we go next.

Also at the moment, being an enforced static body, I tend to reach for the yellow pad to take my mind away from the aches and pains. Shingles is a perfect winter illness. It intensifies the desire to be silent and read and think – no need to converse about music, art, theatre or opera. What emerges from all this profound inertia is a certain awareness that I must, in the next few years, get away from the Met. I will have achieved most of what I set out to do, firstly to organise the technical aspects of the place so that my job would become redundant, and secondly to take that great dinosaur, wild and screaming, into the 20th century. The first job is almost complete and the second is finished, at least in the sense that it will not be possible to say that there is no audience for modern opera at the Met. There are a couple of possibilities, but I am hoping to see you and talk before I have to take decisions in that area.

As neither of us are inclined to go to those places where we might bump into each other, this letter is to claim an appointment for lunch or dinner when I am at the NT in June, squaring off *Galileo*. So don't say you didn't have any warning.

PS: Take my advice and give shingles a wide berth. It's not a gentleman's disease!

Week beginning 3 March 1980
In order to recover I need to take all outstanding decisions: RN [Rudolf Nureyev] Meet JH [Jocelyn Herbert] etc. and *then* vacation. Not before. Stratford is only a possibility. There are others and everything is cleared for any eventuality.

13 March 1980
Fury for perfection makes me, Zero [Mostel] and LO [Olivier] above all, and everyone I respect, difficult to work with. What nobody understands is that one's fury comes from oneself and is directed to oneself. The pressure that people feel is merely the afterburn of that blast off. They have no right to stand too close unless they are insured against fire.

21 March 1980
Give up and go home and rest. I am older than Peter Brook and I look younger. Why? Because I *don't think.*

Week beginning 28 March 1980
NEVER AGAIN MAKE DIFFICULT THOSE THINGS WHICH GIVE YOU PLEASURE. It takes time to explain in detail what you intend but it saves frayed nerve ends.

15 May 1980
Memo to Anthony Bliss
. . . To recapitulate, I had always thought of this season ('80/81) as a culmination and expression of my feelings as to how opera should look at this time and in this place. In addition to the 6/7 productions which have been created during these years, with a view to a more flexible touring programme, there are 4 major revivals and a new production with all of which I am involved. Contrary to your feeling that I should not be criticised for things for which I am not responsible, this is the season above all others in which I would wish to accept that responsibility and be criticised for it if necessary. In short, the artistic proof of the value of the last 5 years' work is to be demonstrated in the forthcoming season and I would ask therefore to retain the titular authority until it ends along with the contract.

With regards to the more personal matters involving James [Levine] and myself, I will make every endeavour to clarify my situation with regard to James, Stravinsky and the future. At the

moment you must realise that my sense of personal disappointment in the failure to create an ongoing creative relationship
dominates most of my thinking. I will be writing to you at length
when I reach England. Thank you once again for your letter and
looking forward to next season, whether it is the end of
something new or the beginning of something new.

Week beginning 19 May 1980
Been approached about taking over Royal Court. Max [Stafford-
Clark] is leaving. I really ought to be at Sloane Sq. How on earth
can I afford it. Why shouldn't the Met pay some of the bill? After
all *they* gained from what I learned at Sloane Sq. therefore I
might then feel justified in taking the 'emeritus' position. Riggs
understands as usual. It could be the end of the worst time and
the beginning of the best *if* I can be honest and *relax* as I work.

23 May 1980
Talk to JH who will talk to Greville [Poke] and then . . .

24 May 1980
Baubourg! A few more days like this and I shall begin to think I
am as creative as I would like to be. If not, then at least I can get
AB [Anthony Bliss] out of the shit in which he has placed himself
and RN [Rudolf Nureyev] out of the shit he deserves.

30 May 1980
Royal Court Theatre March 81.
See if *that* helps the shingles! or brings on the heart attack. That
all depends on Riggs and a first rate staff to whom *everything* has
been explained.

6 June 1980
To Patrick Garland [Newly appointed Director of Chichester
Festival Theatre]
First of all, many congratulations. I can think of no one better
equipped to place a theatrical time bomb in the middle of the
stockbroker belt.
    Unfortunately, with regard to your much appreciated request
that I direct a play for you at Chichester, I'm afraid my answer is
negative, but if you have a moment I would like to give you my
reasons so that you will in no way take this personally.

Several years ago, at the time at which John Clements was retiring, Sir Laurence suggested me to the Board with the hottest recommendation as Artistic Director. I was interviewed and, in due course, found wanting. This in itself presented no great problem. The manner of the rejection, however, caused me to lose an engagement which would have given me a great deal of financial security. In other words, as is the way with all business men dealing with artists of one kind or another, I was left on the hook, and finally, after 3 months of waiting, was forced to ask for information. You will understand therefore, however pleasing my memories of the theatre are, Chichester is not for me, and indeed was largely responsible for my decision to get the hell out of England.

14 July 1980
To Stephen Sondheim
Meetings seem impossible anywhere, any time. However, I promise the third person I telephone when I reach New York will be you. *Galileo* opens here on 13 August. Expect to hear from me shortly after that.

Yes, I did see *Sweeney Todd*. I am sorry it has cost you pleasure and pride, and more importantly two years. I stand by my original statement – it would have made a good opera. That was not what I saw on the stage. Perhaps for that and other Mozartian matters, I have been less attentive in making contact than normally.

11 July 1980
Low but not *so* low. Don't *snap* out of it – ease out of it.

13 July 1980
Not the Royal Court but who rejects who? and do I have a SLIGHT sense of relief?

14 July 1980
If I can save £200 a week, the Matisse is ours! which leaves me £250 which is what I would have to *live* on if the Court happened to happen and I have it just to *play* with. Think! Fool!

2 August 1980
Concorde home for Happy Birthday. Never ask yourself which Perfect Birthday.

5 August 1980
Return London.
Three quarters of an hour with Agatha Bliss. Writing detective stories while Lincoln Centre burns.

16 August 1980
And now for Berg, Satie, Poulenc, Ravel, Dekker, Ibsen and Shakespeare and hopefully security plus a little bit of affection.

22 September 1980
End of six months practising most of the Christian principles. I can relax with Peter and Modest [Tchaikovsky and Mussorgsky].

23 September 1980
Bliss/Levine: Orloffs Restaurant.
Talk about *Queen of Spades*. It's one of my favours to the Met which usually turn out Bad. Take the Risk or NOT. There is a price for JL and AB to pay – it is listening to me without interruption for ten minutes about the last year or as one might say BI (Before Ingpen) [Joan Ingpen, Administrator at the Met], who is incidentally the only justification for their ambitions and indecisiveness. Can I get it all off my chest in clear order? Memo or not?

24 September 1980
Memo to James Levine, Anthony Bliss [during strike at the Met]
It seems there is never enough time to discuss some of the problems that concern me, nor, in the present mayhem and lock-out situation does it seem likely that we shall have much time for discussing other than practical matters, i.e. *Queen of Spades*, the '81 tour, etc., etc. However, before we continue in our relationship, I think it appropriate that I should get off my mind some of the problems which seem most to militate against a creative future for myself at the Met. I would ask you to read this memo in the spirit of an end-of-term report rather than a series of not very coherent complaints. I will try to be as brief as possible, but do remember that I am reviewing a whole year during which I have seemed to be under some kind of attack, more or less day by day. Allowing for incipient paranoia, which goes with the job, I have eliminated most of the more trivial

incidents and concentrated as far as I can on those events which have seemed to create misunderstanding and, in some areas, downright malfunction.

Last Tuesday morning's conversation about the possibility of my taking up the remnants of *Pique Dame* seems to have brought our relationship full circle. I began as Director of Productions by undertaking a production of *Aida* for which I was totally unprepared; an *Aida* whose main virtue was its economy and adaptability to its singers. Much against my better judgement I was persuaded to *Rigoletto* and *Don Pasquale* by James. Whilst I hope they never went over their budget, and achieved a little dramatic coherency, they are not works I enjoyed dramatically or technically and that lack of enjoyment and energy shows on the stage. The only occasion when I picked up material to which I was unsuited and tried to make it work, and partially succeeded to my own satisfaction, was *Don Carlo*. At least in that I believe I was giving the Met a unique artefact for any opera house in the world: a full-length *Don Carlo*, never held up by intermissions, into which any major singer can fit with comfort and ease, and within a reasonable budget.

However, in spite of all the dangers, you are now coming to me once again and asking me to pick up the bits and pieces of a production which is going to be palpably too expensive or too cumbersome. And so, as it often does, the situation has repeated itself and my position is doubly difficult. When I think of *La Traviata*, I feel most strongly, still, that the decision to apply expensive cosmetics to it was arrived at in panic and taken at a time, moreover, when I had neither the physical nor mental energy to argue the case either to you or to the Executive Committee. However, I did understand from the few rumours about *La Traviata* which reached my ears that what was in question was my ability to understand the work, my visual taste, my sense of drama, especially in the matter of the last act. We have also to consider the Executive Committee's dictum that experiments (*à la Ballo*) with major works are forbidden, although no one has yet described to me the difference between an experiment, a success and a failure. (*Abduction* was an experiment and a success, so was *Don Carlo*; *Mahagonny* was traditionalist.) We might spend an interesting hour with the Committee discussing that last sentence to see if I can attempt to understand their reasoning, as it is clear they do not understand mine.

It is curious to me that at this time of great crisis I could at no point establish contact with you, James. In fact it was Tony who raised the subject, not entirely tactfully, in the middle of a final rehearsal of the battle scene in *Billy Budd* when, in addition to medication, I was having extreme difficulty in thinking at all. What we have now is an unfinished *Traviata*, on which more money has been spent than was initially allowed, which is the same in terms of structural planning (exits, entrances, etc.), and which has had added to it a considerable overpaint which, whilst it may add sufficient glamour for Mme Cotrubas, takes the teeth and bite out of the story. However, I accept that it is the Executive Director's right to make these decisions, but I would hope, were we to continue, that these decisions would be made at least with the three parties involved. Jimmy asked me in London what happened to *Traviata*? The truth of the matter is I don't know but I would be very interested to find out, just in terms of making my biography accurate if I ever have time to write it!

Nevertheless, here we are again. You are asking me to come up with a solution to an opera which I do not really like and upon which I can only 'experiment'. However, I am willing to consider this, should the workshop time be feasible, but I must point out to you that it contradicts completely all the strictures I have had laid on me and my work, quite apart from breaking my own rule of long and concentrated preparation. Were it to go ahead I would be expected to produce a rough working model four weeks from now and even were I not doing the musical, I find that an irresponsibly short space of time. The most important thing for you to consider is should I be doing it *at all* in view of the Board's view of experimentation and your own views on my ability to handle this particular style and period of opera. All of which brings me to the most difficult part of this letter.

For the last year, or at least since *Mahagonny* opened, I have become more aware of a rift between James and myself and that my authority has been undermined within the house. Five evening meetings in one year (pre-shingles that is) do not seem to me enough contact, especially when plans you have discussed with Joan never reach me either verbally or on paper, with the result that I have to spend hours at APAC [Advance Planning Advisory Committee], trying (as loudly or as softly as possible) to draw attention to the fact that, for example, *Tristan* will not tour and the '80/81 tour is overloaded with new productions and we cannot service it satisfactorily. Indeed there was a point at which my irritation exploded in front of APAC and the rest of you, which may have been the first time everyone else noticed that there was something basic and deeply wrong with our relationship.

In the period 'before Ingpen', hereinafter referred to as 'BI', I had a feeling I was fulfilling a satisfactory function and indeed beginning to work creatively on the purely practical matters which had to be faced. After Joan's arrival we had less and less contact. After *Mahagonny* I received from Tony complaints about my professional behaviour, reporting rumours of my behaviour in Los Angeles and, of all places, at the National Theatre of Great Britain. Where and how these calumnies circulated I have of course no idea but some of the lines of supply are fairly apparent and give me little pleasure. I do not now intend to change my way of working and I think the fact that I am continually asked back by the National Theatre (if not by Los Angeles, which seems to be going into bankruptcy) should indicate how much truth these rumours contained. Nevertheless, to be greeted every morning with a complaint either about one's personal behaviour or work was somewhat confusing. I had 6 or 8 months of constant and petty irritations of this sort before my nervous system packed up and decided not to allow me to continue.

Tony now proposes a new relationship, and it is this relationship I would like us to define. I am to be relieved of all administrative and workshop matters and to concentrate on planning the future, with reference to wider touring parameters and the staging of new works. I am to be his adviser on artistic matters and my particular duties. This is admirable if we can hammer out the lines of authority. If we do not do so I shall be in the same position as before, that is to say, endowed with responsibility but no power. Now understand, once and for all, that I do not wish or need power; I have enough of that to satisfy anybody. Nor do I wish to enhance my world reputation; that seems to have reached a point which would have satisfied even my father! However, if I am to stay on, we must address ourselves to the question of a working structure.

I am proposing that we should disband APAC which seems merely to have become a convenient unit to sign, in the name of all responsible parties, policy which has already been decided on the first floor. I propose the formation of a very close technical committee: Volpe, Wechsler and Clark, to whom the very first sketchy plans of a season are shown *as soon* as completed, so that they may add their voice to the possibility of, for example, touring with 5 new productions in one season, and prevent us from being in the present overloaded state. In parenthesis I should point out that it will be impossible to achieve any of the standards we have carefully built up for touring in the last three years if tours as overloaded as '80/81 are part of the management's policy. Just as long as it takes to rehearse the orchestra, chorus and soloists, just so long does it take to prepare the stage for each performance. The present plans for '80/81 make no concession to this basic philosophical point and we will not be able to continue to function until a more disciplined work attitude is shared by us all. Therefore this new committee should be empowered, on examination of a proposed season repertoire and new productions, to advise the Executive Director of cost, complexity and viability of the rehearsal and performance planning, just as the Artistic Adviser gives advice to the Director and the Music Director on designers and directors.

On this latter point, Jimmy, I must point out that you have been several times at fault. For instance, we all agreed that Franco Zeffirelli should do a production at the Met once every three years, and I said to you that until we have 4 or 5 productions sufficiently trim we could not afford to ask him and, were we to ask him, we should place budgetary controls in his contract, for him to ignore but for our protection. The result is now that we have a *Bohème* which not only cannot tour in its present state but is costing half a million. This seems to be iniquitous in view of the gargantuan efforts of other directors and designers aiming for economy, style and lightness. The decision to ask Franco was reached without any consultation and presented to me fait accompli: 'I have spoken to Franco and asked him to do *Francesca* and *Bohème*.' Fortunately for us he turned down *Francesca*, but *Bohème* lives with us still as a mark and a monument to bad planning, although as a production I am sure it will be an enormous success with the audience. But it is only one more obstacle to the future and will, like *Trojans*, become a scenic white elephant, with which we will not be able to deal. It is particularly galling to me since one of the first things I mentioned to you as something I would like to do was this particular opera. I remember making an observation to the effect that it is really all about keeping warm in the cold if you have someone to cuddle up to and what a difference that would make to a production. Now it is quite possible that I said something in discussing the opera which you felt was inappropriate, in which case you should have told me and not allowed me to hear second-hand that you had decided to go in another direction.

When we come to the question of *Manon*, we find another kind of interference which to my mind is wholly irresponsible. You will recall the endless parade of Frigerio, Faggioni, Ming Cho Lee and others, whizzing around the world because I quite rightly insisted that if we were having a new and distinguished director we should have a designer who had worked in the house. After several months of Mafioso-like misreportings and in some cases downright lying, Joan had suggested Gian Carlo Menotti and I suggested Desmond Heeley and had to do a great deal of arm-twisting to persuade him to take on another job at that point. The results were successful: the designer knew the house, the director didn't and the fusion worked perfectly.

Unfortunately, the director also brought to bear on the production the acting techniques of the silent movie, allowing the principle artists to indulge in every acting cliché that has been used since Thespis.

Now in the case of *Queen of Spades* we have a comparable situation. I wanted Ciulei as a leading European, now American director, to work with Svoboda. Svoboda was busy but agreed. They met, a first model was produced and was too elaborate (this model, incidentally, I was never shown). Svoboda was two weeks late coming to us with a simplified model and Joan Ingpen told me to get rid of him. The next thing I heard, Tony, was that you had had a conversation with Ciulei and had agreed to Radu as designer. I pointed out to you at the time that the rule about new director, old designer was a dangerous one with which to tamper. However, time was running short and no one seemed to have time to wait two weeks for Svoboda, so we went ahead, with the result that you now know.

Therefore I would ask in the future, if I am to be your adviser and if you are to take the technical committee's advice, that this sort of thing cannot happen again. The rule can hardly ever be broken without producing the chaos which exists at this time. For example, had it not been for the decoration that had to be applied to *Traviata* and the endless delays while we mollified Nureyev, who was not and never would have been my first choice as choreographer, these two productions and *Cosi* would be finished and ready to go on the stage. Now, no matter what the strike situation, I think that is something we would all have preferred. At least it would have given a certain flexibility to our planning.

I have on two occasions in the last year sent a memo to the first floor suggesting repertoire which interested me but have so far received no acknowledgement nor the favour of discussion which, with so many other factors, contributed to my unhappiness at the manner of our so-called collaboration.

However, and not to expand the point beyond the point, I have touched on the main areas which have caused me distress, and downright misery in some cases, and they are things which we must discuss together openly before we can commit ourselves to the future. Understand, I am not asking for power for myself but that you give power to those to whom in future you give authority, so that the Executive Director or General Manager, whatever the title is, has the back-up advice of the most efficient, hard-working and inspired production team I have ever been able to build up in any theatre. If their technical knowledge is to be ignored, as it so often is, we shall lose their services and, more important, their confidence and ability.

I hope this letter isn't too long or too discursive but at least it leaves me free when we meet to discuss positive things about *Queen of Spades* and the future, rather than the negative reflections on the past which are still in my head because they have not yet been satisfactorily answered, let alone discussed.

16 October 1980 [*One Night Stand* rehearsals.]
I left in despair. Orchestrations commonplace and too heavy.

17 October 1980
Next week make decisions on Canada, Santa Fe, NT, Melbourne.

25 October 1980
One Night Stand Previews 7/8. Producers close it. *My* fault. Analyse.

5 November 1980
To Greville Poke
Thank you so much for your letter and the kind words about *Galileo*. I also am sorry about the Royal Court affair, but once [Max] Stafford-Clark [Artistic Director, Royal Court] had decided that he wanted to continue in his present position, I had no option but to withdraw. I too think I might have infused some life into the building, but there you are. The workers voted against us.

The problems at the Met are still not resolved, now the chorus are holding out for more money. God knows whether we will have a season or not but even if we do not I shall have some good news for you.

There is such a stalemate at the moment that Riggs and I are off to the Islands for 10 days of sunshine and swimming. So sucks boo to Peter Hall, Max Stafford-Clark, Norman St John Stevas and the Iron Maiden.

18 December 1980
Canada *out*. There is a world elsewhere.

7 May 1981
To Régine Crespin [re *Carmelites* revival]
A copy of your letter to Maestro Levine has just reached me in London. Please accept my word that until that moment I had naturally assumed that you would be with us for every revival.

Whatever decision has been reached, without my consultation, I have written to Mr Bliss to ask if he can interfere.

If you wish to contact me at all I am rehearsing a play at the National Theatre [*The Shoemakers' Holiday*] and will be here until the middle of June.

I love you, though you never sang the three waltzes for me.

PS: You will note my new assistant is French and I can now extend a courtesy to you that hasn't been possible in the past.

7 September 1981
The triumvirate lacks an apex: JL⟵⟶JD both reaching for

the apex which is not there because the final stone will not fit into place. It insists on flying from left to right base instead of resting on top and getting the money together.

15 September 1981
Discuss: A theatre is a place to grow, to learn, to fail, to succeed and in which neither the failure nor success are as important as the work. The practical problem is keeping a group of actors together long enough to grow, learn, fail and succeed. Money cannot always hold them, vanity *can*.

17 September 1981
A man who never makes a mistake will never make anything. Require from Tony [Bliss] definition of our jobs as he sees them; i.e. JL [Levine], JI [Ingpen], JV [Volpe] not clear on mine. I am. But only following my instincts, not instruction. Define the relationship. Discuss the responsibility and power, once again. You cannot take one without being given the other.

21 September 1981
As AB JL have done it again in the Press, I shall finally have to speak the truth.

7 October 1981
Bliss meeting. All the classic errors in administration have been made. It's my job to advise. Admit it and pay up but *learn* when control passes out of our hands.

10 October 1981
I have learned to read and conduct a dialogue. I used to read to increase my knowledge and only now do I need to increase my mind.
When I was a boy in Derby, masturbation must have reached epidemic proportions.

22 October 1981
The pursuit of the best brings out the worst in me and sometimes justifies the rage.

10 March 1982
Ankle *again*! Sloppy discipline and common sense.

11 March 1982
The Met mist clears all because of a sprained ankle. What a thing for a theatre to hang on to – an ankle. A coherent plan on all fronts.

15 March 1982
Bliss dinner. Can I, should I come to the National Council and make a pitch for Arts Education?

18 March 1982
I would like the Met to lead the world of the 21st century. How much can be done *NOW*?

22 March 1982
When I arrived, the expensive scenic tail was wagging the musical dog. Ways had to be found in which to get the priorities right. Seven out of ten. Adding 2 for the bargaining entailed in offices before the real work began.
1. Never swamp the human scale no matter what the opera demands.
2. Light and air not gloom and darkness
3. Rising costs

22 March 1982
To Professor P.A.W. Collins, University of Leicester
My impressions of Dear Margaret [Maggie Smith] are impossible to put into any coherent fashion, as half the time I want to beat her head against the stage with a brick and the other half, she's the person I most want to direct anywhere and any time. This sort of material seems hardly for dissemination to the general public. Give Margaret my best wishes and if the occasion seems suitable, a kiss.

30 July 1982
Memo to Anthony Bliss
I cannot say I enjoyed our conversation yesterday, but at least some ground was covered. You asked for a meeting next week with Joe Volpe and myself in order to discuss some resolution to this situation, which for me is very awkward and embarrassing.

However, it was my understanding that the secretarial assistance so far rendered on my behalf by Ms Palmer for two days a week would be remunerated by the Metropolitan for three days a week and by myself for two days a week. As Joe Volpe is away for four weeks and you are scheduled to go on vacation, can we assume that Ms Palmer's position with the Metropolitan is established so that when you both return we shall be able to make proposals that will be both sensible and money-saving for us all? As I said, 'the present situation is causing me much distress and for my own sake cannot be allowed to continue.'

Much more important than all this is some positive thinking and planning on our part. Now, with regard to the aforesaid future and in this area, I am willing and waiting to consult with James, Jane and anyone else you will desire who has a positive idea to contribute. Let me repeat that whilst I agree with you as to the importance of the centennial fund, I must point out that a centennial which passes without the firmest and most forward looking plan for the future will hardly be worth memorialising.

1 January 1983
My *preliminary* object: to work and break out, escape the Opera Routine – consider the Met and how it can serve you – it will make a change.

3 January 1983
And I have not been happy at the Met since *Abduction/Mahagonny*. Too much politics and publicity. The individual *before* the house depresses me as a state of mind. At least the computer does not make that mistake. *Heartbreak House* [at the London Haymarket with Rex Harrison and Diana Rigg] continues in freezing theatres. Management nearly succeeded in killing off Charles Lloyd Pack and gave no help of any kind to me or to my legs.

24 March 1983
To Sir Frederick Ashton
Jane Hermann told me in conversation a short while ago that you might not be averse to choreographing the incidental dances in *L'Enfant et les Sortilèges* [at the Royal Opera House].

I meant to respond with great joy at the time but unfortunately dealing with the after effects of diabetes (peripheral neuropathy) has taken up most of my energy and thought. I now am in the hands of a merciless physiotherapist who is pushing and pulling my legs into some form of order.

I feel much brighter and better and very worried in case the delay in my response has reduced your interest in any way. If it has not, I shall be in London in May and hope to be able to talk with you at that time.

If you need more information, I will write immediately, but of course David Hockney is as familiar as I am with the work and moreover has one thousand photographs which may act in some measure as a guide.

Looking forward to seeing you in London and even more to the collaboration in Covent Garden of Ashton, Hockney and Dexter. It will be a wonderful homecoming.

25 March 1983
I want to have freedom from the Met even at the price of security. I could not work with JL in any creative way and I do not enjoy the 'political' atmosphere he creates and the relentless pursuit of popularity in which he drowns himself and the work like a child with a sweet trolley.

25 July 1983
Working at the Met one sometimes felt that one was trying to win a popularity contest and I have no longer the energy for that kind of peripheral activity. We must get to centre ourselves and our work.

19 August 1983
Opera audiences do not know how to look at anything for the first time. They can't listen and look at the same time, who can? But at least ask them to look twice.

23 August 1983, London
L'Enfant et les Sortilèges
Children are wonderful. Twenty minutes only for first block moves. Ended the day feeling better and more optimistic than for a year at least. Frightening. Check the blood pressure.

26 September 1983
The only duty opera I have in front of me is *Traviata*, and now I do know enough to do my duty better, and intend to do as with

Don Carlo, following the book except for the last act which you remember we set in the first act decor, stripped, with a stove in the middle of the floor and screens around the bed.

27 September 1983
SH [Sybil Harrington] doesn't like the idea that Violetta ends up with nothing. She thinks it's too sad. As she's paying for it she thinks she can change it. Bliss, having created a Frankenstein's monster, can no longer control it. If he had not submitted to the *Traviata* backstab, the Harrington monster would have been killed at birth.

14 October 1983
Typical of James that when I hand-write a personal note to him he responds with two secretaries and a press department at his side. No wonder gossip rots, festers and thrives at the Met.

21 October 1983
Leave it to Franco to celebrate the 19th century – it's easy. The 20th is bloody difficult, but we are living it, so let us enjoy it. And now that you have learned how to work, enjoy it.

29 December 1983
Mahagonny is in trouble. None of the three leads can help one another, but they work wonderfully and are happy, which also has its value on that stage.
1pm. Russian Tearoom. Tom Stoppard: discuss future and past a little.
Treasure Island script arrives.
Pollocks toy theatre is ready.
Aubrey Beardsley *Yellow Book* arrives.

10 January 1984
How to make it impossible for the old guard to get a seat for the next hundred years. Marketing: For the next *Parade*, aim your seats at those beautiful, male and female, pre-college bums in that gaudy dust-filled hall. This time let's pre-sell ourselves to the right crowd.

26 January 1984
After ten years spent working at the Met it does not require the

mind of Agatha Christie to know where one or two of the bodies are buried. The question is whether or not to point the finger of Miss Marple in the direction of the guilty parties, especially when at least one of the persons to be accused is, as one should have known, the last to be suspected and had until recently always been regarded as a valued associate. It is not pleasant to see oneself as a wagon on which any band may jump, and the sight can lead to Peter Paranoia. Avoid it.

29 February 1984
Up to this date I still thought it possible to work at the Met and perhaps repair some of the damage done by the last two years' artistic administration.

1 March 1984
Joe V [Volpe]: Bliss, does not want to pay me – Nothing to discuss. After all a gentleman's agreement requires two gentlemen. Now what does this open up?

A very depressing meeting. JV, caught between power and pride, is out of his water but has by his indifference to pragmatics at least forced a decision and released me from the drudgery of security.

3 April 1984
Had I begun my work at the Met with *Carmelites*, the final view of the work of ten years would have been different. But *Aida*, *Rigoletto* and *Pasquale* were needed. Who lost? Who pays?

When can I meet with JL ref *Forza*, *Flute*, and one other work over 3–4 years. Otherwise the deal is off, and in addition warn Volpe – I intend to protect myself artistically as well as financially. I can't discuss the artistic question with him, only with James, but if my productions cannot be maintained according to the original conception and NOT restaged at the convenience of the technical department then my conversations with James are pointless.

16 May 1984
Notes for meeting
I have an ulterior motive in taking on *Simon Boccanegra* under these absurd conditions. I want for all and for once to demon-

strate that economy can mean style as long as the economy dominates the style. No one can do *Simon* for less and with more skill than can I. Not Franco [Zeffirelli] nor Jean-Pierre [Ponnelle] nor Peter la Bouffe du Nord [Brook]. I speak modestly, but if I don't say it I would be lying to you all when I explain what their job is and tell them to get on with it. Economy and Style without cheating.

18 May 1984
Political action: Do not any longer defend your position – *assert it*.

Boccanegra: The theories are on trial – I will abide by the result in future. The economy and style are the same thing – only the accounting is dishonest. Give Joe Clark [Technical Director] authority and watch his every move, but he is responsible in *all* matters to me personally. But explain to him his own position. I must trust him for an honest scrutiny of everyone including Joe [Volpe], James [Levine]. Our findings at the end of rehearsals will be the basis for a final report to the board and Chairman. Joe [Clark] must choose which side he is on. He and I will decide whether to tell Volpe or treat him as the others. There's a moral dilemma Arnold [Wesker] would enjoy – and giving little Joe a chance to become Big Joe.

19 May 1984
Now then tell Clark and *then* decide who else to tell or tell them all at the same moment or after the final dress. Should they know that if the theory is correct they will have helped to save the Met for the next hundred years, and from now on the absolute truth shall set me free. The absolute truth is everything.
And the Theory is
Economy and Style
are cheaper than
dishonesty and guile.

The last two years have been instructive rather than creative. We have seen a season in which Levine/Bliss/Volpe have demonstrated forcefully the preferred visual sense of the mid-eighties. *Trojans, Francesca* and the rest of the upcoming design clones point the way. I had hoped *Boccanegra* could be a signpost for a new direction which might ensure survival into the late eighties.

At the moment we are artistically as well as financially bankrupt. I do not speak now of communication problems (on the artistic problems which confront the Met for the next few years) but of the deepest rift and the uncertainty of theatre economics at this time. Either we all do it or no one will do it. JL cannot have it both ways.

Notebook:
Summary
1. SH [Sibyl Harrington] offered a huge endowment to the Met centenary fund
2. SH likes 19th-century opera
3. AB [Anthony Bliss] chooses the money over policy
4. JL [James Levine] also chooses the money over art
5. (This Hurt.) My own discovery, someone I took from the floor and trained and promoted to an office position betrayed me. JV [Joe Volpe] chose the money over loyalty
6. Not to mention GW [Gil Wechsler]

24 May 1984
Bliss lunch.
They cancel SB [*Simon Boccanegra*]. Sad for us. Tragic for them. The marriage of convenience is no longer convenient. *Now* about the financial settlement.

25 May 1984
It's a pity when I learned so much at Lincoln Centre, that the Met learned so little. It hardly seems a fair exchange for the pleasure of working with [Teresa] Stratas, [Maria] Ewing, [Richard] Cassilly, Hockney, Herbert and Co.

26 May 1984
NY sunny and depressing.
England wet cloudy and cheerful.

27 May 1984
Apart from Chicago there is no *need* to return unless it is for a short space *and* financially rewarding.

21 June 1984
To Anthony Bliss
Bill Fisher has just telephoned my secretary making a request

that I should be sure to make myself available for *Aida* this fall. I am including my reply for your information.

I hope all goes well. I am about to embark on five hours of Jean-Paul Sartre [*The Devil and the Good Lord* at the Lyric Hammersmith] – God help the behinds of the English audience.

20 June 1984
To J. William Fisher, Metropolitan Opera Board
My secretary has just informed me of your very kind telephone call and once again I owe you a word of private explanation.

Of course I would like to supervise the revival of *Aida* as I have some definite ideas for its improvement (no camels!). Unfortunately the derisory *per diem* offered by the Met to non-staff directors would require my drawing upon my own funds, which I cannot afford to do. I have already explained this situation to Messrs. Volpe and Bliss. They are powerless to make any adjustment, as the Finance Committee refuse to countenance any increase in this area. In order to understand my position, the Committee would have to make the effort of living in an hotel in New York and at the same time eating three meals a day on $150. Were their nerves and constitutions strong enough, they would understand the impracticality of such a proceeding. I do not expect them to comprehend matters so mundane, after all they are the group who, whilst willing to spend $1,750,000 for a minor Zandonai, cannot find $750,000 for a major Verdi. Their logic escapes me – as always.

30 August 1984
To Anthony Bliss
This chatty and on the whole cheerful letter is intended to welcome you back from what has been, I hope, a pleasant vacation. Whilst you have been wallowing in beaches and bonhomie, I have been knee deep in Existentialism, God and the Peasants' Revolt – all on a budget of £18,000! We are now one week away from preview and people seem optimistic. The rehearsals have been relaxed and the free time divided between cricket, house buying, the Proms, and visiting the dogs in quarantine! I am feeling twenty years younger and fitter in spite of the Iron Maiden and Comrade Scargill; swimming every morning and meeting up with old friends in the evening is a wonderful tonic and I have finally been able to throw away my walking stick!

'And now', as Lady Bracknell never stopped saying, 'to minor matters'. It seems that we are at the parting of the ways; I could wish that the negotiations had been handled with a little more style and with fewer pathetic attempts at humiliation or intimidation tactics, which, though they will provide a fairly funny Chapter Ten in 'Murder at the Met' (publisher's attention-getting title, not mine!), served very little other purpose.

As you know, I think the Met's *per diem* arrangements are unrealistic and will become even less realistic after November. However, there is the problem of *Aida*. In view of Mr Fisher's personal request that I supervise the revival and of my feeling that the revival will need very careful handling, I have indicated to you and Mr Fisher that I am willing to undertake it at the fee and *per diem* already discussed, if someone will send me a detailed rehearsal schedule I will be able to make plans to dovetail it with commitments over here. As yet no plan has arrived and I think I am meant to assume that management has decided to go ahead without me, but it would be helpful to know one way or the other. So far my only pleasant communication from colleagues at the Met has been your own much appreciated letter and an equally friendly one from David Stivender.

With thanks for all your help in the past.

21 November 1984
To Phoebe Berkowitz [Assistant Director]
At last a cable from AB announcing that due to the shortness of the rehearsal period involved there would be no point in my coming to New York for the rehearsals of *Aida*. I have replied that both he and the technical department ought to be aware by now that minimal rehearsals have never yet prevented my pulling a show into some semblance of artistic order. My only concern is that you, Miss Price and David Reppa should be under no misunderstanding or misapprehension as to the reasons. In spite of the petty irritations surrounding the termination of my engagement, I have not wavered in my intention to put my best endeavours into the work, in view of Bill Fisher's request that I should do so, and had indeed devised a new trial and finale of a simplicity that would have tickled your fancy. However, whoever takes decisions on the first or third floor has decided otherwise and to be completely honest with you I am relieved to bring my association with that plush and

crystal whorehouse to an end. If the Mafia and the Pimps decide on the policy of the brothel, it's time for those of us who enjoy spreading our artistic legs to get back to the streets. At least the air is cleaner and we are responsible for our mistakes.

I have watched and waited over the last months for some recognition that somewhere in the Maestro's head was the idea that he needed help and that what had been accomplished over the few productive years we had together had not been done entirely on his own. The telephone remained silent, the letter box empty. It has been made perfectly clear to me that neither my person nor my ideas are wanted and I am happy to work here [in London], where I belong and have a creative function to serve, amongst people who can take joy in work and give love to each other in the doing of it.

As regards the future, I am happy to feel that those productions which I value most are in the best hands: *Lulu* in yours, *Parade* and *Carmelites* with Max [Charruyer]. For the rest it will sink or swim according to its merit.

Undated
To David Hockney
No news from the Met except a cable from Miss Blisskins telling me that lack of rehearsal time renders my presence unnecessary! No word from the chubby maestro, but that, as Noël C. put it once, would be like 'expecting Clytemnestra to fry you an egg'.

7 December 1984
To Anthony Bliss
Thanks for your letter of November 29. I take note of the points you make. To begin with a negative answer. To give you three months notice on *Lulu* is no longer possible as December 4th has already passed, so the answer must be at this time, regretfully, no. The rehearsal date of the musical is not yet fixed, but I obviously cannot keep you waiting.

For the future I note that you would like a commitment from me with regard to *Parade* on August 4th 1985, (*Aida* should now rest with Bruce Donnell) and *Don Carlo* December 13th 1985. Those periods are now entered in my diary and I will respond at the latest by the dates named and before if possible.

With regard to a future project, and I now write to you in confidence, I do not see the likelihood of collaboration with

James looming very high on my list of priorities. Since my last telephone conversation with him on the subject of *Simon Boccanegra* in March of this year, I have been granted no communication of any kind, neither good wishes nor regrets that ten years work was coming to an inconclusive end. This is not acceptable behaviour on any level, be it social or professional, and whilst as a member of the staff I had to submit, as did we all, to his dilatoriness and lack of professional courtesy, I am now at liberty to express my feeling that as long as the Metropolitan puts itself in the artistic control of such rampant egotism combined with inexperience, the future is not one I care to contemplate, or with which I would care to be involved.

Let me assure you that at all times my personal regard for you and gratitude for your support are and have been constant.

Diary:
Bliss letter re revivals answered once and for all.

In America I seem to have been swimming out of my depth and in quicksand. I may still be out of my depth in England but at least the water is clear.

7 March 1985
Why is it that I can think only in a crisis?

Week beginning 11 March 1985 (in NY for *Lulu*)
Stay in all week. Blinds down. I draw the blinds and New York goes away. Nice for a while, but not as a way of Life.

Oh Lord let me write a book, but not this week.

12 March 1985
Not like Chicago, at least I have the home to return to. Behave accordingly. Not let depression make you totally inert, but still learn how to re-energise from inertia.

14 March 1985
I really have to become my own Mr Wiley [R.B. Sheridan's Stage Manager] and lock myself into a dressing room for 3 hours a day with only a yellow pad. Solitude is not a state to be rejected but used. I have not used myself well this week but in retrospect the

week has been well-used even if I have not written the *Rivals* or was it *Scandal*.

15 March 1985
Tom H[ulce] has as much right to have a go at the moody as Frank Grimes but one has ability, the other has gall and both could do with more of either.

18 March 1985
The visit has been useful in retrospect. I realise that I have no regrets or, better yet, no nostalgia for any part of Manhattan or the Metropolitan but I do find it a very depressing place. Any enthusiasm is so subdued.

But I learnt about betrayal at the Met. Betrayed on all levels – personal, professional, political, you name it.

It's very difficult to find *anyone* ignorant enough for me to teach.

16 October 1985
Volpe called at last. Telex? They understood I was not coming – eventually I had to ask if I was being asked not to come. Volpe said he'd 'have to work on it'. Bet your ass, Joe, you bet your ass you will.

17 October 1985
Volpe to call. If he says no, ask for James privately, before I take advice. Does James want to risk the scandal which would follow leave alone the question of royalties in lieu of the actual royalties never offered.

Soothe the ruffled feathers of *The Times* with an update with an exclusive on developments.

25 October 1985
To Bruce Crawford, Metropolitan Opera
Dear Mr Crawford,
You will, I hope, forgive the formality of my address, but as we have never been introduced, in spite of many requests from me to the management, I feel perhaps you will understand.

There is no question that contractually you are in the right, but in moral and practical terms you are in the wrong, and I feel I must write to you to state my position. Undoubtedly I should have contacted you before August, but I had given my word to Messrs Levine and Bliss that whatever problems (financial) I found with the Metropolitan's stated offer, I would fulfil my obligations to *Parade*, in view of my special relationship to this programme, but that I could not guarantee any engagements beyond that without further discussions. It seems that both James and Tony have suffered, as I understand from your representative, Mr Volpe, from a lapse of memory, and Maestro Levine refuses to communicate with me as he considers the present discussions 'non-artistic'. For this reason I am forced to impose upon your time.

In defence of my failure to contact you before August 4th, I must point out that, having given my word to the then General Manager and Artistic Director, I had assumed that they would pass this information on to the appropriate department, and at that time I would have hoped for some communication from you, not only to discuss this matter, but perhaps to say goodbye to me after ten years of service to the Metropolitan. However, I fully understand the pressures involved in taking over an organisation of this kind and would not wish these matters to come between any future discussions.

I am told that you do not take artistic decisions, and this I understand; but James is refusing to take any decision or to speak to me. I must therefore discuss with you the artistic aspects of the decision you have taken.

I wish to protest most strongly against the appointment of a director who is, in my view, unsympathetic and incompetent to handle the particular problems of this evening, of which I am to some extent the author. Whatever abilities Mr Mills has as a routinier, he is hopelessly out of his range and M. Charruyer was brought in specifically to assist on the revival of *Parade* and more recently *L'Enfant* at Covent Garden. His total understanding of the music and his instant rapport with M. Rosenthal and Mr Hockney gave him advantages Mr Mills cannot, with the best will in the world, hope to attain. Charruyer came with me to Covent Garden and is the only person, apart from myself, cognisant of the changes made in the last five pages of the score, which for the first time complete the evening in the manner in which I had conceived it six or eight years ago. Mr Mills has none of this background, and I must once again protest at being forced to watch an assistant do to *Parade* what another one did to *Aida*.

I intend to be in New York to do my Christmas shopping and, if possible, to prevent the damaging of my professional reputation by any legal means that seem proper. If you wish to meet at that time I would be happy to make an appointment.

4 November 1985
To Anthony Bliss
Sorry to intrude on your retirement from Metropolitan affairs, which I hope is as happy and enjoyable as is mine, which seems to consist mainly of rebuilding a hundred-year-old house and picking up royalty cheques.

However, to return for a moment to Metropolitan matters, Joe Volpe tells me that you have no recollection of our conversation the last time we had lunch at Alfredo (24th May '84). Please let me know if this is the case as I am in a professional dilemma, being very concerned that the revival of *Parade* should be the perfect and final version, representing as it does the high point of our time at the Met and, as the Met are not inclined to think my presence necessary in view of my failure to return a contract in August, I must decide how to proceed.

4 November 1985
To James Levine
Dear Maestro
I am told that you do not remember the substance of our conversation in The Ginger Man (March 25th/26th of this year approximately), toward the end of the *Lulu* rehearsal period. Please confirm this.

Further, I am told that you do not consider my present debate with the management 'artistic'. Really, James, if the decision as to who is the best person to direct *Parade* is not an artistic decision, what is?

I would appreciate an answer, at least to paragraph one, at the earliest possible moment. The rest can wait until I am in New York, which will be some time before the opening.

6 November 1985
Common sense atrophied by expediency as so often in a large and necessarily bureaucratic organisation.

8 November 1985
To Bruce Crawford [re *Parade* revival]
Dear Bruce

Thank you for your very welcome letter, and I look forward to seeing you when I arrive in New York. As to my exact time of arrival, I cannot at the moment enlighten you as I am still awaiting the arrival of a rehearsal schedule. Would it be intruding on your time to ask you to shout down the hall to whoever is responsible and ask them to express a detailed rehearsal schedule to me so that I can decide upon the point at which my presence will be most useful?

Also, before I arrive, I would like some guarantee that the security officers will allow me through the door and that the staff allow me in the auditorium. From then on I will be able to communicate without actually directing the action and incurring working permit problems.

I have written to James and Tony on this matter and shall, I hope, see them during my stay. I do hope you understand that my only concern in all this is with *Parade*, which was, in my view, one of the few creations made at and for the Metropolitan, which was, due to many different pressures, unfinished at the premiere. The ending of *Parade* is particularly close to me in the statement I am trying to make, and I must have one more opportunity to get it right.

8 November 1985
PS: It is very good for the book to finish the work on *Parade* and the Met at the same time.

14 November 1985
When I think happily of my life and work in the operatic field – and unhappily I am not often happy – but on those occasions I think of Phoebe Berkowitz. Try to describe and explain – in Part One or Part Two? Think.

Should be written from the point of view of someone who has been out of touch with himself for years and is trying to discover why.

28/29 November 1985
And whosoever shall not receive you, nor hear your words,

when you depart out of that house or city, shake off the dust from your feet.
Matt. X. 14

If a revolution fails there is no need for bloodshed as long as the first revolution is only the first and not the last. And anyway it's silly to go on playing Trotsky to Volpe's Stalin (if you follow my political and literary drift). So never send to know from whose hands the ice pick cometh, it comes for Thee baby, if you really want to know, and I prefer not to watch the end of the revolution. The beginning was exciting. But after that to end with a whimper not a bang. And so, with reference to Matthew X 14, I leave you as I came without translations.

11

Shakespeare: NY to Buxton

'Learn to live as a community or die.'

14 October 1977
To Richard Burton
Just a short note to let you know how delighted I am at the probability of *Lear* becoming a possibility (or should it be the other way around?).

I am up to my ass at the moment with *The Merchant* and *Rigoletto*, and then am going to North Africa for a vacation, after which I gather from Alex Cohen [Producer], we could meet in London during the period December 15–16, as we certainly need some more conversation before either of us commits not adultery but murder maybe.

In addition to endless discussion of Folio and Quarto, how old is the Fool? Do you like the idea of Hume Cronyn as Gloucester, etc.?
Love to Susie.

3 January 1978
To Richard Burton
I trust you will forgive me for the delay in contacting you, but your addition of *Romeo and Juliet* has brought with it immense logistic problems which I think are now solved, at least in my head.

I must tell you that I think your inspiration about *Romeo and Juliet was* an inspiration – nothing more or less. In addition to giving you the opportunity to look as young as Shirley Temple (or Baby Leroy, if you like), I have been made to see the two plays as a much more organic whole, in fact complementary to each other. The First and the Last, in fact.

Having spent most of the Christmas period in the tiresome cross-plotting, doubling and scheduling problems, suddenly on New Year's Day I was able to step back and look at the enormity of the task ahead of us. For the director it is rather like walking through the Henry VIII Chapel in the Abbey and from that into the Sistine Chapel. The thought is at the same time frightening and stimulating. I am not sure if the two plays bound together by setting, costumes and casting are not the most thrilling I have ever undertaken. I only wish to God I had had the idea and not you.

If, with the stage, we can solve the stylistic problems in both plays (upstairs, downstairs, cliffs, battles and bodies), we have, or rather Alex Cohen has, a stage on which you may play at any time in the next 10 years any Elizabethan or Jacobean play which interests you and, incidentally, the way the design is going at the moment, it can play in a tent or in a barn. I don't know about you but I wouldn't mind storming a barn or two.

Of course, there have been many solutions to the problem of 'Shakespeare's stage'. Tanya [Moiseiwitsch]'s solution in the histories was, I think, the best, but we have to find something else – something which can tour and make its statement no matter in what surroundings it may appear.

What is true of the stage is also true of the costumes and this brings me to my major rethinking about which you and I must have some conversation in the not too distant future. I have always felt that Granville Barker was right in his emphasis of the Renaissance aspect of the costumes. What I am encouraging the designer to work for is a basic early Elizabethan shape (no peasecods, slops or RUFFS!), but I want him to find an attractive but somewhat uniform profile for each of the plays to which we make additions. Wolf skin and leather in *Lear*, brocade and damask in *Romeo*, let's say.

Oddly enough, the two weeks spent on clearing up the many technical problems of staging and rehearsing have left my mind quite clear about the look and style of the two evenings. However, not being graced with the gift of words, I shall explain it all much more vividly when we are together and I can extravagantly wave my arms about.

The whole purpose of this letter is to congratulate you on the inspiration which, as I look back at it, is an inspiration with a splash of genius in it. Please can we start rehearsing tomorrow?

Shakespeare in America
A Reaction

A reaction to what, it may be asked. The initial provocation arose from the irresponsible, expensive influx of English televised Shakespeare. It is true that American actors, under responsible guidance, can do as well as and better than their British counterparts, and this is a subject on which I think I can speak with some authority having worked with most of the pre-eminent English theatrical profession.

Unless we all in America – and by all I mean investors, producers, directors and the actors – react positively and *now*, it will be impossible to produce the evidence of American acting quality in this area in sufficient time to combat the inherent snobbism which dictates the costly importation of not necessarily superior foreign work.

If one works in the theatre long enough, one fails to recognise its almost total lack of importance to the non-professional world at large. An awareness of theatre as something more than an easily available soporific between cocktails and supper is, for the majority, an unknown factor, and yet it is to this unknown majority we must appeal.

Now is not the time for a discursive paper on theatre as a life-enhancing force. Theatre as school and world lies outside this brief, the purpose of which is to raise money. Money for what? Money for a primary school, money for an educational and cultural force. These demands can hardly be met at this time. Nevertheless, the theatrical demand is desperate and immediate.

The gigantic gap in the American actor's vocabulary is 'classic'. Many attempts have been made to close this gap, all of them admirable. But these experiments have tended always to bring the plays to within easy reach of the actors and the audience by reality, to a known modern cultural or ethnic background, instead of taking the actors up the height of the plays. Shakespeare, Sheridan, Wycherley, Webster – all of them partake in the universality of great drama, but, as Harley Granville Barker taught vainly for years, Shakespeare in modern dress does not necessarily increase our understanding: 'Shakespeare plays by Shakespeare means.' This is a dictum of Barker's to which all directors have, at one time or another, paid lip service. Yet perhaps within this phrase lies the economic solution to fulfil a deeply felt need to satisfy a shameful cultural lack within the late 20th-century American theatre.

There are, I know, many, many young American actors and actresses who are desperate for a firm, non-gimmicky Shakespearean training, because they have come to recognise how much the future of American drama depends upon its actors being trained through classic discipline to help change the face, style and future of American dramatic literature.

For some years I have been attempting to create a space in which it would be possible to present *on* Broadway any play from the Golden Age to the late Restoration. I believe this has been accomplished. I know it to be possible to propose a five-year plan for a company to present, on a changeless space, any of these plays, using the same basic wardrobe, properties and lighting. These costs can be amortised over a period of five years. The set, lighting and costumes not only reduce costs by about 60% but drive the actors to attend to the text and nothing but the text. The basic requisite of an actor has always been supposed to consist of 'four boards and a passion'.

Perhaps at last the economy is forcing us to take a step which our artistic consciousness should have forced us to take many years ago. The cultural need is urgent. The time is now. A commitment can be obtained at this time from Mr Christopher Plummer to lead such a company in a repertoire of two plays presented upon the same stage by the same company. The first tragedy and the last. *Romeo and Juliet* and *King Lear*. This project is subject to the resolution of Christopher Plummer's film commitments and is intended to begin rehearsals in early June and open in late July, 1978.

In addition, I have a second season commitment from Miss Diana Rigg to play *Taming of the Shrew* and *Cleopatra* with Mr Plummer, or Mr George C. Scott should Mr Plummer be unavailable. These two figureheads are already attracting more and more actors. The repertoire is extendable and is, in fact, only intended as a guide to budgeting. Should the plan go forward, then conversations should begin with Messrs Pacino, Hoffman, and, indeed, any young leading actor and actress whose ideals lead them in this direction and whose ambitions are no longer satisfied by cinema alone.

If the American commercial theatre does not *now* take an active interest in its training of American actors, there will be no future of any great depth. This 3–5 year investment must be regarded as an investment in the future of American acting.

THE STAGE AND LIGHTING

We need *now* a supple, portable stage and lighting grid upon which, if need be, *all* the plays of Shakespeare can be presented in a manner which catches some sense or flavour of the speed, fluidity and discipline the bare stage demands, so that the actors are *forced* to face the text nakedly and evoke the world of *Lear* and *Romeo and Juliet* from the text and only the text. The mobility of the set and lighting are essential. It must be capable of one-night-stands on a college campus or a Broadway house. Once installed in a theatre, such lights and set need no further addition (balconies, extra lamps, projectors, etc.). The fit-up and lighting must be possible in 24 hours. The lighting grid, once prefocused, is hung in toto, needing only minimal adjustments (special care always to be taken in the packing and maintenance of the grid to ensure speedy, accurate focus in each date to be played). The sketches should, as I have previously said, be judged as a means of arriving at a basic 'guestimate' budget. Do not look for variety of scene. This lies in the text.

16 February 1978
Telegram to Helen Hayes
Forgive the intrusion and impertinence if I ask whether there is the remotest chance you would consider playing the Nurse in *Romeo and Juliet* in a production to be directed by myself, Peter Firth as Romeo, Roberta Maxwell as Juliet, Christopher Plummer as Mercutio. The play to run in repertory with *King Lear*, rehearsing early June, tour and play New York.

You would be involved as the Nurse in a maximum of four performances in one week. Both plays are intended to launch a three year plan, culminating, hopefully, in a pure American company presenting Shakespeare's plays by the simplest means and on the simplest of stages.

Is there a possibility of your interest? Please cable me (your reply is already pre-paid) and I will come to see you, talk to you on the phone or wait for your arrival in New York. Whichever you prefer. Will write to you with further details.

21 February 1978
Telegram from Helen Hayes
My voice would not hold up even for four performances a week.
Miserable to miss the best opportunity in years. Thanks.

14 March 1978
To Christopher Plummer
I've tried and tried. It's all fallen apart but that doesn't mean I've
given up all prospects entirely. Just, at this time, it is now too late
to do it properly. If you have time, ring me and I'll give you the
gory details.

March 1978
In November '74 I made a note that I would have to take care of
myself if I wanted to do the job – I didn't – High Blood Pressure.
Blood vessels in the eye bursting like buds in May.

Pull yourself together. Don't do anything but exercise and
think for two months. Go back to Derby! Walk around then up to
the Izaak Walton walk. Maybe write but *no opera*. Think about the
book. See if the streets of Derby jog any memories, even if they
have changed beyond recognising.

The Burton incident contains enough material for one short
paragraph and that's all.

Think as you remember how your work pattern has
developed and why, and you might find a way to change it
without damaging the work.

April Fools' Day! 1978
After a sleepless night brought about by the Nigel Williams play
[WC/PC], a connection and a pattern and a future of some
purpose emerge.
The clarification of the above is a letter to KJ at the Arts Council.
It seems also to belong in my notebook but why do it twice?

4 April 1978
To Keith Jeffrey
'Nel mezzo del cammin di nostra vita' ['In the middle of the
course of our life']. A cliché, yes, but one to which I have finally
made a personal connection.

To move from Dante to Morgan [E.M.] Forster and Margaret
Meade will involve jump cuts and fades that might tax the

ingenuity of Richard Lester. Nevertheless, that is the trip I would ask you to take with me for I need your help and advice – officially and unofficially – and I need you to take this letter away from your desk and look at it at home. Talk to the Minister if you think it appropriate, but treat it as the most earnest and serious request I have made to the Arts Council. The problem of how to formulate this request is one with which I require both your good will and assistance.

Do not worry, it is not my object to discuss the National Theatre or the state of the arts in London. Rather, to let you know the professional lack of direction which I have felt increasingly over the last years and of the possible resolution of that somewhat despairing situation. Although everything in the Met garden is getting lovelier day by day, I have a profound sense that it is not *all* I should be doing. The Shakespeare Prize [which I had received in Hamburg] came as a jolt, a considerable honour given for work which placed me in the position I now occupy. Just as George Devine trained me for the National Theatre, Hamburg trained me for the Met. It becomes clear to me now that it is time to remember these debts and begin to repay them.

If I were to extend this idea, I would have to write an intolerably biographical letter. Suffice it to say that during two weeks taken up with re-establishing old contacts in Derby and walking over the Peak District I had time to crystalise my discontent and produce for myself a coherent, worthwhile future. Make a few connections, in fact, in the best E.M. Forster manner.

Margaret Meade recently made a statement which has hounded me. It seems the sum of her life boils down to the simplest point – 'Learn to live as a community or die.' And by community I know her to mean small community. One small community fulfilling itself, its past and future, and creating a lively present, can show the way for others.

Of course, this is not new. Britten's work at Aldeburgh, Anna Scher's work in London schools and streets point a clear direction. However, my thoughts for the future are simpler and rooted in another principle altogether. The image of ploughing back what one has learned so that more people may have the privilege of knowing music, painting, poetry, drama as related to the world in which they live, to create a community in which its Sheepdog Trials (which are pure drama) can be related to *The Marriage of Figaro*, *Hamlet* and to its own history. To put it shortly, and leaving the philosophy for later, I want *Aquae Armemetia* (Buxton to you!) for myself and others to attempt a massive conflagration of the arts and the community. To work within the community full-time and to create – a centre based on the old opera house for us all.

For instance, Jocelyn Herbert would teach, talk, show drama groups theatre design, painting, etching, help build sets for their own work, be it Gilbert and Sullivan or Shakespeare. I would, with the advice of the local education committee, direct or help in the presentation of plays for schools or drama groups. Tony Harrison and Harrison Birtwistle would compose an opera on the subject of Eyam in the plague year (the community which sacrificed itself for the country), to be performed as far as possible by the community. This communal opera would be balanced by, let us say, James Levine conducting (if we could ally ourselves to the Hallé orchestra) *Figaro/Flute* at the beginning of the opera season. The animals/children would have made their own costumes in the schools to designs by Jocelyn Herbert. Peter Firth (Pudsey – ¾ hour away) would do his first *Hamlet* and Alan Bates (Derby ½ hour away) his first *Lear*.

Tony Harrison wants to write a verse play for Joan Plowright set in a North Country munitions factory during a tea break during the 1914–18 war. We would encourage a Yorkshire and Lancashire brass band contest in the pump room. Sheepdog trials – everything connecting Yorkshire and Lancashire and the High Peak. Painters, poets, musicians, living and dead.

For example, has there ever been a retrospective exhibition of Wright of Derby? In addition to what is local, we bring the best of the international music and dramatic scene to the community. I know for instance that Domingo will go anywhere if I mount a production of *Christopher Sly* for him. I am sure that Montserrat will at least haul herself up from the spa for a concert if I beg. In short, the Parish pump is beautiful but it is not all. International quality of work related to the community and given back by the community to the rest of the world, or at least to anyone who can take the trouble to make the journey. You can be sure of one thing, if London wants to see us we shall not go to them. They must come to us.

I can't speak of costs at the moment. All I can speak of is a profound conviction that this is what I must do with the rest of my professional career. This is the place I want to be and those are the people with whom I want to work. I am aware that a gentleman is trying to open an opera season with Buxton as the Glyndebourne of the North, or the Oxford of the Midlands. Good, but not good enough. I intend to offer to direct something for him (I hope he will recover from the shock) but opera alone will tend to create an élitism which is no longer acceptable in the arts or anywhere else in the world.

Now, how do I go about it? I shall be in England again in May to talk to anyone you think could be helpful, and I am prepared now to have the whole thing underway by 1980/81. I know that it means very little money for me, but I have made enough and it hasn't made me very happy. I will simply have to work a little harder on Broadway or in the West End to be able to afford to begin this work, but I know we could accomplish something very extraordinary. The names I have used in this letter are, as you are aware, all personal friends, and all of them would be willing to commit to a project of this kind and, indeed, have been wanting to do so for many years. I think they all feel the need to define our directions more clearly.

Forgive the length of this letter but you don't know how much longer I could have made it.

16 May 1978
Before three years are up I will do *Henry 1 & 2* with pros and locals mixed in Buxton.

26 May 1978
H[elen] Montagu phoned re Burton/*Lear*. For the right dates and a lot of money I could be committed – more likely dates don't work, alas.

1 June 1978
One way in which to make an audience pay attention to Shakespeare is to play him in his own period. There is still work to be done in this area.

12

The Later NT

5 May 1974
About the NT.
I don't think I can take money for the use of my name. I can have no hand in the planning, nor do I really find the decisions being taken very inspiring; it's donnish and didactic and not much fun. If a national theatre company exists, it exists through the *company* or not at all.

I don't think PH [Peter Hall] or his literary department have any feelings about actors except as objects.

If I can't be there to argue I shouldn't take the money. If I can't devote myself to the Met, then I should not do that job; but the Met has more creative possibilities (if I can stand the pace) than the NT. At least for me.

20 May 1975
To Keith Jeffrey
It was good to see you in London even if club land proved to be too much for my working-class wits.

A propos of our conversation, I have developed one more suggestion I would like you to put before your lords and masters if you think fit. It seems to me on reflection, the only way to resolve the enormous financial burden which the South Bank is becoming is to adopt Lord Goodman's original suggestion (if indeed it was his suggestion) namely to put three major subsidised companies under one roof. BUT, and this is most important, EACH GROUP WOULD HAVE COMPLETE AUTONOMY. That is to say, the English Stage Company would leave the Royal Court and occupy the Cottesloe, responsible to its own board who are responsible to the Arts Council for their own grant. The RSC would occupy the Lyttelton, responsible to their own governors and for their own grants. And the National Theatre would concentrate on the Olivier, again with complete autonomy. The important difference obviously is, instead of having each of the three divergent groups under one overlord, they each retain their individuality, their ability to spend their grant in the way they think fit.

The profession's objection to the amalgamation of the RSC and the National Theatre was the natural objection to monopoly. Not so much on political grounds but on artistic, which is all any of us is concerned about. Any attempt to bend three companies to work under a new leader would fail, even if the profession was forced to accept it. Three groups under one roof, each with their character and independence totally maintained, having only the workshops and wardrobe in common, could provide that competitive energy which is essential to anything calling itself the National Theatre.

When all of us on the building committee (how long ago was it, 10 or 15 years?) planned the South Bank, we planned it in an economic vacuum, never imagining the present economic crisis, and certainly nobody from the Government or the GLC ever suggested that we should! We were simply asked to provide the best facility for a National Theatre, but events have caught up with us, and if the theatre is not to become a white elephant, it must adapt itself to the times and the economy in which it must survive.

I will keep this letter as brief as possible. If you want to discuss it at further length, I will be happy to do so, either by mail or when we meet in four weeks' time.

I do hope you won't consider that I am stepping out of my correct position in writing this letter, but as a member of the building committee and the English theatrical profession, I do have a great sense of responsibility toward it, somewhat aggravated by the fact that I have an equally pressing responsibility here [the Met].

Anyway, those are my thoughts for what they are worth.

1 December 1975
To Lord Birkett [National Theatre Deputy Director]
As you will no doubt have heard by now, *Equus* has opened in Boston to great acclaim and looks to be settled there for some time. Dai Bradley has been praised to the skies and indeed deserves all the praise given, and more. His performance has grown remarkably in the last six months. It now represents Alan

Strang as I had always imagined him. Apart from the 'dented little face', which after all is inherited by way of a coal-mining father and several years of malnutrition, apart from these accidents of breeding, he has developed his own sneaky, uneducated instincts to the point where they serve the play in a way that Firth never did. Of course, it is more than possible that without Firth's personal presence, glamour, or whatever you like to call it, the play might not have been so publicly successful. But it is now, for me at least, a much less comfortable, darker, and more sustained experience.

'And now to minor matters' – the future, Dryden [All For Love] and Molnar [The Guardsman] and all that. I am enormously tempted by both plays, and of course long to work with Diana [Rigg], but I can't summon up any desire to work at the National again. Please read on patiently and try to understand my problems and some of my needs in the theatre.

I have lacked theory in my work and have operated on instinct. Such intellect as I have has been held in check until my instincts have been given full rein. Not perhaps the best way of working, but the only way I have or am likely to have. In explaining this present decision, I am trying to explain to you an instinctive decision in intellectual terms.

Consider my position with that National Theatre. For something like ten years I helped LO to keep the pot boiling in the Waterloo Road until the South Bank was ready to be occupied. It wasn't always the happiest experience. LO, always inspiring, was often ignorant of the sacrifices of personal life that were made and often cavalier in his treatment and use of the abilities I had to offer. But for all of the time, we shared an unspoken sense of the need for community within the theatre which would enable the company to become a social unit as interloving and hating as a family. After all, if one is to give up so much private life to it then the theatre must give us back another and perhaps richer life and can, in return for our work, become family and lover!

At the end of ten years, the family we had built was dispersed and replaced with another unit, historically and politically necessary. But so far, it has not given me any sense of group life, nor indeed any sense of an intention in that direction. This is perfectly fine and represents what Peter [Hall] wants and what the Board wants, but it isn't what I want in the next phase of my work. I don't believe that pile of concrete will ever become a theatre without a community to inhabit it.

At the moment, I feel that I can find what I want in the theatre in this ugly, gold-plated monster. There is a general music director, of not only musical but theatrical genius, who shares my attitude, superb singers (yes, even singers), and technicians to help interpret those feelings and needs that I have tried to articulate to you. The gigantic financial and moral crises here are the ideal breeding ground for future home and family. A sense of the *necessity* of survival can produce, and indeed is producing, a wonderfully happy, energetic atmosphere so that if it is all to end in divorce, recrimination and disaster, we shall at least have been living together and not the least trying to pull 'the most total form of theatre there is' (to quote PH) into the 20th century. So I think I must become one of those 'unheard and unsung in my own country' in order to grow and live in another one.

There are times when I regret England and have even a sense of failure in relation to it (should I have stayed on and formed another company somewhere?). But, in the end it is my life and work I must think about, and with that international, if extremely selfish attitude in mind, I must decline your kind offer for the future and hope that you will continue as creatively in the new building as we have all done in the old one.

This seems, on reflection, a very personal letter to write to someone I hardly know, but I don't know Peter much better. Therein, perhaps, lies some of my problem. So, perhaps you will pass it over to him at a time when he is not under too great a pressure and assure him and yourself of my best wishes for you and the National Theatre.

20 September 1976
[Royal opening NT 25 October 1976]
To Lord Birkett
How can you seriously open the first theatre of the 21st century (which we all hope it will be) with such a clutter of 19th-century terminology? I lack black tie, carriages, postillion and footmen (though I suppose I can by now afford them) but I do resent having them forced upon me. I find it hard to believe that you insist on the black tie after so much time has been spent in the last twenty years trying to make the theatre more available and less exclusive. May I ask for a Lordly dispensation in this area?

Apart from the social implications for the future of the theatre, do you really want me to appear before you looking like a superannuated cinema organist?

I look for a loving answer, Lord, perhaps 'Perish the baubles, your person is all I desire.' Of course I want to participate in the occasion which represents the culmination of 15 years' work.

28 December 1976
To Keith Jeffrey
I was in London for the opening of *Il Campiello*, unfortunately having seen the Strehler production in Paris the week before. He makes the play seem a work of genius in one of the most dazzling productions I have ever seen, and if Bill Bryden and Peter Hall had any humility at all, they would recognise the genius and realise it was impossible to copy and would have thought of something more original than HM having to watch scenery being erected, although it's probably the only erect thing she's seen in many years (No, that can't be true, can it? Unless . . . but that possibility is too horrendous to think about).

I haven't heard about Comrade Birkett leaving the National but it's about time. The theatre should unload all the ineffectual amateurs and engage all the professionals it possibly can. But that's too much to hope for.

I shall begin rehearsals for *Man and Superman* on April 4th and I hope to see you at that time.

29 June 1978
To Peter Hall
Thank you for your note of 20 June. Of course we can talk any time you like. Whenever I come to London you are up to your eyes in work, and I know how I hate people dropping in on me at the Met.

As regards plays at the National and the future – now that I have been able to help push the Met beyond the mere survival stakes, the prospects for the next three to four years involve a complex exercise involving the community, schools and a general shake-up, not any longer of the technical staff but of the audience now and in the future. As you will imagine, this takes a great deal of my time and in all those short gaps which the tax man allows me in England, I like to occupy myself with something which does not revolve around a gigantic organisation and have plans in that direction which cover the next three to four years.

I have found a play of Nigel Williams' [WC/PC] which I very much want to do and with whom I have put in work on the text for a few weeks now, but I think this does involve the Royal Court or some commercial theatre. It is not that I would not like to direct in the new Olivier. I would, but unfortunately the only three plays that I would like to do with Jocelyn, you are already doing with John Bury.

19 January 1979
Shaffer's soufflé arrived [*Amadeus*]. My play developed. Good day.

24–27 January 1979
THIS TIME REMEMBER IT'S A PLEASURE AS WELL AS A PRIVILEGE. I tried to formulate the style as PS [Peter Shaffer] spoke it, NOT *impose* it upon him for four whole years.

5 January 1979
To Peter Shaffer
I just cancelled my vacation. Dawn broke about 5.30 a.m. on Sunday morning and as a result I am ready to do *Amadeus* now or as soon as possible as long as we can open some time before August 20th.

A weekend spent in the company of Kelly, Jahn, Einstein and the letters has made me realise that perhaps I know a little more about the background than I thought I did and apart from reading the play, the main pleasure is getting around to listening to some of the chamber music I don't know. (Incidentally, Benda and the lesser luminaries are fascinating background music to work with because by listening to them one has an extraordinary sense of the revolution that had taken place. One has always been aware of it but never actually made the musical comparison.)

I have some detailed observations but none that you need think about or worry about until we meet when you return. For example, I think you have under-estimated Joseph [Emperor of Austria] to the degree that the support and observation of that old despot, autocrat and reformer are diminished somewhat in their effect, but anyway I have GOT IT and I want to go *now!* We have never needed stars before. If we get them good, if not, good. There are fine actors who are not stars and we can get them, but the words must be said *now*.

The question of age and the starriness of the cast seems fairly clear in my mind now as I think it has been in yours from the beginning. If we are prepared to think of JG [John Gielgud] and Paul S [Scofield] as Salieri, then why dismiss Jacobi and McKellen? None of these four is exactly expert in the expression of passion for 'tit and slit' but whereas the older suffer either from problems of memory and energy (and saintliness) the other two can produce energy, venom and astonishing vocal variety and are also adaptable enough to be unflustered by the constant changes of text.

I am not sure where I will be when you return or if you will receive this letter on vacation. It is merely meant to cheer you up about the date, which can now be any time between late April and August 20th, and will stop you whingeing around like an old Jewish authoress suffering from hepatitis. Have a good holiday.

7 February 1979
Five weeks from now and where and when and cast of *Amadeus* should be decided.

16 February 1979
PS: if it's not fun and I won't earn a living, forget it!

17 February 1979
This weekend I solved the problem of STYLE in Peter's play, formulated a contract and recognised Mercia as a separate kingdom.

20 February 1979
I am/we are to produce it. HM [Helen Montagu] to do it in the office. Consult me on all points. Budget etc. Peter will have Robbie [Lantz, Shaffer's agent] to intercede with management. I will have Riggs. So we ALL have producers' profit as well as the usual % because we work for it all the time even if we don't get billed like Riggs or Paul or Robert.

Week beginning 19 February 1979
THIS WEEK ENUNCIATE THE STYLE AND THE CONTRACT.

21 February 1979
And tell PS of my personal, as opposed to financial, needs to PRODUCE properly. + NO STAGE DIRECTIONS IN PUBLISHED TEXT. I'll help to do it in an original way at no extra cost.

If you agree to this I'll tell you about the production!! *and* what's wrong with the STYLE and construction, so let's talk about that on the plane.

+ *no* little jewels like 'at this point a magic light begins to glow as the actors elegantly and eloquently stick their fingers up the arse of the audience'.
PS – it's a Baroccoco version of 'getting the audience on stage'.

From notes on the draft script:
Opening page: THE PROLOGUE: NOVEMBER 1823
I had crossed out the date and written: 'A Theatre, now and then'.
Salieri has had himself brought to a deserted theatre. That's the metaphor PS missed.

Act I, page 22
TRANSFORMATION TO THE 18TH CENTURY
'– and then, dear, she wants them to climb the Andes, THAT'S what she wants them to do.' [a quote from Binkie Beaumont, describing *The Royal Hunt of the Sun* while Shaffer was out of the room]

Act I, page 23
THE ACTOR HAS TO DOMINATE *BOTH* SCENE CHANGE AND HIS OWN APPLICATION OF MAKE UP WITH THE DAZZLE OF TEXT, AND TONSILS, LIPS, TEETH, AND TIP OF THE TONGUE.

Act I, page 77
THE MUSIC COMES UP IN VOLUME, AND WITH IT, RELENTLESSLY, THE CONE OF LIGHT IN WHICH SALIERI STANDS – UNTIL HE APPEARS TO BE BLINDED BY THE SOUND.
Peter, please trust your words, the situation and the *actor*. No,

blind him with the light of music, pin him in laser like beams until he is beaten to the ground, writhing his way down between ecstasy and torment.

DO IT IN THE SPEECH. Why repeat it aurally? PS Discuss the whole style in terms of this which is too easy, make the acting and the light create the music.

Salieri speech on I.79: The speed and venom of this needs LO. Alec [McCowen] has no speed and *his* venom has an antidote, this does not. It must be *fatal*.

Act II, page 1: If three acts, the audience will have two opportunities to leave and we can play the last act for ourselves, if we wish, as long as it holds us.

Act II, page 35: I think it would be better if we did it with *NO* music at all except the variation, as long as the actor can play it.

23 February 1979
To Christopher Plummer
Mr Dexter asked me to send you this [*Amadeus* script] as soon as possible. As you know, he is still in Los Angeles, but should return some time during the week of April 30.

Week beginning 26 February 1979
It must be simpler than *Equus* because its text and its mind are in the right place. It's the job of the production to help put its stylistic heart in the right place.

Tell the truth to them all. From *Royal Hunt* to now, from my point of view, and as honestly and unemotionally as I can. *Royal Hunt* rejection and acceptance. Casting stars and actors. *Black Comedy*. John Bird. New York etc. *Woman Killed*. Bradley. *Equus*, didn't like its style, interested in its content. Riggs said read it again. P. Hall became the balancing vote. LO far from certain. K. Tynan against it. New York problems. Division due to lack of contact. Kermit [Bloomgarten]'s use of Paul [Giovanni] as a divisive factor. If contracts had been properly drawn up this would not have happened. Control must rest with us. Give PS personal history. Number of perfs of *Equus*?

Made work for nothing either financial or artistic.

9. Dialogues of the Carmelites. Metropolitan Opera House.

10. (*Above*) *Billy Budd*. Metropolitan Opera House.
(*Below*) *Lulu*. Teresa Stratas (*middle*).

11. (*Above*) *Mahagonny*. Teresa Stratas and Richard Cassilly.
(*Below*) *Sicilian Vespers*. Hamburg production.

12. (*Above*) *Abduction from the Seraglio.* Metropolitan Opera House.
(*Below*) *L'Enfant et les Sortilèges.* Covent Garden.

13. (*Above*) *Pygmalion.* Diana Rigg, Alec McCowen and cast.
(*Below*) *The Cocktail Party.*

14. (*Above*) *Creon*. Robert Fleming, Cathy Finlay, Jackie Dankworth and
Tamsin Olivier.
(*Below*) *Julius Caesar*. Leicester Haymarket.

15. (*Above*) *M. Butterfly*. Anthony Hopkins, Glen Goi and cast.
(*Below*) *3 Penny Opera*. Sting with Teresa de Zarn and Nancy Ringham.

16. *Equus.* Peter Firth and Nicholas Clay.

1 March 1979
The problem goes back and springs from *Equus* and the Florida
company in which both Lantz and Shaffer, not to mention Paul
Giovanni [director in Florida], were involved. At the time of the
last conversation on this subject, I told PS that though I did not
blame him for what happened I had in future to *protect* myself.
Obviously that remark did not register, nor did my attempts to
discuss my needs during the last three years. During all those
free advice lunches PS had with me, his interest never extended
to the director's timetable or future plans. On the plane flight to
London an attempt to discuss a rational producing plan was
dismissed. When I attempted to discuss the Problem with RL
[Lantz] in L.A., again the subject was dismissed. These are the
issues:

1. Subsidiary Rights
In allowing PS to use *every* detail of the production in the
published text [of *Equus*] my feelings were those of affection and
regard. I did not imagine how much income I was giving away
with regard to the film sale (an exorbitant artistic mistake) nor
has PS ever acknowledged any debt in this area.

2. Producers or Directors
The misery of *Equus* in New York I will not repeat, in spite of PS
and RL insisting on selling to the highest bidder *now*. Instead of
retaining control for ourselves. We are all at the mercy of the
property developers.
Lantz = *Equus* film = *Hunt* film = money and artistic disaster.
The play doesn't need me. Even Michael Blakemore could do it.
It wouldn't be as good though.

An agent is about as important to the art of theatre as an
undertaker is to society, and *just* as vampiristic.

6 March 1979
Shaffer blew it!

7 March 1979
Talk to PH re PS and *the facts*!

3 May 1979
To Ruby [Shaffer]! Why do you have to decide *now*. I don't think

the pressure helps. Don't sell before you know *what* you're selling.

AFTER: Beginning here and until Sept needs writing down more carefully if I want to get it clear and fully understand it.

24 May 1979
Ruby Rites a Letter. I return it, unread. I want the *spoken* word. I know his *written* words well enough. PS phoned, says it isn't about money. He's *fucking* right (it's about **TRUST**). What, *apart* from money request, have I done wrong?

25 May 1979
It's *all* about money. If it isn't it's all about *trust*, and when have I betrayed your trust as you have betrayed mine by that one act of moral cowardice all that time ago. I have of necessity, since you would not discuss the matter, had to be on my guard, and if I *cannot* have a contract that protects me we *cannot* work creatively together for I can no longer trust you.

26 May 1979
PS phone call, principle accepted. Now he has to square it with his ancestors!

28 May 1979
If I sit down and read a play to an author I think I may be allowed the presumption that I am going to direct it. If I break into a very complex work schedule to spend a week in London for date and casting discussions I may also make the same assumption.

On Jan 19 PS asked me to direct *Amadeus*. On this understanding I went to London, rearranged my schedule around existing commitments, agreed to direct it. On Monday May 28th he asks to 'beg off this one'.

29 May 1979
When good faith is abused then a firmer more equitable contract is needed.

30 May 1979
I would, oddly enough, have no problem working with him day by day. I can look at him. I have nothing to be ashamed of. He has, and knows it, and that is the root of his problem. He has

taken his decision and left me with the moral problem, guessing that a moral decision in the hands of a protagonist is safe. I should have remembered he learnt his code of theatrical behaviour from Binkie.

31 May 1979
The NT: is it the Theatre of 'Binkie' or George Devine? Byzantine or Honest? Ancient or Modern?

8 June 1979
PH letter arrives. The issue is that of verbal contract and its validity. I believe that without it we cannot operate. He says that we are clearly in a very difficult situation now over *Amadeus*, to which my reply is 'I am not.' He also says that for months he has wanted to preserve my friendship with PS. Preservation was not needed until three weeks ago. He says that the only alternative is to offer the play to the NT with him directing. His alternative is to honour his agreement with me or accept that he is in breach of at least verbal contract if not moral one. Then do it, but do not expect me to remain silent. We have an agreement for *Amadeus*. You [PH] will be breaking it at the author's request.

6 June 1979
Telephone message from Peter Shaffer, dictated to Christopher Beach, my personal assistant, by Robbie Lantz's assistant:
After a horrible week of self-examination, I sent you a letter in which I finally tried to communicate to you the true and most painful reasons which have emerged in me for my increasing reluctance to collaborate with you at the present time. Being unable to wait until December was the least of these reasons, offered literally to spare your feelings. Had you read this letter you would not regard this reluctance as an aberration of mine. However, you have also refused to receive my communication. I can now see no other way to proceed than to offer the play to Peter Hall as he is the natural second choice. I have postponed doing this until this afternoon.

Telephone message from me, dictated by Christopher Beach to Robbie Lantz:
With regard to Mr Shaffer's telephone message, you can tell him that I feel Peter Hall must make his own decision, Peter Shaffer

must make his own decision, and then I will have to make my decision. Please tell Peter Shaffer that had he been concerned about sparing my feelings, it would have been better for everyone had he not offered the play to me in January or indeed not spent the last three years discussing it with me.

7 June 1979
Ruby's message and answer delivered.

8 June 1979
I am willing and happy to do the play now that the principle of my subsidiary rights in the production has been accepted.

9 June 1979
Ruby's 'facts' by phone *all* after work, gossip and bitching.

11 June 1979
Ruby – looking for an out? At least she's come up with the idea of producers pay residuals. Now what will PH say?

12 June 1979
Telcon Ruby!
1. I have agreed.
2. He has agreed to subsidiary rights in principle. BUT we have not agreed as to manner of payment. Now NOW NOW what will PH do? Thinking as Director of the NT, is PH (replacement *Amadeus* director) blacklegging the originally designated director by doing work at a cheaper rate? Is this good labour relations? If PS had arrived at this state of mind on the plane to London we would never have gone to the NT, as under my plan I would have been entitled to producer's share and that would have satisfied me.

13 June 1979
Telegram from Peter Shaffer
It truly saddens me but it is now crystal clear to me that we must not work together in present circumstances. You have every right to demand certain terms and I have every right to refuse them on the principle that as a playwright I am not prepared to pay for the services of the director. You have today made it clear to me that you do not consider yourself committed to direct my

play unless your terms are met by me. I cannot meet them. I truly believe it would be unhealthy to embark on this production with you feeling aggrieved or me feeling similarly. You have clarified for me absolutely that it will be best, especially after the wretched preceding weeks, to end immediately this series of painful conversations and demands. I must regard this decision as final.

15 June 1979
Conversation with PH interrupted by telex from PS, and the telex as a work of imaginative fiction should not be wasted on me. And in all this, tho' I have heard much of Peter's AGONY I can't recall having my feelings considered or even discussed.

There have been moments when I seem to have been playing Mozart to a real life Salieri. A Mozart without genius and a Salieri without charm or grace. Perhaps PH has been rehearsing him in the part!

21 June 1979
And now that it's all over. *Never* again waste your time trying to turn the second rate into the first rate. You can't do it, because it should not be done at all, and because from the second rate there is nothing to be learned.

25 June 1979
To Peter Shaffer (never sent)
This letter is to acknowledge your telegram which was read to me in front of Peter Hall whilst we were discussing the possibilities of reaching a solution to the remaining problems. I do understand that you reject the agreement made on January 3rd and re-confirmed on June 12th that you wished me to direct the play. You telephoned me on June 12th and informed me that you did not wish to discuss the matter of subsidiary rights, to which I replied that I would talk to Peter Hall and attempt to solve the problem and on that hopeful and happy basis I left for England.

I cannot understand the volte face which has taken place. We were, you said, to have a further conversation. However, in the face of your telex, which seems to me a mixture of invention and deliberate misrepresentation, I must assume that something happened after Wednesday 13 June and before I arrived in England which you felt unable to communicate to me yourself.

Now that the affair has ended and apart from the various technical problems relating to the validity of verbal contracts, which must be further discussed by agents, I have only one observation to make at the end of our personal and working relationship. As I look back on the events which have destroyed a friendship I had always imagined to be lasting, my bewilderment increases. Since Paul Scofield became available with Peter Hall in September, and my request for some subsidiary acknowledgement of the contribution I made to our past work, I seem to have been facing a different personality to that which I had previously known.

It was not until the aforementioned events had taken place that you first mentioned that we had emotional difficulties in relation to our work. As you know, and as you admitted, these emotional difficulties were not in fact connected with work at all but with gossip and if they exist, they exist upon your side alone.

Had you been direct and honest at this point, you would have saved yourself a great deal of agony and lying and would also have saved Peter Hall a great deal of time. Had you indeed been honest enough to tell me that the play had already been promised to the NT in the first place and not played that shameful game with Michael Codron and Helen Montagu, both Peter and I would not have spent those days talking at cross purposes and almost endangering the relationship which was, I believe, important to both Peter and myself and developing along a creative line into the future.

This future now seems to stand on shaky ground but of course cannot concern you. The truth would have helped us all. The truth and maybe some sense of obligation to the honour and nature of friendship. It is the loss of this friendship that distresses me more than the loss of the play, and I suppose the fact that it would not have emerged in its present form were it not for the time and work we have expended together for the last four years. This I suppose must be my consolation for the many little petty betrayals beginning in Florida and continuing to this date.

I have heard much in these last months both from your agent and yourself of your 'agony'. My feelings have never been discussed. I trust this short résumé will help to clarify them for

you and for the few people who have been unfortunate enough
to be involved. You may rest assured that it will be the last you
will hear from me.

Peter Hall's Diaries, which included sections on *Amadeus*, were
published in 1983. My annotations are in capitals:

25 October 1978 'I think Dexter is much better for Shaffer than I:
sweet with sour, and plenty of bitch.'
WHICH YOU, OF COURSE, DO NOT POSSESS.

25 January 1979 'I want Dexter to stage *Amadeus* at the National.
But he doesn't like the place – the new building, I mean. He's
spent the last four years saying he will never work there. So it's
going to be difficult.'
WRONG. I SAID NOTHING OF THE SORT. IT WAS YOUR
COMPANY I OBJECTED TO.

30 January 1979 'Spoke to Shaffer. Dexter won't do *Amadeus* in
the summer as we hoped; won't do it in the Lyttelton; might do it
in the Olivier; and will anyway only do it when Jocelyn Herbert
is free to design it.'
QUITE RIGHT.

1 March 1979 'The centre of the day was taken up with John
Dexter and Peter Shaffer. They came for lunch. John fizzed, and
talked nineteen to the dozen without ceasing. I sat and listened.
Peter looked troubled. When Dexter went to the lavatory, he –
Shaffer – gazed out at the Thames and murmured through
gritted teeth, "My dear, during these last few days every one of
the hairs in my head has gone white." '
BECAUSE YOU KNEW PETER FIRTH HAD NO CHANCE
WITH ME OR WITH *AMADEUS* AND POOR SHAFFER
WROTE IT WITH HIS CURLY HEAD IN VIEW. RIGGS AND I
THOUGHT CALLOW WOULD BE BETTER. HE WAS.

16 March 1979 'Robbie Lantz has formally offered the National
the rights of *Amadeus*, providing either John Dexter or I direct it
before April next year. I am still trying for Dexter.'
BUT NOT VERY HARD.

28 March 1979 Shaffer: 'I would never hold a pistol to John's
head. At the moment I would use a pistol to blow his head off.
But I wouldn't hold it to his head.'

TOO COWARDLY AND AFRAID OF A KICK IN THE BALLS.

25 May 1979 'Spoke to Robbie Lantz, who told me that Dexter has returned Shaffer's letter unopened, attaching a note to it saying they shouldn't be communicating by letter at this stage of their relationship.'
FAIR ENOUGH I THINK.

5 June 1979 'Dexter told me this afternoon that if Shaffer were really dumping him from *Amadeus* he would not go gracefully, he would go with all guns blazing publicly.'
HE DID NOT. HE SAID 'MR SHAFFER HAS THE RIGHT TO CHOOSE HIS OWN DIRECTOR'. WHY LEAVE THAT OUT?

13 June 1979 'I am sure my productions of Pinter have had a big influence on the way he's done all over the world, perhaps too much. But I wouldn't, as a result, dream of asking Harold for a percentage of his receipts.'
BUT HARD AS THOSE PLAYS WERE, THEY WERE FINISHED AND *HE* DIRECTED THEM. CHECK THE BLACK SCRIPT OF *EQUUS* FOR COMPARISON.

13 June 1979 'It's off with Dexter. Shaffer then rang, but I said I will not be involved personally any more.'
PILATE YOU'RE JESTING.

20 June 1979 'For years I have been praying for a sincere radical right-wing play, and this is it.'
THAT'S THE PROBLEM, IT WASN'T RADICAL. HE CAUGHT HIMSELF IN HIS OWN TRAP AND MISSED THE REAL PLAY ABOUT THE ENVY OF TALENT FOR GENIUS, I. E. BECKETT AND SHAFFER.

Diary:
Shaffer moving out of my work has left room for Shakespeare and Brecht, so who gets the best of that bargain?

Shaffer's being a twin makes it impossible for him to maintain a creative relationship with me. He's too competitive. So am I. He with me. I with the play.

18 June 1979
Rehearse *As You Like It* at the NT
1. The audience is there. USE them. We are performing. They

are watching. We talk, they listen. If we shout, they won't listen. We do not orate, we discuss. We argue with them and each other.

2. Go away, work alone or together and bring it to me. Don't discuss. Do.

On going through my notes I discovered this letter from Paul McCartney on my first attempt at AYLI.
Dear John
This is a very awkward letter to write, because I want to explain honestly why somebody else should do the music for *As You Like It*.

When you first suggested it I wasn't sure, but later it seemed that it would be a 'good' thing to do. Challenge, new horizons etc. The trouble is, though, that I don't like the play, or Shakespeare, enough to do something good.

I could probably do something, but it's silly me doing it when there are so many other people who could either do it better or enjoy it more than I would.

Everything you said when we talked about it obviously made it more attractive, but I still haven't got the basic feeling of 'I love the play and can do something with it', which anyone doing the music should have.

I must say I do feel a bit of a cunt not having said this before, but I think I'm right.

I would love to write music for a play that I'm not so far removed from, because then it would be instinctive and not a question of forcing something to come out that is probably not there anyway.

I'm bad at explanations, but I suppose what I mean is that there are other plays, and there will be other 'productions' of yours that would be easier, better, and more obvious to me. These reasons may not be good reasons, but I think I would be stupid to do music I didn't *mean*, and I haven't got enough love for Shakespeare to be able to do it naturally. I'm sure the result would be forced, and therefore would be bad for everyone concerned.

The trouble is I've taken a long time to work this out, and probably fucked up your plans. I'm sorry.

It's not an easy matter writing letters like this I can tell you but

I'm sure it will be better eventually, Mr Dexter, Sir. Could your secretary ring my secretary and fix it up for you to come and see my new house? Mind you, it would be easier if you rang.

Notes on *As You Like It*.
A PRIMITIVE SEXY, MUSICAL MYSTERY PLAY for the OLIVIER. IT'S anti Brook and Kott.
IT'S pro 1588–90, or as close as imagination will let us, BY THE POOL! L.A.! [where this was written]

Just remember it's some time considerably *pre*-R. D. Laing and more than somewhat post-Kott.

The geography of Arden is theatrical – so ask no further questions about lionesses and palm trees.

Arden is an escape.

In this forest everyone except the country folk is/are in disguise including Touchstone, the Senior Duke and all of Rosalind's servants.

As You Like It as a social comedy as well as a Romantic one! Touchstone as a broken down touring mixture of Sid Field and Lindsay A[nderson].

There will be no lite cues.
There may be shifts in balance.
Plumb white lite.

NO effects.

NOTHING FLOWN

Try to visualise The Primitive as the Elizabethans (1593) imagined it.

A stubble field at harvest time. *New reaped*.
STAGE COVERED WITH CUT CORN
PRE-CURTAIN BINDING CONTEST
ORLANDO BINDS LAST SHEAF
HORN MUSIC.
Lunch break in the hayfields begins the play as a 'workers festival' into which Law and Rigidity enter with Oliver.

From the point of view of the COUNTRYSIDE PEOPLE let them

observe as much as possible, and keep them separate from the COURT *AND* THE MOCK COURT.

The country and court are separate, so is the false court. 3 different worlds of TRUTH.

AMIENS: A wild old mad Welsh harpist, probably pissed all day, but sings like an angel at 60. P. Pears sort of.

As You Like It opened in the NT's Olivier Theatre on 1 August 1979

8 August 1979
To B. A. Young, critic of The Financial Times.
As yours was the only newspaper handed out on Concorde, yours is so far the only notice I have read. I imagine it will be fairly typical of the reactions.

I would like you, as a favour to an old friend, to take your own suggestion and see the play again. It will, I think, bear close examination both in its interpretation of the text, which I will defend line by line if you ever ask me to, but also in its use of the Olivier space, which is something nobody seems to have observed. Before you go again, read the play without the footnotes or the stage directions, as the only published text is the Folio and I know you are aware how unreliable the stage directions are. Read the scenes just for the text and tell me for instance how you find any merriment in Celia and Rosalind's first scenes. I know they are always interpreted with a kind of idiot gaiety which is totally at odds with the actual words used. One woman is desperately trying to cheer her dearest friend who is distressed, rueful, lonely but not, I repeat, not ever merry. She has spirit and imagination, but happiness and merriment come in the forest, not in the court.

I won't waste your time defending the interpretation scene by scene and line by line, but will be quite happy to do so when I get back to England should your second visit not have convinced you of the integrity of the point of view springing as it does from the text and nothing but the text. Also, I think you have done much less than justice to the extraordinary performances of Callow [Orlando] and Kestelman [Rosalind] who have dared to lay open veins of sexuality in the play from which the Vanessas and others have always shied violently away.

I have been thinking about this play for 10 years and preparing this production for the last eight months, so perhaps another visit and a few more words on the subject might not be uncalled for.

PS: And incidentally, why shouldn't there be a kudu in a forest with a lioness and a gilded snake? But of course you're wrong; they're not animals at all. They are the people of the village preparing for the May, the high summer festival which Rosalind joins as she transforms William into Hymen and indeed just as every character in the play and the audience should be joined in the end with the Duke.

PPS: Admit one thing. You did see the worst performance and the slowest performance of the first act the company had ever given. Intimidated by the codsheads in front of them, they slowed down to a degree which would have made even Klemperer lose his temper.

PPPS: Peter Hall has just telephoned to tell me there has been a great rush at the box office and that we have a truly 'controversial seat-filler'. But in any case, whatever we have, please look at it again. I was fairly convinced that you, more than anyone else, would have understood our attempt to take the play seriously on all its levels – dramatic, poetic, sexual, even anthropological. I don't think I've often written to you, but I do mind passionately about this production and about this play and have for years. Never mind whether the play is highly controversial or whether the seats are filled or not, but I do mind that it should be understood by those people for whom it was intended.

12 September 1979
To Riggs O'Hara
After talking to Jocelyn about the problems at the National, the stage, the company, the management attitude, etc., I think the two of us have something quite important to put into the place.

I believe the shape and architecture of the Olivier, if used properly, can change the style of playwriting for the next 50 years and I do not mean the theatre of gesture so beloved of the late lamented Ruby (not too much lamented by you, I think). But a space which is just an empty space (note to P B [Peter Brook], read, listen, can any space be empty?), just a space until the actor inhabits it. *As You Like It* was the first step in that direction; David Hockney on that bare platform doing *The Tempest* is the climax of an experiment. At least in *As You Like It* we proved that a great play can still present itself clearly within the architecture of a theatre as long as it accepts and takes it into the body of the play just as Shakespeare had to accept the architecture of the Globe, accept it, use it and enhance it. The Olivier space is capable, as I said to Peter Hall, of changing local from outer space through the word, the gesture, the actor and those things alone and it lies within the word, the gesture, the space. It is within this area that the future lies. I feel strongly about it. Obviously because I was a member of the building committee but remember also those conversations with George [Devine] about the nature of the theatre and my evolving for myself the theory of the disciplines of any theatre at any time in history, from the pageant wagon to the amphitheatre and the effect of the opera or drama itself.

To digress for a moment, did I ever tell you that the first theatre I ever saw was an amphitheatre on an island headland overlooking a glittering sea. Romantic yes? Perhaps not so romantic if you remember it was Douglas in the Isle of Man. Every holiday in the 30s was taken on the Island and I can only remember it raining once, on a Sunday I think, when I saw *Snow White and the Seven Dwarfs*. In the last week of August we would go, leaving Derby at 5.30 in the evening and getting onto the London, Midland & Scottish Railway train, changing at Chinley and catching the midnight boat from Liverpool to the Island, arriving at 6.00 in the morning, having spent the night sleeping on deck chairs or walking around the ship which my father loved doing. Once on the island, luggage left at the 'digs' (rooms not ready until the afternoon), we would go for breakfast in a café. Then, on a small ferryboat – which was still going when I last went over, for my father's funeral – we would take sandwiches and go to Douglas Head and sit on the cliff looking down onto a fairly natural-shaped amphitheatre onto a little stage where at 11.30 in the morning the minstrels were due to entertain. And I tell you when the minstrels came on I focused on them, because for me they dominated the space, including the sea around them. Now maybe I brought something special to that particular environment in my own barely wakening feeling for theatre, but that space was as strong as you can get and a small human figure in a white costume and black make-up could dominate it. The Olivier is as strong a theatrical space as that clifftop, but it is just as disciplined as the open air, whether the open air were in Bankside or in Douglas Head. Now I have to find the theatrical equivalent of the Irish Sea on a Saturday morning.

It is a space for the entertainers to dominate as was that amphitheatre; that is why I like it. But then you know all this rubbish and I am rambling from the point. But you also know that I believe Bury and Koltai have no understanding for the nature of the space that has been created, and why should they? They were not involved in the early stages. Flytower and drum revolve came in with the Bury and the Hall (and I think I could substantiate that if I had reference to the minutes of the meeting). Larry was fascinated by anything mechanical and G D [Devine], W G [William Gaskill], J H [Jocelyn Herbert], and J D dissenting, he opted for a simple 'one room' space with Lasdun's agreement [Denys Lasdun, NT architect], which would create, because it had no flytower, its own discipline and those disciplines to be accepted by the designer and the director as part of the contract. There it is, it's built, and since it opened, everybody has spent most of their time covering it with silk, satin, canvas, anything as long as it covers it up.

I believe, as I hope you noticed in *As You Like It*, that one must use the architecture, the 'brutality' as some people call it, of the place, one of its most exciting features. That is, I'm afraid, the face of this time: brutal, hard and aggressive, but in the middle of it a theatre should be a space which can take you away from that harsh, brutal world around, transport you into another world and bring you back to the world in which you must live. But it must bring you back. This is a roundabout way of reinterpreting the Brecht theory about learning from seeing and playing. The audience must leave the theatre asking questions, not bathed in a forgetfulness. For some people that happens even with *As You Like It* in its unfinished state. For those who don't, there is no hope. There is, as simply as I can put it, a compulsion to finish the job I helped initiate and though I know I am very immodest, I have a strong feeling I am the only one practical enough to make it possible to solve the aesthetic problems. But that's another theory and another letter and I must close now, otherwise Jean will go crazy.

14 September 1979
To Irving Wardle

Thank you for your detailed and encouraging letter. I have been thinking a great deal about *As You Like It* and the future plans for the National. On reflection, I think it is possibly one of the most interesting, but least finished productions I have done. I had asked for a measured driving pace in rehearsals; I allowed it to slacken during the previews into a merely 'measured' pace with the result that the first night lacked a great deal of the tension which had emerged in rehearsals.

And why did I let that happen you may ask. Because ever since we have been in the Olivier, I have become obsessed with the problem of the space, which I find more exciting than anything I have so far experienced in the theatre. My head was full of plans for future work . . . *Galileo, Shoemakers' Holiday, Henry IV*, etc. I think the future of this production, if it has one, lies in the fact that the audience at least leaves the theatre thinking about the play instead of about their dinner. I have realised how necessary it is to take the architecture of the theatre into the design of the play. It is not a space for 19th-century proscenium illusion and I don't ever believe it can become that. I intend spending the next three years, if Mr de Jongh [second string drama critic of the *Guardian*] spares me, in continuing the experiment. De Jongh, if he is still alive in a few years' time, will have to eat his words, and those costumes will return during *Shoemakers' Holiday* and some of them during *Henry IV*. They, in fact, form the basis of a 'full Elizabethan wardrobe' which I believe is essential for all the plays in the Folio, including the Roman ones.

Thank you for the note about Koestler and *The Sleep-Walkers*, which I haven't read but which I shall be doing in the next week or so. I hope to be in England some time in November or January and have a crack at removing some of the more pompous moments and reshaping Audrey and Touchstone. I hope to see you at that time.

8 August 1979
To Peter Hall

Firstly, thank you for the support and opportunity and let us hope that the production is sufficiently 'controversial' to put behinds on seats in large numbers.

With reference to *Galileo* and the future, I have only one problem in this area, springing from your remarks about establishing a permanent set for the Olivier. Firstly, I did not appreciate at the time the irony of your asking me to direct Brecht on a stage designed for Shaffer. When the idea did penetrate, I found it amusing, but also worrying. You described to me a raked stage. Now I have to tell you that one of the things I dislike most about the Italian theatre is the rake, however slightly graded it may be. It is one of the encumbrances from the Theatre of Illusion which seems to me to have nothing to do with the space of the Olivier and I am writing to ask you please talk to Jocelyn before she leaves for New York and arrange for her to see the model. Also, does this stage remain for the histories and the *Shoemakers' Holiday*? I feel I should make it clear that for those particular projects I have only thought in terms of the stage 'with those expensive additions which you made at the last minute.' If it had not been for the thought of continuing to develop that stage, I doubt if I would have insisted quite so strongly on that extra expense. In short, dear friend, I have reservations about *Galileo* on any kind of rake and I don't want to see the stage sink lower than the present *As You Like It* point, and I hope I made it clear during our brief discussion about the histories that I did intend to continue to pursue the ideas that came to the fore in *As You Like It*.

I am sure Jocelyn can resolve all our problems, but it is urgent that she meet with you before she leaves for New York on 18 August as she will be with me on *Entführung* and *Mahagonny* until 16 November and we hope during that time to have *Galileo* in preliminary model form shortly after she returns to England.

16 August 1979
To Michael Gambon [re *Galileo*]
Can you yet draw the epicyclic orbit of Venus according to the Ptolemaic assumptions? I think you had better learn to do that before you learn the words and I had better do it before I start to think about the moves.

At the moment I am just starting to think about casting. Jocelyn Herbert arrives next week to begin technical work on *Mahagonny* and I imagine we shall be beginning to exchange ideas on *Galileo*.

Don't bother to answer this, but if you have any questions, please write.

9 August 1979
The Party contained a gem of great polemic and didactic acting and directing – LO and JD. Note to Gambon and *self*. How did he do it, Gambon? Not by reading Deutscher, Marx, Wilson but by pacing the speech as an actor. Responding simply to sound and rhythm and letting the sense take care of itself. And if it does it will be because the sound and rhythm are right. MG [Gambon] understand *first* as an actor *then* as a physicist and only *then* as a politician. JD *note* understand first as a director, second as an astronomer physician, last as a politician.

16 August 1979
To Gillian Diamond [NT Casting Director]
I am writing to you with some preliminary notions about casting *Galileo*. I am also writing to one or two members of the company, i.e. Bryant, Cruickshank, Kestelman, to put an idea before them and see if they will cooperate: the great problem in *Galileo* being casting the heavyweight roles, i.e. philosopher, mathematician, Clavius, Vanni. It is my hope that we shall persuade leading members of the company to play smaller roles, and sometimes not the role for which they would regard themselves as most suited. For instance, I would like to ask Simon [Callow] to play the Little Monk and not Andrea, and offer Andrea to Dermot Crowley. I would also be asking Simon, along with Crowley and possibly Needham, to become acolytes or priests (mute) in the Pope robing scene and I am suggesting to some leading members of the company that when we cast them we will be asking them to play a role and do at least one mute scene. Of course if I can persuade Andrew [Cruickshank] to join in that exercise, the rest will follow. The reasons for this tactic will be perfectly obvious to you . . . to create an appearance of an ensemble rather than to make the appearance of an ensemble and as there are 56 speaking roles in the play and one massive crowd scene, and as I don't wish actors to use false voices or noses in the speaking roles, the question of doubling becomes more complicated than usual.

Just to get the outrageous requests out of the way, do you think there is any point in asking Sir Ralph if he would consider playing the Barberini Pope? Or if this is too much for him, would he consider the very old priest in the council chamber. I hope you know the one I mean. If so, I would have him and Andrew play the Pope and the Inquisitor. If not, then I would ask Michael Bryant to play the Inquisitor and Andrew to play the Pope. As another example, the old woman in the plague scene really ought to be Patience Collier. I don't in any case want to be fobbed off by a young actress acting old.

PS: Ask Sally [Sara Kestelman] if she has read Virginia and how does she feel about ranging from 15 to 40. I WANT HER!

16 August 1979
To Simon Callow
Thank you for your letter; you are a fool! I am only as interesting as the people I work with. But taking you up on your offer, I am not asking you to follow me to the ends of the earth, but to play a smaller role in the *Galileo* rather than Andrea, which your position in the company might warrant. I want to ask you to play the Little Monk, and if that weren't enough, to be a mute priest (castrated if you like) in the Papal robing scene. I shall be asking other principal artists, i.e. Bryant, Cruickshank, Kestelman, at some point in the play, in addition to their speaking role, to take on the responsibilities of a mute. As I pointed out to Gillian Diamond, it is sometimes necessary to create an appearance of an ensemble rather than to make the appearance of an ensemble, and support from the leading members of the company would go a long way to help establish this working situation.

As to the year after that, obviously when I do *Henry IV* I want you to do Hotspur, but in Part Two I don't think you should do Larry's double with old Shallow. I want to save Shallow for Nora [John Normington] to double with Poins. But you have your pick of all the other roles in Part Two. Have a look and tell me what you think. I am writing to the others somewhat along these lines, so you will be free to discuss all this with them.

30 August 1979
To Peter Hall
Jocelyn and I have been working on *Galileo* with the ground-plans of *Richard III* and *Amadeus* and we have hit a number of problems which I am not sure that we will be able to solve on the telephone.

Forgive me if I briefly restate my opinions about the Olivier as a theatre space, but it seems very important to do this before we arrive at an impasse or at the very least, a collision of tastes which will prove an insuperable barrier. When we first discussed *Galileo*, *Henry IV*, *Shoemakers' Holiday*, etc., I felt and still feel that I wanted to pursue that work on Hayden [Griffin]'s basic platform with the lighting grid which is to me an essential component of that set. It seems to me the most authoritative, dynamic and flexible space I have so far seen in the Olivier, and one in which I would like to work and develop the ideas which were coming to the fore in *As You Like It*, i.e. direct address to the audience and only the simplest elements of scenery, placing the emphasis on costumes. I think the Bury/Koltai solutions are fascinating, but I also think they are still not facing up to the inherent discipline which Lasdun has most excitingly imposed on the space. Having said that, I should add that I believe the experiments you and they are making are just as valid as any experiment Jocelyn, Hayden and I might want to make. I don't think any of us are convinced that we have explored all the possibilities, but it does seem to me odd that in the Olivier, with all that mass of space backstage, it is not possible to make two permanent spaces – i.e. the Bury/Koltai, the Herbert/Griffin –and truck them in and out. But of course what we really need is, I think, a head session between ourselves to talk theory for a day or so, but that seems to me well nigh an impossibility, given your schedule and mine. And I am not sure how to resolve this problem. I very much want to be part of the National Theatre again and become a close collaborator in the future. However, after two weeks work on the groundplans, I can see no effective compromise although, of course, we would still keep working at it, but with all the various technicians and designers we have around, I think it should be possible to continue the exploration of the Olivier without limiting ourselves to one permanent set. I would like you to consider whether we might not reach a two-stage compromise which would allow both lines of inquiry to continue to interact upon each other.

I still have your very generous first-night note, which has now been stuck into the much battered variorum and will be treasured in moments of despair.

10 September 1979
To Peter Hall
Dear Lear,
Since our last conversations in London, obviously I have been

thinking a great deal about the future and of how I can help in the years ahead. In my letter to you the other day, I touched on the subject of the Space and how I imagined the Olivier to develop in the future and the restrictions which I thought this placed on us both in our two seemingly opposed points of view as to its treatment. However, that debate can continue (indeed it has just done so. Thank you very much for your phone call this morning. You are always most welcome, and I still think I'm right. I am the pessimist and you are the optimist.) I would like to take a little of your time and mine to try and pass to you on absolutely equal terms some personal feelings, and I would ask if possible that these feelings remain private between us except of course where they affect policy and planning. But the distance between us, and indeed between Riggs and myself, means that I have to spend a lot more time writing and much less talking!

Firstly, the plays we have discussed: *Galileo*, the two parts of *Henry IV*, *The Shoemakers' Holiday* and *The Tempest*. I will first address myself to the space in which these plays will appear and trust that you will understand that, speaking in these broad planning terms, it is very difficult to avoid being dogmatic. And therefore, if it needed saying, I would like to state emphatically what I feel is my attitude to the Olivier now, at this time, and so without concern for the fact that what I write looks like a takeover bid. But I have at last become so bored with power play and the games I'm forced to play in order to deal with it in this house [the Met] that I no longer wish to have it part of my working apparatus. I will, therefore, speak more directly than our acquaintance seems to justify and will say, 'I do not want even one-third of your kingdom.' What I want is to develop myself. Your kingdom happens to be the only place on earth in which I can do that. I speak, of course, of only one part of your kingdom, the Olivier.

It is the Olivier which is for me the challenge, the inspiration and what has given me a sense of direction for the first time since I left the National Theatre. To explain, I think I'm doing a reasonably good job at the Metropolitan, but it is a feasibility study and not a passion. What I feel for the Olivier is a passion, or as near to it as anything I know. Excuse the passion if my terms and manner to you are expressing a friendship which does not exist and cannot exist just yet. It's very difficult for me at the moment to accept the idea of the combination of friendship and work as essential to organise growth and which can turn a Space into a House. Recently, I had thought to put friendship into the deepfreeze. I do not ever wish to go through the sense of betrayal, delusion and finally disgust which have dominated the last two months ever, ever again. It is a terrible thing to imagine for several years that a friendship existed whereas nothing existed, not even a working relationship. In future, if I am to be used, I must be used to some better purpose and so, knowing perfectly well that I am again taking the same risk in reaching for a personal relationship with you in order that we may work together, I am taking that risk with much more confidence, for at the beginning of the other relationship, I was not even aware that friendship offered could ever be rejected with deceit, malice and greed. But with my reputation for directness and yours for duplicity, both of course totally undeserved, we can take the risk confidently. (If I needed any encouragement to open myself up to a friendship when a friendship has just recently been thrown back into my face, Jocelyn [Herbert] more than anyone else justifies another beginning.) So, softly, softly . . . here goes.

The Space of the Olivier. It is the outer and inner space of the theatre in the 1980s and I want to explore it or at least open up a launching pad. I feel that the space itself can change the space of the mainstream of British Drama within fifty years. As for the poet and dramatist who sees the space as his, there is a new territory where very few people have been since Sophocles or Shakespeare.

Specifically, with regard to the physical production of *Henry IV*, I would like to ask Hayden [Griffin] and Jocelyn to cooperate and collaborate; and Hayden alone to do *The Shoemakers' Holiday*. My reasons are twofold. Obviously Jocelyn is the mainspring of most of the best work I have done. Jocelyn initiated our experiments with an overhead grid. It developed during our preparatory conversations to doing the first Sunday night of *The Kitchen* at the Royal Court Theatre. I asked despairingly for a light which would define the actor and separate him from the space and said I thought the direction could only be from overhead, but didn't see how to solve the problem. Jocelyn, within ten minutes, had solved the visual problem and years later Andy [Phillips] came and, with his peculiar genius, put the grid to its perfect use. The light he creates with it defines the space and forces the actor to dominate it. It has a clarity which gives weight to space and has the effect of giving the actors height and stature, *kothurni*, surely much-needed in the Olivier. In the introduction to the Prefaces, Granville Barker defines the position of the actor on Shakespeare's stage and its relation with him. The stage is the actor's instrument, responding to his needs, being without a breath of a pause an open space or a closed one. I believe Hayden has got, with that rough scaffold [for *As You Like It*], very near to what is needed to achieve this. It thrusts into the auditorium. It states its relationship to the auditorium and the architecture and it challenges the audience to imagine and to listen, not to dream for two hours, but to listen and think.

For all these reasons and for many others, I would like to ask that we maintain this stage for *Henry IV*, *Shoemakers' Holiday* and *Galileo* and towards this end, I will begin to work with Jocelyn. In addition, I would like to continue my conversations with David Hockney, which have skirted round *The Tempest* at the National in a few years' time. I want him to be able to take a puritan stage and make it magical in a totally modern and totally romantic way. You and I have already discussed the approach to *The Shoemakers' Holiday* and there is nothing much to add to that, except to say that I would like to open the plays in the following order: *Henry IV Part 1*, *The Shoemakers' Holiday* and finally *Henry IV Part 2*. I think you will understand my reasons for this, without my going into a boring explanation. In short, as far as the stage is concerned, I am asking you to consider a two-stage state for the next three years. Stage 1, Koltai/Bury, Stage 2, Griffin/Herbert, plus a modified and acceptably adaptable Andy Phillips/Jocelyn Herbert grid. I think the Olivier needs two stages at the moment, just as for the last three years it has needed to experiment with every possible decorative device available to the stage, and it is good that now we are all accepting the disciplines of the space itself. I hope that before long it will reward us, as it is already a superb space and will become a superb theatre.

As to the company and its development. Actors: for instance, Callow. I wrote to him the other day to suggest that he should expect to be asked to do the Little Monk in *Galileo* and not Andrea, because I think it necessary to create the appearance of an ensemble before you actually have any such thing, but that one can only make the appearance apparent by casting, so that whoever plays Andrea or the Little Monk will be required at the same time to lead the acolytes in the Pope's robing, hooded, invisible. I think it appropriate that we can begin to build an interior life for the company on *Galileo* and let the actors develop a responsibility for each other and to each other, that when it comes their turn to be robed, crowned or killed as Pope, king, usurper, each will have a sense of the difficulty that the acolytes, bishops and conquerors have in performing the sheer mechanics of those ceremonies which give him his crown or sword. If we can achieve some of this interdependency during *Galileo*, then we might be ready for the Parts 1 and 2 of *Henry IV*.

Dominating this sprawling canvas of a play (and watching all the drama from his throne throughout the performance) is Michael Bryant as Henry IV, with Prospero to follow and the Cardinal Inquisitor [in *Galileo*] to begin with. This has a recognisable pattern and contains a challenge, but I would like to ask him, in return for that challenge, to be a 'mute' senator in the Venice scene. I expect he will enjoy this idea, I would look to him to lead in its acceptance and execution, and would like with your permission to write to him along these lines.

Now, that Henry needs an extraordinary Northumberland, as much as he needs a Falstaff, a Hal and a Hotspur. I want Frank Finlay, who alone has the right granitic power for this mighty opposite, who as I have always thought was as much an iron rivet between the two plays as Falstaff and Hal. In order to persuade Frank to this role, we should offer him Simon Eyre [the lead in *Shoemakers' Holiday*] and in turn remarry him to Joyce Redman (divorced since *Othello* alas!) and ask her to give up Doll to Sara Kestelman and take Mistress Quickly to herself.

The Fat Rivet we have already discussed and will, I imagine, continue to discuss for the next year. The Thin Rivet, 'eelskin', 'tailor's yard', 'starveling' to balance this Falstaff's fat, Peter Firth please; who could be offered Hal, Rafe in *Shoemakers'*, Ariel and, to begin with, Andrea in *Galileo*. Some may ask, 'Why Firth?'. For two reasons, one personal and the other a question of interpretation. Prince Hal, who is not King Henry V, is never required to be seen at Agincourt and that little touch of Harry in the night, vanishes forever after the butchering of Hotspur, and for the rest of the play transforms from Dionysius to Apollo. (The journey for Firth and Hal ends as Ekkehard Schall, bullet-headed politician, bully and pragmatist.) We must not, in this play, work from a salvationist's point of view of the Prince. Personal reasons for wanting to use Firth I think you can guess. It has always given me a sense of personal failure that Peter had not been given by me the sense of responsibility to his talent and that he has allowed others, including his agent, to persuade him to dreams of instant stardom. However, I think he is now ready to move forward, and if you force him by the scruff of the neck to accept this offer and be worthy of it and his talent, I think it would set my mind a little at rest in that area.

I hope these notes will give you some sense of what I think my contribution might be, and I offer them to you as a basis for discussion when we meet (and in some cases for casting action fairly quickly I think).

In short, if I say to you I am thinking along these lines, you will know I'm thinking also in the future of asking you to let me direct Joan Plowright as Cleopatra (gypsy, overblown, Veronese), against the wreckage of Robert Stephens or Blakely, to the Octavius of Callow, the (ageing companion of Antony) Enobarbus of Bryant, and the Octavius of Peter Firth, in conjunction with an *All for Love* with Maggie [Smith]. Or, say I have a passion to do an Elizabethan *Much Ado* with Alec [McCowen] and Diana [Rigg], you will recognise that while I am satisfying your needs, I am also satisfying my own, namely to do more Shakespeare. And I tell you, if you hadn't said that to me after the run through of *As You Like It*, I do not think I would have dared to do anything so all-consuming. So you see, you have brought this diatribe upon yourself, making me believe that I am 'onto something', but for the first time in many years I am sure of my direction. It's odd, because it is all summed up in something George [Devine] said after a performance of *Royal Hunt* at Chichester. I wonder if Jocelyn remembers the conversation, the essence of which was that though everything I had done at the Court was good and sometimes original, sooner or later I would have to face up to authors bigger than myself for my own sake. Recent events have given me a distaste for living authors, as you might imagine, and anyway they've had enough of my time. I want an author who gives me something other than money, and to do only those works from which I can learn and grow for the *next* fifty years.

12 September 1979
To Simon Callow

If you're sulking or if you're wanting something to work on or if perhaps you think the Little Monk is beneath you, just let me advise you in my most fatherly fashion, that I do not expect too much of you in the role. Simply I expect you to be as good as, no, better than LO in the same situation in Trevor Griffiths' play *The Party*, except that he had to do it for twenty minutes. You only have to do it for maybe three; but whatever the stopwatch time of your performance finally is, you will do what you have to do standing absolutely still from beginning to end or sitting absolutely still from beginning to end. You see, as a director I am not inflexible; I give you a choice.

There were some tricky technical problems on *Galileo*, and it was highly pressurised. Simon kept doodling around with the part [of the Little Monk], because that's what he enjoys and I hadn't the time. The great moment came when he decided that he wanted a limp. A limp and a crutch. Or was it a humped back? I can't quite remember. Well, all I could say was 'when are you going to get Long John Silver's parrot?' I love Simon. I'd work with him any time, and I think he'd work with me probably – if the part was big enough.

25 October 1979
To Laurence Olivier

Saw Henry Plantagenet again last night. It is having a special showing at the Regency and they have given you an absolutely new, clean print (and the arrows *are* visible). So this is just a fan letter I might have written 20 odd years ago if I had known you well enough. It seems now, as it seemed then, one of the most extraordinary, daring, imaginative pieces of film making I can remember and in your performance I now see details that I never spotted before. I could drone on for several hours, but rehearsal of *Mahagonny* awaits. This is just to let you know the audience gave your name a standing ovation and as far as I could see from looking around, it consisted of 'tout New York'. I was very proud to know that I had worked with you.

PS: I even noticed the patch in the cyc this time!

29 October 1979
Rules in the theatre and laws in life, both are mere conveniences, and can be broken and remade for our convenience. But this does not obviate the need to make new rules and new laws CF OLIVIER.

Galileo – shape decision, square solution.

I like what people call the brutality of the Olivier. It makes its laws which we must *establish* before we can break.

We have not advanced since sixteen hundred, only elaborated on perfection and destroyed it. The Olivier both inhibits and releases, just as the Globe must have done. Work to the discipline of the space, allow it to make its own rules and laws. Once law and order is established it is easier to break rules.

19 May 1980
To Peter Hall
This letter will be unsigned as I am about to get on board, but I must say, I have never embarked on a boat for a production with more misgivings. Cunard will deal with the first problem and I hope you will be able to deal with the second one.

Not to waste time, I am frankly shocked that your technical and accounting departments have introduced the word 'budget' at as late a date as this. How can we be over a budget when no one has told us during the last year what that budget is? Had you said, a year ago, 'I want the *Galileo* in the Olivier for fifty pounds', I would have thought of the production differently. I would have thought of it differently, but probably would still have engaged myself. Incidentally, I wonder what budgetary arrangements can have been made in the past for some of the baroque extravaganzas which I have seen on that stage. I will of course do my best to abide by whatever budget now appears on paper but I must ask you to now realise that continual badgering, especially with regard to projections and music, will be counter-productive. I would ask in future that I am at least forewarned of the kind of restrictions that will be imposed.

With regard to *Henry 1 and 2*, I think further discussions should take place only when we meet. The present experience has somewhat cooled my passion for working in the Olivier.

PS: I have attempted on four occasions during the week to

contact Gillian Diamond to discuss casting. On the last I was told
that she was not available. No calls have been returned and I am
assuming therefore that the casting of the Cardinal Inquisitor
and Cardinal Barberini/Pope will be discussed on my arrival.

28 May 1980
Galileo. JH [Jocelyn Herbert]. Set crisis solved. A white surround! A white stage! i.e. if they want 'drapes' and *no* steel doors
they can have them but WHITE. One huge step to making BB
[Bertolt Brecht] joyful.

The Life of Galileo opened in the NT's Olivier Theatre on 13
August 1980

14 August 1980
Galileo notices v. good, esp. Billington who compares with
BB's!!! Hubris beware.

Notebook:
I was totally satisfied with the production. Next to *Woman Killed
with Kindness* I was happiest with *Galileo.* I felt we hit the style
dead centre.

Jocelyn and I thought the height and size of the Olivier stage
were wrong and in *Galileo* we tried to correct it. The key to that
space is to thrust the stage forward and raise it up. The National
Theatre were thrilled, but they didn't take it any further which is
why it's still slightly out of kilter. It's always difficult in an
institutionalised theatre because everyone is protecting their
own position and trying to do it the easiest way which isn't
always the best way.

3 September 1980
To Keith Jeffrey
With regard to future plans, I have had a second meeting with
Peter Hall, and he is trying to reach a situation in which I should
join him as co-Director of the Olivier and the Cottesloe (leaving
the Lyttelton to go its own Shaftesbury Avenue way), and that
we should have two separate companies who would inter-
change theatres, which, after all, is the principle on which those
endless corridors of dressing rooms were designed.

We have agreed on the sort of repertoire I would like to do, and he knows what he would like to do. Unfortunately he has a gap between the beginning of 1981 until I can join him in March of that year, so he must first find a director who is willing to do a stopgap job. He has suggested to me that I might prefer to work in tandem with Peter Gill, to which I have replied quite firmly 'no' because whereas I feel no imbalance in my working with Peter H. in collaboration, I certainly would in the case of Peter G. for reasons which I think will be apparent to you.

I am actually free and available to the NT from March of next year, and I am not sure what the internal problems are which prevent me from joining at that time, but I am hoping to have some sort of answer from Peter. If he ever puts anything on paper I will pass the gist of it on to you. So far it has all been pleasant and conversational. I suspect he is in a bind and wants to get out of it to do less work at the NT, certainly less administrative work, and be more confident that the stage itself will be receiving proper attention. I do not mind doing adminis-trative work to this end, but I have no intention of being an administrative dogsbody for that think-tank he has developed around [John] Schlesinger, [Harold] Pinter, [John] Russell Brown, and all the other 'caterpillars of the Commonwealth'.

I have written a nice, I think, thank you letter to the Minister [Norman St John Stevas, Minister for the Arts]. I wasn't sure whether I should invite him to dinner in New York but hope he will let me know if he is around.

3 September 1980
To Peter Hall
My situation has resolved itself, in spite of our present strike, and the Board [of the Met] have offered me a very generously paid position, which does not tie my legs to the desk or the rehearsal room, and I am in fact available to you from March next year to March the following year, during which time we would, I imagine, be discussing future plans. If I interpret you correctly, you want what I want: to get on with the business of directing and not to be administrating a theatre so that other people can do the plays we ought to be doing; quite apart from a desire to keep certain colonials [Michael Blakemore] out of the corridors of power.

All goes well with the musical [*One Night Stand*]. Casting is

finished and I have a two week delay before starting as the dear
script needed tearing apart. The unspeakable Andy Phillips
seems to be on very good terms with all the professionals of his
class around Broadway, and I suppose that is a great comfort to
him after the rather black character reference given to him by
your technical staff. If we ever have time for something more
than a breakfast, lunch, or five minutes in the office conversation, I would like to talk to you very seriously about that area of
the theatre, not with a view to a Night of the Long Knives, but
rather to sharpening up the talent which exists but is either not
being allowed to use itself with sufficient imagination or has
decided that the easiest way to do something is always the best
way.

I found the objections to Andy's behaviour at rehearsal
somewhat startling as you must realise that I was attendant at
every rehearsal, and close to the lighting board. Were I more
closely involved, I would ask for more specific accusations from
the parties involved, and for Andy to defend himself, should he
feel so inclined. However, this letter is going on for too long, the
musical waits, and I wait to hear from you.

I am certainly trapped in New York for the next three or four
months but, as you will appreciate, being a working director
yourself, I would like to be starting to make plans for next year at
the earliest possible moment.

25 September 1980
To Keith Jeffrey
The enclosed is a photostat of a telegram received this week from
Peter Hall. I had, as is usual in all National Theatre matters,
digested the information in the *Guardian* several days before. I
am bringing you up to date on this as a post scriptum to the
excellent lunch we had with the Minister [for the Arts]. In the
unlikely event that he should ever ask what happened to
Dexter's promises to return to England, you may bring him up to
date.

I had several exhaustive conversations with Peter Hall in
London and one here, the essence of which was that I was ready
to come and work with him for as long as he wanted in March
next year, but I thought certain changes, i.e. in the technical and
casting area were essential, and moreover I outlined a programme on which we could both collaborate. Since then I have

heard nothing until the *Guardian* article. My feelings at the moment you can imagine. I will give you more information if and when I have any.

1 October 1980. NY.
To Michael Gambon
I haven't been able to write before. As you know, I came back here to finish auditions and begin rehearsals for the musical. However, that seems to be going quite well and everyone is very happy. I have been made slightly less happy by a telegram from your ennobled leader announcing that he couldn't wait for me to be available, so had to go ahead with Peter Gill, which means, I am afraid, that my plan to bash you through Henry V as your last juvenile has gone somewhere up the chimney. Being an instinctive paranoid, I cannot believe that immediacy of need was the motivating factor in PH's action. As you are aware, we created a fair amount of, not havoc, but extra work for the technical and electrical staff who, I am told, have complained in a body to PH. Which does not surprise me; what does surprise me is his reaction. Or maybe the words of Jonathan Miller are, after all, true: 'Peter is only interested in other directors failing in his theatre in order to prove that he can succeed. Success is not allowed.'

God knows I have tried to be fairly direct and honest with him in all my dealings during the period when we were doing *Galileo* but he baffles me. For instance, the telegram he sent to me giving me the news, although sent from London, must have been dictated in New York where he was at that time, and I believe is still, rehearsing some play about a mad musician written by an English author whose name for the moment escapes me. I hope you are enjoying the performances you are allowed to give, they seem to me miniscule in number. I registered a protest about that before I left but obviously nothing has happened. So I suppose the best thing I can do at the moment is wind up this somewhat confused letter by saying how much I enjoyed working with you and how much I look forward to, somewhere in the future, working together again.

7 October 1980
To Peter Hall
My only surprise on reading about the appointment of Peter Gill

in the *Guardian* was that you of all people should have followed the traditional English theatre establishment's path in communicating information to your colleagues and equals.

17 October 1980
To Joan Plowright
In the middle of a lighting rehearsal yesterday, Andy Phillips handed me a copy of *The Times* of October 15th. The picture is wonderful and you might send an old friend a signed copy if you really cared!

Derek Jacobi has opened here [in Nikolai Erdman's *Suicide*] to splendid notices; he is now a star but nobody is quite sure whether the play is going to run. I haven't seen his performance because I am in the pre-preview week of *One Night Stand*. The composer, Jule Styne, is ecstatically happy and I should get a Tony award for that alone! The lyricist and book writer is a pocket sized Arnold Wesker who combines the vagueness of Diana Boddington with the laziness of Bill Bundy.

It was so good of you all to come to the preview of *Galileo*, and I am glad you enjoyed it, but I hear on the grapevine that Sir PH was somewhat miffed as Father [Olivier] hadn't been to one of *his* previews. I was delighted, naturally, and especially that you and he liked it so much.

There has been an interesting development over the last few months which I think you ought to know about. During the period of rehearsal of *Galileo*, Sir PH and I had many conversations about he and I sharing the Cottesloe and Olivier, as two separate companies but each company using both stages. I had given him lists of plays and casts including yourself (*Little Eyolf* but I don't expect you ever got your 'good, useful eyes' to read it). I had given him the dates at which I would be able to give him all of my time, and had even suggested that we split my cherished production of *Henry IV Part 1 and 2* so that we established, at least on paper, directorial parity. On returning to America, I put my dates formally in a letter, and three weeks later I hear, via *The Manchester Guardian*, that he has appointed Peter Gill to this position. One week later he himself, who is already in New York and rehearsing in the same building as myself, sends a telegram from England.

On reflection I find it fairly predictable. I am finally forced to believe that the man does not want any creative talent around in case it takes the shine off his shoes, but once again the English theatrical establishment has announced its intentions to one of its members through the aegis of the popular press. I know a little of how Larry felt a few years ago, furious at being hurt but nevertheless hurt.

What a wonderful idea a Sloane Square book would be, for while Irving's book was excellent and John's we know will be vitriolic, no one who had the pleasure and fun of working there has said a word about it, and that I do think we owe to Georgie. However, I do have to warn you I have been making notes for such a book myself, without Jocelyn's knowledge, but sneaking information from her day by day, so if the burden of a book ever becomes too much for you on your own we could sit down together and write one called 'Conversations in the Square', and I think between us and with a little more help from Madam, we could produce an original, well photographed and documented history of what has become historic. On the other hand you may want to write your own book. I do too, but not about Sloane Square, about directing.

How is Dickie [Richard Olivier] getting on in Tinseltown? I have several friends there whom he might find it amusing to meet. Apart from David Hockney they're not in the star bracket of the entertainment world but I expect he may be exposed to too much of that, much as he loves it. However, I do know David Hockney would welcome him to the studio and for a meal, as would another friend of mine out there whom you've met, Dennis Erdman, who is a struggling – but at the moment quite successful – actor; also Dennis Christopher whose film *Breaking Away* you probably saw. Larry met him in New York on his last visit. I am aware in suggesting this, Madam, that you may say 'I'm not 'aving my lad mix with a lot of poufters.' However poufteresque they may be, Richard is a perfectly normal young man, quite capable of dealing with that sort of social situation, and you can take my word for it that no attempt on his somewhat dubious chastity would be made by any of them.

So, to finish up, we begin previewing on Monday, my leading actor twisted his ankle last Monday and is wearing a plaster cast. Andy Phillips and I have invented a most simple but therefore diabolically difficult lighting plot which is in no way resolved, and the orchestra moves into the pit tomorrow. Therefore I shall maintain a golden silence until I hear from you. Don't get too optimistic about the musical; although we all love it it's a bit tough and sad and visually sparse, for a Broadway musical that is. Furthermore, its title is *One Night Stand* (no exclamation point).

Love to Father.

30 October 1980
To Jim Hiley [author of *Theatre at Work*. On the production of *Galileo*]

I am sorry to have been out of touch for so long. It was the strike and the musical (which has just been closed in preview! by three mad, manic producers, to the utter consternation of the cast and, not least of all, the director) but now the strike seems to be resolving itself I can bring you up to date.

During the period in London, Peter Hall and I had several conversations about mutually running the Olivier and Cottesloe as two companies side by side. I had very much hoped that this would come to fruition as it would enable me to continue working with some members of the National company on two different stages. However I was not contractually free until March and Peter, for his own reasons, needed somebody immediately, and chose Peter Gill. With the usual dashing style of the English theatrical establishment, I first read of Peter Gill's appointment in *The Guardian* and was informed a week later by telegram by Peter Hall. You will imagine I am not particularly pleased by the situation at the moment and it doesn't really make a very interesting wind-up to the book as it seems that nothing will have developed from *As You Like It* and *Galileo* in the management's basic understanding of the Olivier space. However, it is a subject for a long essay and most of my thoughts on the subject I think you probably caught in conversations at another time.

So you haven't got a nice romantic finish to the book and I am now fairly definitely going to take up the other Stratford [Ontario], though this is not for release for some considerable time yet. Now I go into a three-act *Lulu* and probably will have to pick up Gaskill's *Cosi Fan Tutte* as he has arranged to take on other work.

5 November 1980
To John Osborne

Someone took the trouble to clip out and send me your buggery note in *The Guardian*. It gave me immense pleasure but also reminded me that I owe you a letter. It has been very difficult to think of how to write to you after so many unattractive things have happened to me since I rather euphorically grabbed you on the telephone and announced that I was offering my body up to the Royal Court. I presume you know what happened and have heard all the details. (Did you know I had a wonderful letter from the Chairperson of the Royal Court Workers' Committee asking me to present myself for an interview?)

What made the whole of my stay in England even more humiliating was that at the same time Peter Hall was begging me not to go to the Royal Court but to join him and run the Cottesloe and Olivier, which also interested me as I thought it was about time for me to come back to England and put back some of the energy I had taken from it. However, Peter Hall decided that Peter Gill would be more readily available and, I suspect, more acquiescent. Hall is a man who is impossible to talk to in any ongoing creative sense. He knows his organisation is all to fuck but resents any criticism of any members of his staff. As I had made it clear that I would not come unless there were considerable changes in the technical and casting areas, I suspect that was another reason for choosing Peter Gill. I wonder if he will be able to cope with Peter's ulcers as well as George could.

Does all this sound rather bitter and resentful? Well it was a couple of months ago, now it is all past history. Although the Met is on strike, there is plenty of interesting work to get on with here and I am just off to the Islands for 7 days of sunshine and swimming.

Week beginning 6 April 1981
Rehearse *The Shoemakers' Holiday*
A period spent with the head set on in order to shut out the noise of gossip and complaint from all at the NT. The production finally gained 99.9% from the critics and 50% from me. So, do it again and *get it right.*

Make them listen as to John Arden in *Armstrong*. Trust the prose, the verse.

I am not coming out of the closet, I am coming out of the cellar where the body is buried.

Week beginning 13 April 1981
Shoemaker space. How good I left space (and how self important) for a good clear look at the NT and my involvement.

By April 13 we had completed a first week or what felt like a first week. I was already in the rehearsal room retreat, gossip having driven me to the depths of Lasdun's inner space (inefficient, not sound proofed) and Stravinsky.

How much longer do I have to clear up after Peter Hall's endless parade of white elephants, they leave shit behind just like any pachyderm of another pinker colour. Advice for PH, if he ever again *deserves* advice: *If* you fuck as well as you're supposed to do, then give up a bit of your fucking or give up the National altogether.

Undated
To Peter Hall
Dear Friend. I would have been delighted to have told you of the sorrows and miseries of your company 'face to face'. Unfortunately, I hardly ever saw your pretty face, hidden as it was in darkest Sussex. (Happy you!) I, however, reported to the staff members in whom I believe we both had confidence and on whose confidentiality we both rely.

I recounted to Bill [Bundy, technical director] and Michael [Hallifax, company administrator] the rather disturbing atmosphere which led to, what was for me, an untenable situation.

As you may remember, on my first night in England, I spoke to you in your office, having just escaped the clutches of a member of your staff, who had proceeded to attack the management in no uncertain terms. I shortened the conversation, with as much humour and tact as I could, but did report it to you. You did not seem overly concerned and I did not discuss the matter again. However, after two weeks' rehearsal, the situation had become embarrassing and unnecessarily distracting from the creative work. I reported to Hallifax and Bundy that in the Green Room and Canteen I was continuously being assailed by the actors, senior, junior and middle'range. All concerned with telling me how unhappy and miserable they were made by the lack of any, and I quote 'any', coherent management. After two weeks of this, I retired to the Rehearsal Room and did not use either the Canteen or Green Room again.

I may attract dissentious people but I do not invite them.

You must be aware there are many actors in a company, and in any company, who will use any opportunity to create attention. My unnecessary retreat into the Rehearsal Room robbed me of some period of relaxation, but I was by no means unhappy or miserable. The company were working well as actors, even if not as politicians. Why do you not talk to [Andrew] Cruickshank? He made a speech at the pre-preview party, which apart from embarrassing me out of my mind, gave me an absolute sense of a wonderful working relationship which had developed. I would abide by his judgement as to my state of mind during rehearsal.

I must say I do rather resent having to defend myself against a charge of disloyalty, also company politics. Ever since *Amadeus*, and for years before, I have demonstrated my loyalty to the institution and to you in so many ways, I would hardly have thought loyalty came into question. I told Hallifax and Bundy that your actors were demoralised and miserable. I only passed on what *they* had said to *me*. And realising this sort of situation might arise, I have removed myself from the area of controversy.

PS: I will answer your letter about audibility after I have finished the Stravinsky technical.

The Shoemakers' Holiday opened in the Olivier 19 June 1981

1 July 1981
To Alfred Lynch [playing Simon Eyre in *Shoemakers' Holiday*]
Well I hope you enjoyed the process and are now enjoying taking over the part. You came beautifully to the boil on the first night; I couldn't have asked for more from you or the company. If there is any confusion in the notices it's the fault of our old friend time, and prejudice. We didn't have time to fully develop the reality we found in Eyre, as opposed to the traditional 'Falstaffian' view, but that will grow with each performance, the bitterness, the sadness, and truth in fact.

I shall make a point, whatever I am doing, of trying to see how you have developed it in a month or so's time.

Again, thank you.

PS: Please, please, no Falstaffian joviality from you and the production will receive no goosing up from me – we got it right, they don't know their Dekker.

8 July 1981
To Michael Gambon
There is not much for me to say at the moment as I was not able to speak to Peter during my period in London and my enquiries about *Coriolanus* were answered in a Private and Confidential letter, but I don't think I am betraying any secrets if I say that at the moment Peter is incapable of making plans as far ahead as next year. Where this leaves us, I don't know, but please don't do it [*Coriolanus*] with anyone else as I have more than half the production mapped out and it's modelled on you, *providing* you can lose some weight on the left tit.

PS: You would have been wonderful in *The Shoemakers' Holiday* – cunt!

8 July 1981
Write Caryl Brahms – she gave me my first good notice, *ever!*

9 July 1981
To Caryl Brahms
How wonderful to have a postcard from you. I have heard nothing from the NT at all but have read, I think, *most* of the notices. I'm glad it worked so well but I'm not sure whether I'm up to the stress, strain and lack of joy on the South Bank. If the working atmosphere isn't happy the work can't be, and creating happiness in a depressed company is too exhausting at my time of life.

Notebook:
The National Theatre gave a lot of us a home for the first five years, which were magical. You had the world's repertoire to choose from, only five plays to do a season – and with certain exceptions the people there wanted to be there. It couldn't ever be like that again.

We were a very well matched, argumentative group. Sir Laurence was an incredible chairman. We worked in what were really just huts, which meant that we all had to get to know each other better. If you wanted some information from Ken Tynan you simply pottered into the office and said, Ken, what's a decent version of Ostrovsky? It's no longer possible; you have to write out an inter-office memo. Bill [Gaskill] and Ken and I didn't really know each other at all before we started. Ken was a critic and Bill was suspicious of him. But Larry came out with his great phrase about it being better to have him inside the tent pissing out than outside pissing in. A very good move too – the wisest thing he did.

One of the first things I felt about the new building, and still feel, is: this is too big. It doesn't need an artistic director – it needs three artistic directors. Otherwise somebody's going to destroy the place under the wrong kind of pressure. It needs another way of managing – which is what Aukin and Eyre [Richard Eyre and David Aukin, appointed Director and Executive Director of the NT in 1988] are going to do, I hope.

For me the high point since the National has been at the South Bank was *The Mysteries*. All-star revivals of Ibsen *are not* what it should be about. I would like to see a literary manager of Ken's flair, irritation value and resource. With no disrespect to any of the dons who are in the place at the moment, it has not been very bright. Bill Bryden has his own ideas and his own style, which he communicated to the company – and that's what it's about.

The problem is that in the last ten years the National Theatre has not developed its own stars at all. Gambon, McKellen, Jacobi – they were all walk-ons at the Vic. There is nobody walking on now who looks like a potential Romeo or Hamlet. The lower level of casting has deteriorated very badly with this modern approach: that we have stars, television stars, character actors, then the rest. It means that the rest are a limp wagging tail, sitting in the green room getting drunk and complaining. That's got to be tackled. In a large company (and it's too large) there is so much space for the tail to wag in – and if they're not employed there's nothing worse than an actor on the moan. There are actors who might as well telephone in their performances for all the commitment they've got. You can't get them out of the green room, and you can't get them out of the dressing room because they are playing bridge.

No, I am not enamoured of the place. It's ready to be occupied, but somewhere it needs a man of genius. We had one, two – but they haven't now. I like Peter Hall and we have great respect for each other's work. I just can't stand what he's done to the place for the last ten years. Yes, I had an invitation to the 25th anniversary party if I wanted to pay. You're paying for a handshake with the Queen. £250 was the going rate. I'm not going. They'd have to pay *me* to go and see Shakespeare at the NT.

24 July 1981
To Andy Phillips
Thanks, or as my teenage friends write, when they CAN write, Thanx!

I see little or no hope of my returning to the Olivier and I do not want to return to the NT, if indeed I have ever been there.

Andrew was right, it *is* all about love but if you give it out as work you do expect something back. Not love. CERTAINLY (CEEERTAINLY) not love, but good work. But when can we do it again?

13

Return to Europe

Summer 1984
Notes from the last Concorde pen for the first days back in Europe.

I return to Europe with yellow pads, notebooks filled with aborted plans, salesman's rhetoric and self-justification and yet what is there to justify? I have worked for ten years with the usual successes and failures following each other, as usual. In the long term, nothing has been gained but a few short-term indications of possibilities emerged only to be ignored. The loss is for the Metropolitan to bear, the profit in experiment and experience is mine. For a while I was able to 'live better' than ever before and derived very little stimulus from the life style but a great deal of pleasure, travel, David Hockney, and a fourth Folio, and most important, enough stress to make me seriously ill and in recuperating to discover more about myself than I had ever noticed before, and in so doing find a real relationship with Riggs and perhaps give him more of the happiness he deserves.

Now, explain why I only worked at half-strength in Lincoln Centre? Does security deaden the imagination? Certainly, and need sharpens it.

Freedom of movement is what I need. I've spent many years basically in subsidised theatre, from the Royal Court to the Paris Opera, the Comique, the Metropolitan, the National: they're all subsidised houses. And to me – this is entirely personal – there is something very deadening about that atmosphere. I want another one to do the next years' work, if spared.

Let me try to define what I expect of company style and how that style will affect the Sartre [*The Devil and the Good Lord*]. From the first line, to be whispered by a near naked Prophet, when the landscape has been fractured into the broken images, and which remain to suggest location and mood, to the last line, which is to be spoken by Goetz putting on his iron gloves as he stands under the high broken wheel on which lies the decaying body of a man. Between these two points we are to create a series of pictures with the company which, in addition to theatricalising the drama, contain the outlines for a company style which might give some guidelines on the real cost of economy and style.

The Devil and the Good Lord can be the beginning of a popular theatre by exploring the possibility of an artistically economical People's Theatre.

Will the mixture as before work for the next time or can we make it the last time and can we make it last?

Sartre as an Epic Dramatist.
Define this on a bare-board stage.
Would modern dress assist or intrude?

I said that the only difference I wanted from *A Woman Killed with Kindness* was that we should use building planks and make it very rough looking. I didn't envisage the crucifix being vast, that was Jocelyn. I nominate the space and Jocelyn supplies the object in space which tells you what you need to know about the scene. *The Devil and the Good Lord* looked wonderful. It's obscene what is being spent on scenery at the moment, but this production cost only about £4,000.

6 August 1984
Rehearsals Sartre begin.

First days are much worse than first nights. At least I can change my mind on a first day. And will.

7 August 1984
Watch it!
All very Sanderson, these notes.

Suppose I keep a proper journal, would it help clear my mind. If so, be truthful and do not edit. Write it so that only I can edit it. In other words take the trouble to write it, don't dictate it.

10 August 1984
Like Shaw in *The Man of Destiny* and *Good King Charles*, Sartre is

using the myths which have gathered around historical characters to express his own philosophy and, like Shaw, he finds wit, and the laughter it induces, to be the greatest aids to making an audience concentrate. The wit and the philosophy are a gift to the actor, and, if he adds his own wits to its delivery, four hours can seem like two.

13 August 1984
This week, find the comedic centre by observing your characters first and afterwards humanising them.

20 August 1984
Third weeks are the worst. All slog and no pleasure until Sat. when it paid off. A different drummer this week.

24 August 1984
Existence before Essence.
We have the existence of the play, now to find the essence.

25 August 1984
Now the play exists, we now establish the essence of its greatness. I think it's the most modern play I have worked on.

13 September 1984
SARTRE open.

14 September 1984
Rest day.

15 September 1984
Times, Guardian, Telegraph, v good. *F. Times* foolish, silly, and not important. The *Observer* says all I could ask for.

18 September 1984
Lindsay [Anderson], the distressed divorcee's director, talking to Adolf [John Osborne's name for Jill Bennett] all through Sartre. I should have been there to talk to him.

If transfer happens, cut Sartre by half and lose three actors.

'As far as I am concerned, the London Intellectual is a wash out.' Thus, George Devine upon his retirement. 'In ten years we have not managed to build an audience who have enough confidence in our work and will support it even when the Press does not.' Now it seems that the London Intellectuals will not support a theatre of ideas even when the Press is good and better than good.

Has the situation deteriorated, or are things just the same? Having taken the decision to return home and commit myself to working again in 'dear old, bloody old England', it is alarming to find the audience for the kind of theatre in which I take greatest pleasure vanished, and after having also persuaded Peter James at Hammersmith that in England there is always an audience for a theatre of ideas. The question must be considered, even if it cannot be answered. Smiling in the face of almost unanimously favourable notices for the play, production, and for Gerard [Murphy] and Simon [Ward], the smile fades rapidly in the reality of empty seats facing the stage night after night. During the first depressing week and after a number of jokes about Le Bon Dieu and his speed to an angry response in Durham [where the cathedral had been struck by lightning after the Bishop had expressed doubts about the virgin birth] – 'Well at least He didn't burn the box office down.'

He might just as well have done for all the use it is. During this week it has been easy to blame the length of the play and the difficulties experienced in getting to Hammersmith for six thirty and only leaving after eleven, but I cannot believe that the London Intellectuals are less dedicated than London Opera-lovers who prepare in advance for Wagner at Glyndebourne. Certainly the elitists have more time than the intellectuals in which to prepare the dress and the hampers, but Hammersmith gives them food and does not insist on uncomfortable costume. I find it difficult to believe that food and dress would keep an audience away and am left with the conclusion that the English do not come out to think about religion except in Church. However, at the end of the second week, the enthusiastic response of the happy few atheists who were interested enough to brave London Transport at rush hour raises my hopes that the future we have planned is possible. After all, I have always been told that God in the theatre is death at the box office, and have time and again found that to be untrue, much to my pleasure and profit.

However, all the God-haunted plays and operas I have

worked on in the past have affirmed man's need for Gods of some kind, which this play denies. Here is a play which affirms, on the other hand, that man has no need of God and that life without the myth, though tougher, is richer, and man stronger (an optimistic thought) and to look at the way men destroy in the name of Gods of one kind or another (a practical thought for today). An atheist's Thought for the Day might be more useful, but perhaps there are too few theatrically inclined atheists amongst the London intellectuals. Even if you allow fifty per cent reduction in capacity to be caused by time and distance, and divide the remaining fifty between Christians and atheists.

Would Sartre have fared better under the wing of the NT or the RSC? Better used in a repertory of Feydeau, Otway and others? Have the subsidised theatres destroyed their mailing lists to the London Intellectuals? Is there nothing left for those of us who cannot or do not choose, for one reason or another, to work on the South Bank or in the city? What about the suburbs of the theatre? Are they to be denied all traffic to the Epic and Classical theatre? To answer only the last, and to me most important, question. Certainly not.

One of the motivating forces behind the lunatic decision to attempt the Sartre at Hammersmith sprang from my personal desire to continue to develop, with Jocelyn, a stage upon which the actor and the epic could face each other on equal terms and which would give us an economic platform, not only for Sartre but Shakespeare, Brecht and many other modern playwrights whose imagination cannot be contained within the four walls and five characters of the theatre of murder, sex and farce upon which the economy of our theatre seems to rest. The RSC and the NT cannot develop every actor who needs to exercise his muscles, nor can they present all the work of modern playwrights which deserves to be seen. This responsibility now falls squarely upon the smaller theatre, and if experiments of this nature are to be met with such blank indifference, how can the Royal Court and Hammersmith, let alone the King's Head and the Bush, hope to continue, and how long before each season they must fall back upon the one-set, five-character play? Moreover, if the younger actors cannot cut their teeth on the classics, the standard of playing in drawing room comedy, tragedy and farce will soon fall below its present excellent standards. There seems to be no choice at all. If Hammersmith have the time, we have the stage and the actors, and the plan for the Hammersmith Historians, with Gerard and Simon, Finlay and hopefully Gambon joining us, must go ahead, and perhaps with the greatest box office playwright at our side the London Intellectual may respond. But what of the other play – [John Osborne's] *A Place Calling Itself Rome* for example. Can the management take that risk, or should I recommend a triple bill of those well known seat fillers of my repertory days, *Love's a Luxury*, *Bed Board and Romance*, and *Honeymoon Beds*?

I know that Sir Peter Hall and Trevor Nunn would be the first to acknowledge the need for more actors working in the Classics, but even with the number of theatres and the amount of subsidy at their disposal, they cannot satisfy the needs of all the talent that is around at this time. We are lucky that Mr Branagh and Mr Sher have been brought to the forefront in so splendid a manner, but for every one of them, there are others who cannot be so happily exposed but for whom a new production of *Henry V* and *Richard III* is impossible, financially and artistically, and to expect an actor or director to recreate in a revival the same sense of discovery and excitement, presented to the public and critics in such a lavish and splendid manner is, in my view, impossible.

Draft letter to David Hockney
I could write you a long letter about how good I feel, but as I am not a poet I could not make goodness real. So avoiding the rhyme, not committing the rhythmic crime, I break out of the rhythm I'm feeling and talk of the passing of Time, of passing the time without writing of joy I am feeling at last, in doing the work I was meant for and being at peace with the past.

To save your embarrassment and my nerves, I will resist and desist from committing the Harrisonian debauchery of verse and try to confine myself to the prosaic.

I threw down my Sartrean calling card complex but dazzlingly clear and as austere as I could have wished. I made one star and revealed an old one and gave myself the infinite happiness of making new friends, young enough to work out of love of the work, without regard for any other reward. It was exhilarating and, moreover, I can now be taken for forty-three in the dusk with the light behind me. I am making an amalgam of these new children, with some of the old gang, and by the middle of next year maybe we'll have something to show you and anyone else who cares for theatre, of intelligence and economy of style.

Not just my own sense of physical well-being after two years of illness and convalescence, but an exhilaration at finding so quickly a group of performers whose concentration never obscured their sense of the fun of work and who make work the best kind of play.

If I single out Gerard, it is not because his success was more obvious but because, whilst with Simon I was sure he could rise to the unusual demands made by the part of Heinrich, with Gerard I had no idea if the sleeping tiger would roar. That he did was a welcome reward for the joy of the thrust and parry of the rehearsal process.

So now we have a platform which will fit in any space all over England.

23 October 1984
Man and Superman: Gerard [Murphy], Simon [Ward], Stephen [Boxer] at the Mermaid.
If it works followed by commercial Sartre. Discuss plan, then present to [Jerry] Minskoff. The Company of Dialectic.

9 November 1984
What about a comic double bill *Under Plain Cover* [by John Osborne] and *Black Comedy* [by Peter Shaffer] for the future box office.

11 November 1984
Phone John O. and P. Shaffer and Thank God for the ideas? or would that be hypocritical?

15 November 1984
Selling England and the English language then and now – two views of history – Shakespeare and Osborne. Shakespeare: *Richard II*. Osborne: *A Place Calling Itself Rome*. After tour return to Mermaid with edited Sartre and introduce some old friends to some new ones. See what happens! Osborne, Shaffer, Herbert, Rigg, Murphy, Wood.

19 November 1984
If you think of Duncan Weldon [West End producer] as the Peter

Hall of the unsubsidised you will be able to understand his motives more clearly. The barrow boy's Binkie.

25 November 1984
75 days to dogs home from quarantine.

4 December 1984
For years I have been learning about musicals from the best: Rodgers, Styne, (Sondheim). Now is a chance to show what you have learned.

8 December 1984
SWET Olivier award dinner. Do we go? NO. Too expensive a price for humiliation.

1 January 1985
Riggs – please translate my diet into practical terms so that I can cook when I have to.

For August/September: Jocelyn, Hockney, *Othello*, *Shrew* for the Aquinas Street Players [former NT company members], followed by *Iguana*? Think about bringing all of the past into the present but without living in or on the past.

4 January 1985
Vanessa for drinks. NO SHOW!! Kidnapped by the PLO.

7 January 1985
Gambon. Othello. No.
Seems production would suffer by comparison with my first *Othello*. Actors are dumb.

26 January 1985
After months I have to admit that the theme of any company must come from me and I must call it my company – not Lilian's or Larry's or Guthrie's – and take the consequences.

9 February 1985
Move in to 142a.

1 March 1985
One year ago today we took the decision to leave Manhattan and we are in, with the dogs, Alex and Liza, and it's home already – with a routine.

21 March 1985
I do not understand the compulsion to write down even the most trivial observation.

Alex is 'untrainable'.

25 March 1985
Stop searching for the worst of the past. Try to think the best of yourself rather than the worst. To do this you either have to atone for guilt or get rid of it altogether. For God's sake disentangle God and Guilt, at least, even if you can do nothing else – and without professional help, literary or psychiatric.

17 June 1985
Ring LO re two parts at Her Majesty's. 'As long as you are directing, my dear, anything!!'

18 June 1985
To Richard Luce, Minister for the Arts
Returning to England after ten years at the Metropolitan, I have formulated a plan of work for the future which I hope will interest you, as it involves revitalising the Buxton Festival without involving the Arts Council more deeply than it is at present.
  I wonder if I might ask for a brief meeting with you to inform you of the details, and for such guidance as you would think fit to give me?

19 June 1985
Is opera to be considered as elitist all over the world, or only north of the Trent? At least in Verona, Rome, Vienna it is a populist art which assembles thousands in a collective life-enhancing experience with no violence of any kind. Why is this unthinkable in Derbyshire?

Week beginning 15 July 1985 (Buxton Festival)
A week of working with hard-working, well-meaning amateurs,
and I am not referring to the children. A woolly headed artistic
team and an overworked, underpaid and badly led cast of
craftsmen, stagehands and artists, all falling over each other and
willingly overworking at non essentials, whilst central authority
vanishes. Nevertheless, a healthy experience, and I must think
of the influence of Bea Lillie on the Marchioness. The return
home hysterical – describe it some time.

25 July 1985 [*Gigi* Rehearsals]
Another amazing day. Rest work and play – but both work and
rest are play – can this be right? This time I established an
authority by doing my job gently and living beautifully.

29 July 1985
Think about Buxton: De Falla, Dexter, Hockney, Stratas,
Harrison *Nights in the Garden of Spain* Festival + *Yerma*, if it is
ready by December, with D. Atalantia directed by me as a back-
up or, if desperate, *Man of La Mancha* (Broadway supports
Buxton). Produce a budget.

30 August 1985
Management meeting [*Gigi*] at which point JPA [Jean-Pierre
Aumont] should have been sacked, and HM [Helen Montagu]
took his side.

4 September 1985
Lerner told to leave the theatre.

5 September 1985
To Alan Jay Lerner
Lerner,
(Since you seem determined to ignore the customary civilities.)
It is sad that a man of your years and experience should react in
such a petulant and adolescent fashion to a politely expressed
and perfectly normal directorial request – i.e. 2 days of free
rehearsals.
    What you see on Friday will depend as much on your
objectivity as on the deficiencies of your director and cast. I shall
not be at the theatre on Friday (as the Management already

knows). Your, no doubt, copious notes will be delivered to me before Monday, unless you and the Management have decided to replace me, in which case, I am sure that in 7 days, you will be able to return the play to the San Franciscan form in which I first read it. Stoll Moss will, I assume, advise me if my presence is required on Monday.

The tone of your note is on a level with your behaviour since music and sound came into the theatre: hysterical, rude and out of touch with reality. Whatever your skills as a lyricist may be, your skills as a director are minimal, and have, for the last week, confused and divided a company beyond acceptable limits. As to your statement that you only attended rehearsals in order to prevent people from leaving, I have polled the principals of the company and your statement is inaccurate.

The 'or else' subtext of your last sentence would be irritating if it were not foolish. So Friday it is, or else what? Perhaps you and Jerry [Minskoff, New York producer] would like to take the show, in which case we can all 'Close a little faster' [reference to Lerner's previous musical, *Dance a Little Closer*].

10 September 1985
Sound sense and personal pride. The latter butters no parsnips. The former might, and I have many parsnips that need buttering.
AJL [Lerner] reveals himself to all.

12 September 1985
Freeze day? No wait for one more day on JPA [Aumont] and pace. Lyric Hammersmith to the West End and Buxton – can the 60th year be as good as the 59th? Yes, I think it can.

13 September 1985
Freeze. And the first good performance.

14 September 1985
Mr Lerner seems to find humble pie highly digestible. Understudy on. Panic in Hogarth Road [where Lerner lived].

15 September 1985
Buxton 3 year plan.
1. Kurt [Weill] in Manhattan. 2. De Falla. 3. Lehar & Berg.

Gigi opened at the Lyric Theatre, Shaftesbury Avenue, on 17 September 1985

18 September 1985
Press – [*Gigi*] Those who like the play don't like the production. Those who like the production etc.

I didn't like *Gigi*, but that was my fault as much as Jocelyn's. Bits of it were beautiful, but it wasn't quite the right atmosphere. We thought we could do it as a small boulevard piece and concentrate on the story, but it didn't work well that way. I didn't want to begin with 'Thank heaven for little girls', so Alan Lerner rewrote the first scene about being in a theatre and recreating the past; the opening worked very well, but it wasn't followed through enough.

19 September 1985
Get it right for its own sake, and my 'motive' was the same as Sir PH [Hall] when doing *Seberg* – to earn an honest buck for myself and others.

23 September 1985
For years I was convinced that I had to work in order to earn a living. Only since my illness do I understand that I work to live.

9 October 1985
Sutcliffe interview [Tom Sutcliffe, *Guardian*] in this morning. Wait one week for reactions.

16 October 1985
Cocktail Party – how about Alec [McCowen], Di [Rigg], Anna [Massey], [Barry] Foster. Try for that!

I thought there was a need for a company on a small scale to attempt work which is not normally considered 'West End'. At present the commercial theatre seems to be totally devoted to attracting the tourist trade, which is one thing to do – but maybe there is something else to do as well. Our plans for the future are entirely dependent on how the first one works. We have to find out whether there is a public left in England for classic plays in the commercial theatre. Everyone says there isn't. There used to be, in the days when I was growing up, when Tennent's were virtually controlling the West End and the English audiences were quite capable of filling a theatre for six or eight months of Shakespeare, Shaw, *The Family Reunion*, Gielgud, Scofield, all that. There was no limit. But where have those English audiences gone? Where were they when I did *The Devil and the Good Lord?* No West End management was interested in a transfer unless we brought in a star, and as I thought we'd already created one in Gerard Murphy, I wasn't willing to do that. Then John Higgins of *The Times* asked me about my reaction to a situation where something of enormous appeal was incapable of transferring – he asked me to write an article about it. But I found that instead of writing an article I was laying out a plan whereby such things *would* be possible in future. Then it took about two years of permutating plans and plays and people to arrive at *The Cocktail Party*.

25 *October 1985*
To Diana Rigg and Archie Stirling
Dear Sir and Madam, or Dear Madam and Sir,
Forgive the general address, but two sincere letters saying the same thing would strain your credulity and my nerves. But as I have to talk about life, love and work, I must overcome my natural reluctance to pontificate and writing to you as one will, I think, prevent that catastrophe.

Sir, I have recently rediscovered Thomas Stearns Eliot, and particularly his *Cocktail Party*, to which I can explain my response in detail when we meet, with a hope to persuade you to produce the show, even if Diana, for any reason at all, finds the part or the play not to her liking. And you, madam, if you do not like this play, then we will put our hearts together and find another one. But, please, before you say no let us have one more meeting and, if need be, read some of the play together. (This is a subtle way of asking for another week-end at Manderley.) I believe this part would be something which would not only be different from anything you have done before, but one in which you will find many reflections of all our lives. I only wish that Eliot had written Lavinia and Celia to be played by the same actress, for they are two sides of Viv [Eliot's first wife]: one person the reality, and the other the spiritual woman which no one but he saw. But over and above the extraordinary character of Celia, there is my strong personal reaction to the theme of guardianship. We are, all of us, guardians of our profession's reputation and future, and frankly I do not think our generation has accomplished much. The conveyor belt bureaucracy of the Barbican and the South Bank produces dead work and dying people. I know we are all dying, but I intend making more of a fuss before I go, and some time in the next twenty years perhaps I shall find an economical, stylish and profitable way of presenting good theatre.

It is with this hope and because I am tired of discussing the horrors of the South Bank (and I have long held the belief that letters to *The Times* are not effective), that I feel the only way to demonstrate the economic truth in future is to do it, demonstrate it beyond argument, and let the public make the choice.

So please, dear Sir and Madam, a meeting as soon as possible.

PS: Available and interested at this time: Anna Massey, Alec McCowen and Barry Foster. Comment please?

4 *November 1985*
To Robert Burns [Producer]
In the absence of jungle drums or messengers with cleft sticks I am taking up a secretary in order to establish contact with you. This reckless proceeding became necessary when on Wednesday last at lunchtime at the Savoy Grill the Big H [Helen Montagu] cut me dead!

We need private contact because I am about to come to you with phase one of the plans we have discussed: namely *Julius Caesar* and *The Cocktail Party*, involving a group of players who will present few problems for you except in the matter of billing, and two authors of the very best kind. Dead.

However, before we can discuss this in committee (assuming that the project still interests you), there are some personal matters arising from Mr Lerner's extraordinary dismissal of my services the week before last. I have asked Peter [Baldwin, Burns' partner] what procedure the management proposes to adopt in order to prevent such a farcical proceeding occurring again.

Perhaps you will have lunch with me at the Savoy Grill as soon as possible, as I have a few other less serious and hopefully more enjoyable stories to tell.

19 November 1985
To Alan Jay Lerner
Remembering the speed with which you rushed to your Remington after an inadequate performance, I am dismayed that I have not yet been sent notes on the performance given at sparrowfart on Monday the 21st October. And so, in the absence of any word from you and with a view to the future, I will try to imitate your style. No, perhaps 'manner' would be a better word.

NOTES TO BE READ:
Firstly: never ever deliver what is intended to be a crushing cataclysmic message from a subservient position. Standing three steps below the Laird is all right for Seyton, but Tiresias would not stand a chance in that position.

Secondly: Casting. I am amazed that a man of your experience should consent to play with a Bus and Truck Company [Lerner had arrived with Mrs Jerry Minskoff]. After all, Jocasta hardly lies within the reach of Tamara Desni, nor would you accept Dulcie Gray as Lady Macbeth.

Thirdly, and most important, never appear with an improvised script.

Enough, parody is not my line.

On a more serious note, I am still waiting to hear from Mr Minskoff after having written him a friendly letter asking for some statement from him as to my position as director of *Gigi*. You told me you were speaking for him, but I think, under the circumstances, it would be mannerly if he spoke for himself. I hope to be able to see him in New York during the next few days, but when I return I think we should meet and discuss any problems we have and thereby save an inexperienced management further embarrassment and, hopefully, keep a constructive eye on *Gigi* together. This, after all, is what matters if we are going to continue to attract audiences for some time to come, for which devoutly-to-be-wished consummation all our accountants will give thanks.

Week beginning 4 November 1985
New York – No
Instead absolute pleasure at home thinking. This home was

bought by ten years' hard labour from both of us. It was worth it, including the illness. A modestly introspective week plus a few reasonable letters and work-in-progress.

And on Sunday??

Discipline for us both so that we can enjoy it longer if we deserve it.

7 November 1985
At a moment of crisis he arrived as always when needed. He is balanced in every subject except me, and I cannot blame him for that as it is only in the last four years that I have found I had lost balance years ago.

13 November 1985
Ring [Stephen] Spender, *Billy Budd* Dress Rehearsal and Trilogy [*The Theban Trilogy* of Sophocles in a version by Spender]. Diana – Jocasta, Alec – Creon, Mikhail [Baryshnikov] – Oedipus. What about DH [Hockney] for masks and, eventually, set.

Read TSE [Eliot's *Cocktail Party*], discuss company.

From Becket Street [in Derby] onwards, I made a home in my work and have been trying to do so ever since. Now I have a home of my own for the first time. I have to, must, make a home for other people.

15 November 1985
Don't spend too much time deciding on the form. It's a way of avoiding facing up to the content – or just the work.

Becket Street, Samuel French and weekly rep. Put the furniture where the actors cannot possibly bump into it. Use the work of Guthrie, Devine and all the others who have been robbed blind of even a minimal reward.

16 November 1985
Arnold [Wesker] and John [Osborne] supported me at a time when I could not possibly support myself, mentally or financially. The work was the only happy return, and were either of them to ask me to direct a play which no one wanted to do, I believe we would find a wooden hut somewhere.

20 November 1985
To Michael Billington
A whole article on the style and economics of the British theatre and no mention of Miss Herbert.

For the sake of your soul I think I should give you luncheon at the Savoy Grill, so that we may discuss this matter without raising my voice or your blood pressure. Please choose a date. I am 'Parade-ing' at the Metropolitan from tomorrow until December 5th, but if you will ring me at the above number I will look forward to hearing from you.

I've got 18 months of work planned and I don't know whether we're going to get through all that. I have to go through my knowledge of repertoire and suggest roles to the actors, ask them if they'd like this or that, and build up the programme that way. But I'm not going to start planning the next section until we've done a couple of the first. They're all reading the *Oedipus* now, seeing if there's anything that appeals to them in it. Because that will be our second play – *if* we survive.

14

Butterfly

Notebook:
I know people have stopped going to the theatre. They go to see *Starlight Express*, but are they seeing *any* theatre as such? With TV and movies and the two big conveyor belts [the NT and the RSC] playing to everyone's brows, should we just *give up*? I'm doing Eliot because Tony Harrison hates him, and I think that I'm trying to show Tony that there's more to Eliot than the private mystic.

But it's also great that I can get people like Joan Plowright, Simon Ward, Alec McCowen, Sheila Gish, Di Rigg at co-operative rates because they care so much about this kind of season. There was a big bias against Eliot when I started at the Court too. But to me *The Cocktail Party* is a funny and moving comedy about the reconstruction of a marriage and about spiritual love.

You can either take it as a comedy of manners, in the fashion of Maugham or Wilde or Sheridan, or as a philosophical discussion about the nature of Christian marriage, the disinte-gration and reconstruction of a marriage, the need for us to make choices and be guided in our choices and accept them. It says that good living is as important as good dying, which seems to me as relevant now as it was when the play was first staged in 1949, and possibly more so.

I think probably Eliot himself was very much in search of a good life. He'd been through marriage of one kind and was desperately unhappy. I think he's reflecting back on that in comic terms: the extraordinary thing is that he could see it like that, and the last act seems to be pre-figuring the very happy life he had later with the second Mrs Eliot. The last act is suffused with the yearning for a happy life with a woman.

There is a current cant that he stopped writing poetry after he married again. This seems to me totally unimportant: how much poetry is a man expected to have within him? And is a poet to be denied a happy life, a good life, which is just as important as writing poetry?

Beginning of 1986
The primary motive force behind the Eliot/Spender programme is fury at the patronising reception given to Spender's celebration by the literary journalists, most especially Waugh junior, limping drunkenly after dear old Dad, and indulging in the Sling a Sneer at Spender game. But this force is reinforced by the need to see a discernible style and theme for the coming year's work. Affirmative Theatre Company, ATC, can then disguise itself as ATC Avenue Theatre Company.

1 January 1986
Try in this year to earn a little company credibility via Bourdet, Eliot, to Spender, Shakespeare. And if I see myself as DH [Hockney] sees me I will do no harm. So act up to it (it's an easier part than the other).

23 January 1986
I think, all things seriously considered, I have been a model of restraint for the last six months, but the time has come to set the record straight in relation to Britten & Thatcher [B & M = Peter Baldwin & Helen Montagu, producers]. And tell Irving [Wardle] why it is important. The design must respond to the economy if the commercial theatre is to serve as a creative force. So who cares – Stoll Moss?

1 February 1986
[Notes for Irving Wardle]
What was wrong with you that you missed the point for the first time and why in two pages of Shaffer discourse no mention of the director? Is it bad PR or what? Who else can I ask? Is it paranoid at sixty to feel underestimated in the light of the above?

10 February 1986
After years of not taking myself seriously, I am now in danger of taking myself too seriously if I am to push the company together. If I am pushing, it is the work inside that is producing the muscle.

21 February 1986

1. Di [Rigg] can do until June/July but we have no theatre.
2. How much does Eddie [Kulukundis, producer] trust Tom [Eliot]?
3. How quickly can Bourdet [*The Unicorn*] be ready as a back up if I am wrong about TSE[liot]. 1936–1986. Myths, masks and the whole theory of poetry. Now with the need for Mythic theatre? Let alone economy and style, to say nothing of survival of all of us.
4. From now on the play comes first. Di was an invention to justify a compromise which I would make again if it would get things moving.

24 February 1986

Bourdet is a good stable-mate for *Othello* if Maggie [Smith] and Michael's dates work with Spender.

From now on DR [Diana Rigg] will be used if she is useful, and only if. In short she is Miss Do As You Would Do Unto Others and I am Mrs Do As You Would Be Done By.

26 February 1986

I do not know why Michael [Hastings] bothered writing his play *Tom and Viv*. It's all in *The Cocktail Party*.

As we are obviously never going to own a Cottage in the Country and would probably go mad in it if we did, The Fairly Furious Garden in London should begin from the Church door down a primrose path of Dalliance by Ophelia's wreath and Fortune's flowers, that only Riggs and I know.

6 March 1986

King Arthur in Buxton, Handel, Purcell? I'd rather do a dramatisation of *The Sword in the Stone* with the local kids.

22 March 1986

Sixty is no age at which to try to build the Crystal Palace out of shit.

31 March 1986

Paris. *Italian Straw Hat*. 'Scandalo' – even Peter Wood could do better. Is this the NT in fifty years? Dutiful audiences, large subsidy, total apathy.

8 April 1986

Play it in three acts [*Cocktail Party*] as written. If we get it right, the audience will need a mental as well as a pee break. Shakespeare time – years into decades. Quantum Time as DH will surely say. Time only exists because we measure it.

Alec as Sigmund F. had he been able to afford Vienna in London and had had a vestige of a sense of humour. And *no* wigs. No Jewish.

Imagine an Anglo-Christian Sigmund, if such a thing were possible. It would only be tolerated were the characters aware of the effects of humour and temperament on his clients.

9 April 1986

Miss [Nicola] Pagett will not give to Miss [Sheila] Gish on billing. Nor will Miss Gish give to Miss Pagett. Miss Pagett goes.

16 April 1986

If anyone wants to know what's wrong with subsidy, find out the reason why neither the ESC [English Stage Company], NT or RSC can find the time or the money to celebrate Sam [Beckett]'s birthday. Eighty for God's sake and unarguably the greatest dramatic poet of our time. The answer to the question is for the Arts Council to discover. Indifference or money? 20th-century dramatic poetry moves between Beckett's pessimism and Eliot's despair turned to hope.

2 May 1986

Should the TSE [*Cocktail Party*] not sustain itself until Bourdet and Maggie are ready, take an option on Priestley for the same company + Plowright and the Bourdet girl if poss. Parts for [Stephen] Boxer, [Sheila] Allen, [Sheila] Gish etc. if they agree.

15 May 1986

DH [Hockney] is building a contemplation tower – to escape from his groupies?

26 May 1986

Spender trilogy for Jan. if Maggie not ready. Di, Alec, Alan [Bates]? Hockney has promised time for Buxton then – ? Ask him and JH [Jocelyn Herbert] and explain.

30 May 1986
PS: for Bruce Crawford at the Met.
Quite apart from the financial rewards, the news of a *Carmelites* TV does of course interest me greatly. To have at least one production on record of my own visual aspirations for the Met in a modern economy as opposed to –. I leave you to fill in the blank yourself, and make it possible.

5 June 1986
[Alan] Bates available Jan. Sophocles Spender and McCowen. [Simon] Ward. Rigg, [Robert] Eddison, [Rachel] Kempson, [Stephen] Boxer if they feel like it. Write DH for dates using Buxton and the future as a lever.

6 June 1986
The Unicorn Act 1 arrives [the Bourdet play]. Othello and Iago play Francois and Georges. Emilia plays Coco, Desdemona Germane and so on. *Othello* with a cast of 20. Understudies from Bourdet. One Doge, four senators, six rioters, and Cyprus is a small place.

Phoenix Theatre becomes a possibility. Foyles, Waterstones, Collets are natural centres for our audience.

16 June 1986
BLOOMSDAY
ELIOT REHEARSE. GOOD FIRST WEEK.

25 June 1986
Persuade Sheila [Gish] to face up to the ghost of Maggie Leighton, whom Mrs Eliot did not like as Celia.

27 June 1986
RT [run-through] 2.
Alec brilliant, the others only dazzling. It could work as an allegro with occasional andantes and scherzi.

You can only take your pace from Eliot's verse. It's just as musical. It requires consistent exercises each morning in order to get your tongue round the metre. Exactly like warming up for an operatic performance. It's a text in which the rhythms and metres are constantly changing. Out of the metre comes the character.

30 June 1986
I have been accused of trying to run a company along Stalinist Puritan lines -- I might accept Methodist.

3 July 1986
It took GD [Devine] some time to realise that, although homosexual, I was as much a theatrical puritan as he, and, once we had discussed grandfathers and the Boy Scout movement, we became friends and colleagues.
Not a good afternoon.

5 July 1986
If PH last sentence is true [*Peter Hall Diaries*: 'I don't believe life begins at fifty, but I mean to try and make it'] then it is only true because he has made it so with his opportunistic attempts to drag theatre into Show Business. Has PH forgotten GD's advice which he so regularly quotes in his diaries? ['You can think of the theatre as a temple or a brothel.']

7 July 1986
Let the audience supply the tension. NEXT WEEK.
THIS WEEK RELAX AND ENJOY THE RUN-THROUGHS.

9 July 1986
Bourdet 2nd act arrives and very good and a different balance.

12 July 1986
The fact that I am the son of a plumber still seems to arouse faint wonder. I wonder why? (ask Hopkins). Why is it easier for the actor to be the son of a plumber?

23 July 1986
The work has been a synthesis of the time spent on Molière, Racine & Harrison. Very odd bedfellows to be tucked in by TSE [Eliot]. Like *Woman Killed* a good play to re-examine and learn from.

28 July 1986
'Mixed' reception to TSE but the box office is booming.

30 July 1986
Billington *v.* good for the company. Use 'Racine enters the drawing room.'

1 August 1986
When work is well life is well.

2 August 1986
Birthday party lunch for cast before matinée.
Whatever the notices!!
And made the Sundays!
TIMES RAVE enough for a Royal Court hit.

Week beginning 4 August 1986
Hang Out the Flags for the New Theatre Company this week.

21 August 1986
Playhouse Theatre, near Charing Cross Station, possible home for New Theatre Company, Aug. 87.

22 August 1986
Therefore, Bourdet open Feb., run to July, at which point transfer to new Playhouse with *Othello* to open thereafter, to run in rep with *Cocktail Party* and Bourdet.

25 August 1986
Alec: Iago, like Othello, driven by vanity. The difference is that Othello never thought himself capable of anything as trivial as vanity whereas Iago's vanity is cultivated.

29 August 1986
Godson found!

4 September 1986
Discovering a godson and a company in the same year is a real reason for writing a book.
There is still one pavement in Derby which can for me evoke what seems to be a true memory of my life until my twenty-fifth year. Begin at the Drill Hall.

Week beginning 15 September 1986
Take Down the Flags for the New Theatre Co (keep them in store).

Week beginning 20 October 1986
CLEAN UP THE DESK AND THE BOOKS AND GET THE FLAGS READY.

25 October 1986
Explain Malvern casting plans. Iago in the end of next year. Gambon? Alan [Bates]? Colin [Blakely]? And then tie in with the three choirs.

Week beginning 27 October 1986
NTC – The Malvern Festival presents the New Theatre Company in a new play by William Douglas Home.

28 October 1986
To Malvern – and I promise there will be many little touches of lunacy in the night. To begin – Fraser Simpson sung by the company. Dominic Muldowney to arrange for mixed voices.
We all seem such a drab lot in comparison to Shaw and [Augustus] John and even Cecil [Beaton].

3 November 1986
From Sloane Sq. to Malvern should not be too difficult a leap for a dedicated Shavian.

5 November 1986
To WDH [William Douglas Home] (who has agreed to *Portraits* as a title).

6 November 1986
Can we finance one trial season of six plays – May/Oct '87 with options on both sides, and aiming for a full length [*Man and*] *Superman* for '88. I would like to put myself and the New Theatre Co. on offer to the Malvern Festival for a six month season each year until 1990 which will be my sixty-fifth anniversary. The possibilities are endless, from Shaw to Shakespeare and many stops on the way Home. Brenton, [N.F.] Simpson, Bourdet – alas not Spender [Peter Bogdanovich had got the rights].

7 November 1986
I object to the factory aspect of subsidised theatre. If I am on a conveyor belt it is one of my own making, so let's hope it only turns out Formula Ones and not Bentleys.

1 December 1986
My dear Diana, you are 'about as vulnerable as the North face of the Eiger.' 'Alec only two paces, count five and then move again.'
Sheepdog Trials are very like directing but which one is, or should be the shepherd? The dog makes it impossible to be both, i.e. when the sheep are all poised for the pen and the wind shifts, one of the silly sheep bolts and the rest scatter. So it seems when trying to pull the right group together.

5 December 1986
Phone [Sheila] Gish, [Peter] Froggat, [Ros] Chatto, [Robert] Fox, [Michael] Gambon. We are now talking about offers of definite dates and wanting to ask for commitment to one thing at a time – all trusting to certain objectives. Iago for Alec [McCowen] Cleopatra for Joan [Plowright], but one thing at a time – Take my word.

10 December 1986
Discuss Arts Council position. Subsidy – censorship – must be discussed in relation to the NTC if we're to avoid the trap in which I have spent most of my working life. Check Budget. And why not take Bourdet to Paris for a week?

20 December 1986
JO, LO. If the radio could eradicate George VI's stammer, I can surely edit Larry's mistakes and it will keep him busy.

December 1986
GURNAL seems so much less literary than JOURNAL but gurnalising is much more enjoyable than writing so what better way to begin . . .

A bloody awful year professionally, unproductive, with more time spent in the company of accountants than authors, more plans discussed than activated, the New Theatre Company almost sunk without a trace, and the will to keep it floating, although still as strong as ever, needs nourishment. We need not expect it to come from the Arts Council, unless they take the common-sense step of throwing the Royal Opera House to the Tory wolves and spreading the thirteen million pounds worth of fertiliser north of Watford, but who expects common sense from that group of superannuated stage carpenters, any more than we expect commercial managers to recognise responsibility to anything other than the hopeless or hapless angels. In '87 the NTC must earn a space in which to work as we did in the Eliot play, for the work was good, even if the rewards were not. The wrong play or the wrong place matter little and will matter less by this time next year, for we are unlikely to survive to next year unless the place and the play are more artfully chosen, to say nothing of the management.

At a time when the Arts Council, the boards of the NT, RSC and ROH are locked like Laocoon on national strangulation exercises, it may be possible to divert a small amount of investment money, but subsidy with the certainty of censorship and general interference would be simply to place myself and the players on the old treadmill. Or find a commercial play which does not insult. Subsidy can strangle.

4 December 1986
M. Butterfly arrived!

8 December 1986
Be glad David [Hwang, author of *M. Butterfly*] did not use *Turandot* as a primary subtext for a play in which East confronts the West.

The place in which you live is bound to be a metaphor for the life you live.

9 December 1986
M. Butterfly would be the climax of an experiment that began with *Royal Hunt*, through *Woman Killed*, *Equus*, and *The Devil and the Good Lord*. So as usual I am subject to all the doubts: They don't want me, I am too difficult, expensive, or homosexual. The techniques of the Eastern theatre were for me what they seemed for Brecht – freedom which equalled that given by Sunday nights without decor in Sloane Square.

Of course I am not the first or only director to be fascinated by the freedom offered by the discipline of a stage as simple as that of the Noh. I imagine Brecht's response was like mine: first a burst of possibilities and then hours of joyful study. But Brecht was not merely a director but a playwright of genius (does this still need saying?) and the use he made of his freedom will always be part of our dramatic repertoire. My productions will not, and that is the pleasure of them. They are usually made for one place at one time and move with ill grace, but on the occasions when they work for one group of people on one night, that is the director's greatest joy and no film or video or record can catch it in the can, nor can the players themselves reproduce it in exactly the same way. It is perhaps a selfish and solitary pleasure but one with which I continually indulge myself and never more than now with a new manuscript in front of me.

M. Butterfly, an East West cultural and sexual confrontation, is, like *Royal Hunt* and *Roots*, a glorious first read, propelled by the thought first of what is to happen next, and second how on earth can it be made to happen. In the case of *Royal Hunt* the words 'They climb the Andes' gave the key. In *Roots* 'Pause. Silence'. But in the case of David Hwang's play, the key is given by the language of the text, not the stage directions.

When I was young I assumed all authors intended their stage directions to be read as intently as Shaw. (For GBS they were witty, precise, but instructions to be ignored at peril.) I was wrong. For some they are merely shorthand for a director whose theatrical tastes they know and share, as with Arnold Wesker and Peter Shaffer, and sometimes superbly enigmatic, unchangeable and carefully selected, as with Sam Beckett. I have spent very little time in Mr Beckett's company, in spite of having watched him rehearsing with ears open, but with Arnold and Peter I have spent a great deal of creative time and energy, and having watched them at work, I judge Mr Hwang to be in that class at least. Mr Beckett is of course alone and unclassable.

So perhaps my attempt to clarify for myself how I came to know my directors and directions will be a record of a kind I have never kept before. A working journal should not be beyond my limited literary powers, but these limited powers must be explained if my haphazard working life can be understood, if not by me then maybe by others. At least the record of the work will remain and record the process for intending Stage Directors, who, it is to be hoped, may be a little more highly regarded in the future than they are in the eighties.

23 December 1986
David Hwang is like John Arden – an enquiring mind which can turn fact into drama and in doing so makes the same demands of the story – absolute freedom of Time, Space, Place.

Gurnal
The present is so much more interesting than the past and never more so than when I attempt to write about the past. The daily journal takes whatever writing time is at my disposal. This particular project so bursts with possibilities, in addition to the already planned *Portraits* by William Douglas Home.

19 January 1987
Just as now the idea of style for *Portraits* has clarified itself, I know the cast I want and fuck the Arts Council. Augustus John: [Joss] Ackland, Dodo: Pamela Lane, GBS: [John] Osborne, Monty/Baxter/Jo: [Simon] Ward.

One black screen for final portrait in each act and [Augustus] John uses three canvases at once, ref Holroyd; and all this after five days in New York. Write about the oddness of that.

20 January 1987
JO [Osborne] as GBS in more ways than one. Bourdet is out as the money needs a name and we need the money.

21 January 1987
We may lose Ackland!!! But I think Donald Sinden makes up for it and the company is the happiest mix I have ever had. I want Donald to be seen this year as the money stars may not be available till the year after.

10 February 1987
Remember when the local Derby literati discussed Disney's Pre-Raphaelite period in relation to the design of *Dumbo* – On the whole a good time, apart from the total dependence on seven shillings and sixpence a week, discounting pension and my incredible parents.

2 April 1987
Note for David Hwang. The Brecht productions were the most glorious things I had seen in the theatre since Gertrude Lawrence in *Private Lives* and she was an act of God.

12 April 1987
Garden Ravel. [Rehearsing *L'Enfant* at Royal Opera House].

21 April 1987
Double rehearsals until May 1.

21 April 1987
Malvern – Rehearse *Portraits*
The actor is not concerned with photographic realism any more than was Augustus John – the impression, the spirit is all he needs.

27 April 1987
Two weeks of double rehearsal and I feel very good, if only the work was. A week dominated by the ROH can only be depressing.

4 May 1987
Ravel/Stravinsky open. [*L'Enfant/Rossignol*].

14 May 1987
The emergence of the play. Music works – needs re-recording. Shape emerges and is not half bad. KM [Keith Michell] needs to take over. PL [Pamela Lane] to concentrate. SW [Simon Ward] to enjoy. And [Stephen] Boxer to speak up. [Richard] Wordsworth is uncanny.

18 May 1987
Malvern: *Portraits* First Night.
Performance steady but dull.

20 May 1987
Surprisingly good press.

2 January 1988
To New York.

4 January 1988
Begin rehearse *M. Butterfly*.

1 February 1988
Washington.

7 February 1988
Let me get this down before I forget.
Yesterday Riggs, with his usual clarity, solved the problem of
Helga. I immediately called SO [Stuart Ostrow, producer of *M.
Butterfly* in New York] and was shocked by his reaction. He
refused to accept the idea or even discuss it because it came from
Riggs. However, he agreed to meet for breakfast the following
morning. He walked into the breakfast room, sat down and
proceeded to repeat everything I had told him the day before –
what could I do? I just agreed with him and when I got back to
my hotel, Riggs and I laughed about it. Producers.

10 February 1988
Official opening.

11 February 1988
All press except *Post* raves.

20 March 1988
MB open NY.

28 March 1988
NYT [*New York Times*] acid: *very* comforting.

30 March 1988
Stuart Ostrow phoned. Advance up. Celebrities in. House seats
out.

24 May 1988 Creon.
JH [Jocelyn Herbert] no time – postpone? I would suggest a long
postponement but I would like S[tephen] S[pender] to be alive to
see the end product.

5 June 1988
Fête Dieu.
Tonys – Best Director, Best Play, Best Supporting Actor.

9 July 1988
Dinner [Anthony] Hopkins and Jen [his wife] re *MB*.
V. good. He seems keen! End of Jan.
GBS makes me feel bloody lazy.

14 July 1988
Blood Pressure a *little* down. Increase dose 2/2.

2 August 1988
A good day.
Apart from the fact that Riggs took against the sunset.

IF I HAVE TO CHOOSE BETWEEN THE GREAT AND THE
GOOD I WILL CHOOSE THE GOOD. THE GREAT ARE
USUALLY SHITS.

My generation are much too famous and busy to work with me,
so I'll work with the next generation, their children, Tamsin
Olivier, Cathy Finlay, Jacqueline Dankworth and William Key,
George Devine's grandson. That would please George.

Most young actors now are deficient vocally, in variety, tone,
range, projection. It's appalling sometimes. Bad breathing, bad
phrasing, unclear. As long as ten years ago, Sir Laurence was
saying that we had allowed audiences to stop listening. They get
so used to turning the volume up on the TV. And every time you
go into a theatre now you see support mikes all over the place.
People have become lazy. Some student actors are interested in
improving their voices and some are not. Some drama schools
have a capable staff, some haven't. I've come across two people
recently who have done three years at a drama school, on a local
council grant, and they came out with nasality, no reserve of
breath, and a total inability to speak what we call standard
English. That's the state of things at the moment. Some actors
think they don't need it: they can get into *EastEnders* by speaking
yob, so why should they bother? Well, it's their choice. If they
don't want to extend themselves in that region they don't have
to. But it has created a deficiency of actors who are aware of their
responsibilities to their voices, and to the audience.

8 August 1988
Haymarket [Leicester]. Begin JC [*Julius Caesar*].

Creon and Julius Caesar
I've had this in the pipeline for about two years. *Creon* [Stephen Spender] I've had in my hand for four years now. The relationship between the two plays is getting more interesting as we get further into rehearsal.

It is always more interesting to work with an ongoing group of people on two projects rather than one. It makes casting easier and the work harder but more stimulating.

We came up with ideas for a few programmes which would have probably closed the theatre – certainly emptied it for a few days – but suddenly these two plays came together and they spoke to each other in a rather interesting fashion.

It uses a lot of the forms of classic Greek tragedy but it uses them in a different way; I won't say a modern way.

I've been looking for a new space to work in. I've tried to work within the confines of West End management but I found them a bit too confining. You need to be left to get on with your work and it is difficult to do that in the commercial area. Leicester made advances to me, asked me if there was anything I would like to do.

16 August 1988
!!! Go away pain.
Prepare to work.

31 August 1988
To Joe Harris, General Manager, Jeremiah Harris Associates, NY
If we are going to collaborate with the Leicester Haymarket in the English production of *M. Butterfly*, it is essential that arrangements are completed before the end of September as production plans must be presented to the Board of the Leicester Haymarket by that date. In addition, due to my commitments in the Far East [*Julius Caesar*, *Creon*, Indian tour], all casting decisions must be taken by the end of November and design decisions by the end of October. For the months of December and January I am totally unavailable. Furthermore, this is to advise you formally that I am no longer holding time in the fall of this year and unless I hear to the contrary, I shall be engaged for most of

next year after March. I would appreciate anything you can do to expedite these matters.

The great thing about the theatre is that it never gets any easier. Once, when Charles Marowitz was asking a group of RSC players to come out on stage and say the most shocking and terrifying things they could possibly think of, Doris Hare came out, aged about 70, and said, 'This production opens on Monday night', and that's all you really have to know about fear. Just because *M. Butterfly* has been the most tremendous award-winning hit in New York, there's absolutely no guarantee we can repeat it over here although of course I hope we can.

Anthony Hopkins was one of the young players I brought into Olivier's National almost 30 years ago to play a messenger in *Othello*, and apparently all he did this time was check that his character appeared on the first and last pages and that I was going to direct. So then he said yes, and here we are rehearsing in Leicester, which of course is home. Its backstage facilities are the best I've ever come across, and besides the Midlands was where I started.

20 March 1989
The changes have worked.
They must have worked because Stuart [Ostrow] said he was going to put them into *his* production in New York.
Was it a Freudian slip?
No. He believes he did do it.
As long as he's happy.

25 March 1989
MB open Leicester.

9 September 1989
JC [*Julius Caesar*] Preview 1.

14 September 1989
Creon read.

13 October 1989
Creon Preview 1.

27 October 1989
REST AT HOME.

25 December 1989
Christmas is a week of leonine indolence!

15

3 OP.

Diary:
11 July 1989
Larry died, and when the realisation has sunk in I might manage a tear, at the moment I feel a gigantic space which no one can occupy.

7 May 1989, Venice
Writing by intimidation. Constructing a paragraph, even a sentence, as elegant as the paper on which it is written is at least a challenge and a discipline to which I might respond. Perhaps also the need to explain myself to Natasha Makarova and Tony [Hopkins] (and moreover to myself) as we begin to plan for a working future together, may be enough to give some semblance of intellectual discipline to a purely emotional and instinctive need to make another working family. Family – the word loaded with sentimental over and undertones. Ensemble – even worse. And Company now rendered meaningless by Lord Vestibule [Peter Hall]. Between the pretenders and the Lucksters there has to be a working space.

And pat on his cue at ten thirty in the evening comes the big Luckster himself: Schonfield. 'John, we go back a long way' (how long?) 'I want you to direct *Yonadab* in New York, no one else has been asked.' (Hall? Blakemore?) 'We all want you.' (Lantz? Shaffer?) 'Will you read it and meet Shaffer?' 'I will read it and meet you in New York.'

The time has come to review the situation.

Theatre in the 90s. Using Shaw's book, doing the plays that came to light in the 1890s in the 1990s, encompassing the journey from melodrama to naturalistic drama, starting with *Misalliance* for Natasha [Makarova].
Krasnikov time 6.55 – Somewhere at sea [Adriatic].

10 May 1989
The Asprey bedside clock that Gertie gave to Noël has its counterpart in the Krasnikov watch Natasha gave me. The daily winding a constant reminder of the promises made to a simple Soviet woman, and of the difficulties ahead. Firstly her agents, Lantz and his English parrot [Bernard Hunter] making the shark with the pearly teeth [Duncan Weldon], thrashing around in the waters, snapping up any tasty morsel he finds in his vicinity, unattractive to deal with and totally timewasting. But if I am to be of any use at all to Natasha and Tony, deal with them, I must (hopefully having learnt from the past), and so: –

The Krasnikov Story

Midnight. Natasha phoned . . . perhaps I should go back to the beginning. Went to see *On Your Toes*. Natasha wonderful. Riggs said I must find something for her. By the end of the play I thought of *Tovaritch*. Duncan Weldon has the rights. I went to see Duncan. He liked the idea. I suggested Paul Scofield, and invited him to see *On Your Toes*. I think he was frightened by Natasha. Too much competition. I was sure he would say no. He did.

Stage 2:
My agent calls. Says he has received a call from Duncan. Natasha doesn't want to work with me.

Stage 3:
Four years later. We receive a midnight call. Natasha has been sent a play about Sarah Bernhardt that has been written for her. Would I read it? I read it and arrange a meeting for Natasha and me. At this meeting I discover the truth. She never said she didn't want to work with me, and in fact wondered why I had never been in touch. We agree that someone must be working against us. I invite her to lunch.

Stage 4:
I convince her it would be better to start with *Misalliance*, following with *When We Dead Awaken*, continuing with *The Seagull*, finishing with *As You Desire Me*. Leave for Italy. On the train I realise we must get the rights before anyone else. Especially Duncan. I arrive in Venice, call my agents and arrange for the rights. 24hrs later my agent calls back and tells me that we just made it, that Triumph Productions had also applied for the

rights but were too late. How do they know everything that I am going to do? Discovery of secret. Natasha's London agent fighting very hard for Triumph to produce *Tovaritch* with Natasha. Without me naturally. He must have been the one to tell about the season. Lots of political nonsense to sort out, but Natasha sure. Bought her a present in Venice – a beautiful Fortuny dress.

Three thousand sea miles later.
And so . . . nothing, due to the intervention (via satellite) of the hucksters and whoremasters which disturbed many happy hours between Alexandria and Santorini and which for once gave rise to as much laughter as irritation. And so once again, in Venice:

The Battle of the Temple and the Whorehouse continues.
GD[evine]'s dictum that the theatre represents a choice between the whorehouse and the temple has been an inspiration and an irritant for years. After all, temples have always had a need of professional whores as well as professional virgins. My problems have in the past always been with the amateurs (civilians) in both categories.

Don't forget the shrimp at Aboukir and the row in Venice.

15 June 1989
[Terry] 'Grubby' Hands rang – RSC *Coriolanus* – start in two months. No actor as yet. No decent director would undertake a *Coriolanus* with only two months' preparation and no actor to hang it on. This call was thirty years too late.

20 August 1989, New York
Twelve thousand more sea miles.

So much for good paper producing good writing. Here I am in a wet August. The Krasnikov Company is a little nearer reality – but not much. Robber Lantz to be dealt with this week.

Last Friday Run Through [of *Threepenny Opera*] only modestly awful but at least laying out the objective for next week. Textual clarity.

Ginger Man Restaurant, and a good lunch with Willie Cameron, fresh faced, bright eyed, as though nothing stronger than

Perrier ever passed his lips, eager, full of ideas and talking positively about the company and the years before the Leicester Haymarket. Maybe serendipity or luck but at least practical and pragmatic happenstance.

Best news of the day – Holst wrote *The Planets* at Thaxted!! So much loss and gain since May.

An intelligent director could have written a three-volume novel on the events of the last months with alcoholism, DTs, AA, and broken promises as the theme.

On the positive side, Bob (diabetics anonymous) Stephens seems ready for the Ibsen-Shaw-Chekhov plunge and if he commits to only six months in *MB[utterfly]*, he can have it all (and why not). He has more than paid his dues and the tiny Semite will have to swallow a little pride.

The Story of *The Threepenny Opera*

'John is going to interpret the play and I am going to do what he says.'
Sting

25 October 1988
To Riggs O'Hara from Eric Glass [JD's agent]
I had a telephone call from Joseph Harris [producer] to say that his friend and associate Jerry Hellman would very much like John to direct *The Threepenny Opera*, rehearsing in August and performances probably at the Kennedy Center in September and on Broadway mid October/early November.

1 January 1989
Threepenny Opera. Sting, Stratas: God's casting because only God could sort out the billing.

7 November 1988
From Kim H. Kowalke, Kurt Weill Foundation, New York
We are delighted to hear from Jerome Hellman that you are considering directing the production of *Threepenny Opera*. He said you were interested in familiarising yourself with previous English versions and their history. With this in mind, I'm enclosing the following items:
Vesey/Bentley translation, Grove Press Edition

The Threepenny Opera in America, an article which will be published next year in the Cambridge Opera Handbook series. Vol. 6, No. 2 of the Kurt Weill Newsletter. This issue, devoted to *Threepenny*, includes special articles and a chronology.

It is our understanding that Mr Hellman will furnish you with the other English translations. However, should you not be successful in obtaining them, we would be happy to send them also.

If you do decide to direct the production, we would welcome you to the Weill-Lenya Research Centre, where we have a great deal of material, both audio and visual, that would be of interest to you.

6 December 1988
From Jerome Hellman

Sting rang last Thursday to tell me that he had been delighted with his first meeting with you, and to express his continued enthusiasm for our project. I gather you two are meeting again this week, and I do hope that someone will call and let me know how that goes off.

I've had a look at Michael Feingold's lyrics. I thought the ballad of the Prisoner of Sexuality was terrific. I was less impressed with Solomon's Song. I wonder how you felt about it.

17 May 1989
From Jerome Hellman

I regret that it's necessary to impose upon your holiday with anything other than the best of news, but we have been confronted with a problem regarding the Shubert Theatre, which must be brought to your attention.

From the very start of our discussions with Bernie Jacobs and Phil Smith, they have assured Joe Harris and myself that there would be 'No problem' getting Joe Papp to move *A Chorus Line* to another one of their theatres, from the Shubert where it has been running for the last thirteen years.

This specific point was raised with them repeatedly and their response has always been the same: 'No Problem'.

They have now informed us that Joe Papp has categorically refused to move and, despite the fact that they are within their legal, contractual rights to insist, they are terrified of the 'Public

Relations' and 'Image' problems that such an act on their part could provoke.

In other words, John, at the first sound of musket fire they ran from the field of battle, and we are outraged!

It is only by a stroke of very good fortune that Jujamcyn can still offer us the St James Theatre, across the street from the Shubert. They have wanted the show from the very outset and are prepared to do virtually anything within reason to get it.

I know that you did not want to go to the St James and it grieves me to have to propose it at this time. However, with our first newspaper ad and television spots already committed for Sunday June 4, we are up against the wall and the St James is far and away the best alternative house available.

I very much need your help and cooperation in dealing with this matter and it would be my hope that you could accept the change without feeling in any way compromised, since putting on the best show possible means everything to me, just as I know it means everything to you.

24 May 1989
From Jerome Hellman
As might have been expected, the news of our planned production has brought on a small tidal wave of applicants for some of the choicer roles.

Among them are some whom, because of their prominence, the fact that they have worked with you in the past, or both, leads me to believe that you may already have some fixed notions about them.

In order to spare you, them, or ourselves, the potential embarrassment of bringing one of them in, to absolutely no purpose, I list their names and potential roles herewith. As you can see, I have provided three categories for your response, which will remain confidential:

N.I.   'Not Interested'. Obviously for the people you don't want to see or consider.

I.   'Interested'. For the people you do want to see or consider.

N.S.O.   'No Strong Opinion at Present'. On these, Johnson, Liff, and I will make judgement calls on a case by case basis.

While a small number of these candidates might prove to be out of our reach financially, before we do anything further, I'd like to have your thoughts about each.

I would also like to know how you might feel about 'Colour Blind' casting, that is, black people in roles not usually cast that way. I, personally, am in favour of it so long as we don't violate the interior logic of the piece. There are some supremely gifted black performers out there, and if you agree I would love for us to see them.

PS: Does this remind you a little bit of school days?

TIGER IS MACKIE'S CONTEMPORARY. Has anyone read the SCRIPT? Black, Green, Yellow, Blue. I *am* colour blind.

2 September 1989
It's very tempting, at the beginning, to turn it into a show with electrical gadgets and turntables and whatnot. But I don't think that is the best way to get the most juice out of the piece. I think the way Brecht himself suggested staging it is probably the best way – the half-curtain, the orchestra on stage, the exposed mechanics give it the improvised look of an opera as only a beggar could imagine it. It has to have that look without being boring. Brecht's directions are almost as specific as Shaw's, and you had better follow them. It's very simple, but then the simple is always difficult.

Andy Phillips has finally been dragged into hospital with raving DTs just as technical rehearsals begin in Washington and I am working with Brian on a new lighting plot. JH does not like the staging in Act One but has no helpful suggestions to make. Sting is still the personification of hard work. Georgie and Alvin are beginning to show signs of having absorbed some elements of style. For the rest, including me, it's very curate's eggish. Moreover, Aunty Nellie tells me the Watson Players of Derby are in trouble with Cinderella – the director wants her to marry Buttons and not the Prince; can there be a Marxist mole in the Guildhall and if so how will Nellie (Madame President) deal with him? (Must try and write to her.)

25 September 1989
Sting. Absolutely brilliant. Tough and wiry. This is not a musical, it's a play with music. Something like nine-tenths of it is

spoken, with the numbers, wonderful numbers, scattered through it like machine-gun shots. But these numbers don't spring out of the action, so we have to follow a fairly traditional line with the staging. It's rather like being in a cabaret. You exist totally while you are there on stage, and when you come to a number you say, 'Right! Song' – and then you sing it. You don't emotionally glide into another key and pretend that you are drifting into singing. It's the ability to switch from the internal truth to the external demonstration and the truth behind it. Any good actor can do it, but it's not a technique for beginners. You have to have solved all your technical problems with your feet and your arms and your legs and your hair. It's not apprentice work.

26 September 1989
Humiliating day. Went by the Eugene O'Neill Theatre [where *M. Butterfly* was playing] to find all references to the production or mention of my name mysteriously missing from front of house. Phoned Stuart Ostrow only to find he was as bewildered as I. Come off it Stuart, who else?

27 September 1989
The rehearsals suggest to me that I have lost my touch when it comes to physical staging. Think hard and clear and persuade the cast to do the same.

4 November 1989
NY. Open 3 *Op.*

5 November 1989
The trouble with 3 *Op.* is the more you get it right the less they like it.

6 November 1989
I always said Clive Barnes was the best alcoholic critic in NY. Terrible press but up 5,000. So cry all the way to the bank and go home. Think about 1890–1990. Trudie, Natasha, Di Rigg, Tamsin, Boxer.

14 December 1989
Riggs and I in Rome doing *M. Butterfly*. We went to our local café

in the Piazza for cappuccinos. En route we bought a *Herald Tribune* and on the back page in the 'People' column, read that *3 Op.* was coming off on December 31. This was the first I had heard of it.

1 January 1990
3 Op. came off yesterday.
  'Fail Better' S.B. [Samuel Beckett]
I don't care what they say. I got it right. Now *get to work* and prepare to enter Europe with the New Playhouse Co. Ahead of Mrs T., with a rep from Shaw, Ibsen, Pirandello, Strindberg, Brenton and Ali.

4 January 1990
Opening *M. Butterfly*
Spoleto. Chilly but pleasant. Theatre wood and plaster. Perfect acoustics. 1876.
Healthy backbreaking, ballbreaking hill – to and from work.

5 January 1990
Ugo [Tognazzi] in a panic state.

6 January 1990
Dress Rehearsal. No public. Crisis over, Ugo placated. Lighting beginning to work. Still no chest mike.

7 January 1990
Spoleto opening. Morning in bed!! Lunch Sabatini. Performance tentative and technically disaster. Hysterical reception. Much screaming. At the end of three days I climbed the hill from the theatre and still had my breath intact. Work at it!

8 January 1990
Visit St Francis at home. Lunch and on to Napoli?
Brother Sun absent, Sister Mist and Rain present. We arrived in Missioni and stuffed with the greatest meal ever. The saint punished with five hours of hell and indigestion on the autostrada – Serve us right.

9 January 1990
To Napoli. Tech. Lights. Act Two. Stage calls. First Naples preview. Missioni umbrella stolen during rehearsal.

10 January 1990
Napoli preview, performance better. Audience piss poor and panic sets in. Wait until it's worse then panic.

11 January 1990
Pompeii. Good guide. Good lunch. Good day.
Ugo stronger in first act which was all I saw. Still in love with Tosca.

12 January 1990
Capri. Apart from one hour on the south side, sheer freezing hell. ROH turned snotty after lunch. Jamie turned dopey while I froze. Performance confident and vulgar. Face up to collision with Tognazzi – leave early.
Confused news via Glass re Lee Menzies, The Playhouse, theatre in the '90s. Who lies most?

13 January 1990
Re-light 11–5. Rehearse Tog and Brack. Good rehearsal of four pages. Tog less porcine. Jamie toothache!

14 January 1990
Day off. Ischia, even as a free holiday, is not acceptable, tell JP [Joan Plowright].

Riggs' Italian blood comes to the rescue, eyes blazing, whites visible at fifty yards, stands off a pig driver. V. impressive. Jamie toothache continues.

Porky strikes again, this time from the wings; call Ardenzi showdown Tues/Wed.

15 January 1990
Day off. To Capri – one good meal in the sun. San Michele closed. Grotti Grotto closed. Decide about Venice.

16 January 1990
3.30 Lecture (good) and rehearse.
Telegram to Alan Bates. Love and thoughts. [Alan's son had died.]

17 January 1990
Rehearse. Fix trains and travel.

18 January 1990
Rehearse 3.30. Having at last got Tognazzi to rehearse in a proper frame of mind; the electrical dept (Napoli div.) arrived two hours late and caused us to do about half of the intended changes.

19 January 1990
Italian Press Opening. Do I take a bow or not? Yes I do, to great applause, v. gratifying, even in Napoli. But do not let it become a habit.

20 January 1990
Night train Venezia.

21 January 1990
Venezia 8.55. Pearly and perfect coming out of the mist, immediate relaxation; Danieli thanks to Porky. Perfecto. Lunch and walk to Schamane. Plan Jamie's time-table. Lunch hotel – collapse for remainder of day. Check Leoncavallo *Bohème*.

22 January 1990
Try to get Jamie to Doge's Palace and San Marco before Florian's Bar. Glorious in the mist and the square empty, silent, the deserted drawing room, lacking Lowe or Porter is much more enjoyable.

23 January 1990
Sunrise: one third of San Giorgio Maggiore rising out of the mist, a sliver of moon above it. Turner in watercolour – Venice submerged. Pink and pearly.

Leoncavallo *Bohème* at the Fenice. Pas mal. But you come out whistling Puccini!

24 January 1990
Grey and misty but pick up the lights from Delphos. Night train to Paris.

25 January 1990
Paris – London 4ish. Phone Eric [Glass] re Willie [Cameron].
Phone Tariq [Ali] or Howard [Brenton].

Trapped in Boulogne by 12 force gales, all of lights out, power
lines down, and a pretty mad juggler sheltering from the wind.

26 January 1990
D-Day for Willie [Cameron], Lee [Menzies] and Natasha
[Makarova]. No news. Wait till Weds. *MB* coming off in NY.

Sugar low. Panic. My own fault. Menzies on Holiday!

27 January 1990
Great Sampford? No news from Willie or Menzies. So much for
Jan 1. All we are left with is Sam's instruction to fail better.
Contact Natasha.

28 January 1990
Low sugar due to *me*.

29 January 1990
To Doctor – BP 170/20.
Think about TV Ibsen using Svoboda space.

30 January 1990
Sugar High! Ready for TV Ibsen.

1 February 1990
Howard Brenton phoned, invited us to *Iranian Nights* [at the
Royal Court]. He and Tariq Ali have an idea for a play.

Went to *Iranian Nights*. Enjoyed it immensely. Enjoyed even
more Howard and Tariq's idea: a play about Gorbachev which
they have tentatively titled *Moscow Gold*.

Howard and Tariq come to lunch to discuss idea in full. I finish
by telling them not to say any more but to go away and write it.

Brenton & Ali. *Moscow Gold*. Could be. Must be. Do the NT have
the nerve? They have a gap in Sep. and so do I and also time to
prepare. Piccoli notwithstanding. Get in touch with Svoboda as
soon as Eyre gets in touch – if? If not, what?

2 February 1990
Rotten night. Chest. Shoulder wrenched.
Thought about heart attack. Dismissed as melodramatic rubbish.

3 February 1990
Pain continue and increase.

4 February 1990
Into hospital. Have had heart attack. Fri/Sat 2/3. Pace maker inserted. Into cardiac arrest ward. Not much sleep.

5 February 1990
Wonderful nursing. Pig of a night nurse (male). Odd to wake up connected to so many things; more wired than John Belushi but to better purpose.

6 February 1990
Not much fun. But Riggs present through the small hours, which helps.

7 February 1990
As for 6th. Sleep, when bent at forty-five degrees, is not possible, especially when wired and fearful of breaking connections.

8 February 1990
As for fifth.

9 February 1990
Possible move to Private Patients Clinic under Dr Buckland. Sorry to leave the staff but nothing else. Looking forward to convalescence and enforced rest but not as much as I am looking forward to *Moscow Gold*.

10 February 1990
Into Private Patients. Better. Under Dr Buckland. Not bad for 7 days. Learn from the nurses how to deal with crisis in theatre: humour and efficiency.
Watched *The Great Ziegfield*. Glorious rubbish – worth it for Fanny Brice.

11 February 1990

Better sleep last night. Begin Coleridge *Early Vision*. Good stuff –
need Book of English Verse and Shelley and the Godwins and
CD. David Hare is quite right. Compared to playwrights,
novelists are a pampered and overpraised bunch. Think of Bond
and Bragg, Arden and Burgess.

14 February 1990

Good morning. Planning move to Sampford. Make lists for
Riggs and plan ground floor. Fun and absorbing.

16 February 1990

Ask for Shelley and the Godwins + Anthology of English Verse
and hopefully CD. Begin chronological Shostakovich
Symphonies – followed by chamber music if the NT cannot
afford the LSO.

Dr Buckland suggests leaving on Thursday for London Bridge
and a room with a river view (same price as the Savoy?).

17 February 1990

Crummy night – awake from three. Resisting the third pill is
silly.

The CD works at last! ORGY TIME. About Ben Elton, Robbie
Coltrane and most of the Alternatives (alternative to what?): Jack
Benny, Bea Lillie, Sid Field were funny in themselves with
material which was, to say the least, ageing. Frank Randle,
Norman Evans won laughter from the audience with vulgarity.
Elton et al. can only sink to obscenity. Am I turning into Mary
Whitehouse?

18 February 1990

Mozart K80 *Before Breakfast*. Shostakovich Op47. Two daffodils
in bloom outside my window. Not enough for Wordsworth
perhaps but plenty for me even in watery sun. What's happening in Great Sampford?

Odd but explicable dream. Reviving *Royal Hunt* at the NT. Full
company assembled in a rehearsal room but no one knew who
was to play Atahuallpa or Pizarro. Called on Shaffer to withdraw
the play which he did! NT boss looked like Alan Lerner at his
most Machiavellian.

19 February 1990
Discuss discharge possibilities. Home or away?
Richard Eyre does not like *Moscow Gold*. Terry Hands does. Meet
soon discuss Hopkins, Klaus Maria Brandauer.
We may leave on Wednesday according to Dr Buckland.

20 February 1990
Begin the day with Patience.
Crummy night.

21 February 1990
Moving to London Bridge 10ish for eight-day deal. Gloom on
arrival dispelled by the view and the staff.

Phone Hands. Howard phoned.
Blood twice ECG etc.
Miss Nickers [Claire Bloom] has a bad press as does the Director
[*When We Dead Awaken*]. Can't help feeling smug. Have they
killed the play for Natasha?

22 February 1990
Transfer to London Bridge.
Watch the morning rush into yuppie land.
Identify the Hays Wharf Custom house. Venetian. Who did it?

23 February 1990
Three times round the Atrium. Work on MG [*Moscow Gold*]
ground plan diagram for Joe or whoever! Riggs 12-ish.
Tariq and Howard 6-ish + Terry Hands. Bollinger! In memoriam
LO. Pulse 88 afterwards. V. good. TH to contact Svoboda and
Hopkins with offer.

24 February 1990
Riggs in a shitty and totally negative mood, rubbishing all the
RSC actors, not one of whom he or I have seen. What to do about
this if he has made up his mind forever I don't know, except not
to do the play; and that would be foolish. No sign of Jamie or
Shostakovich.

25 February 1990
Jamie supposed to be here at 4, not arrived at 5. Medication and

doctors rounds intrude. 5 Jamie and Riggs. ECG check pain, everything OK.

27 February 1990
Moving day for Riggs to Great Sampford. Dr Buckland would like one week more of enforced rest and rehab. Gloom for a couple of hours then sleep with a very pleasant dream and no pills.

28 February 1990
Riggs phoned. Move done. My quarters beautiful.

Svoboda in Vienna – Rembrandt symposium. Can he come to England even for two hours?

1 March 1990
Filthy day. Buckland says 10 more days + op (minor).
Row about diet.

2 March 1990
Greek noise all night interrupts all pills. *MB* [*Butterfly*] selling out in Italy. Riggs 11.30 and if the atmosphere is good, talk about stress. Riggs talked, I listened. Will he do the same tomorrow?

3 March 1990
Good night's sleep, no Greek farce. Walk round the hospital outside!

4 March 1990
Phone Billington before 10 [re *When We Dead Awaken*]. Riggs and I walk to HMS Belfast and back.

6 March 1990
P. Shaffer phoned. Angiogram wonderful for confidence.

8 March 1990
Svob. has problems with the play. Get him over here.

9 March 1990
Dr Buckland advises surgery – 90% success.

10 March 1990
Home after lunch. Garden perfect. Dogs wonderful. Slept well due to Riggs. Cuddle deals with the blues in the small hours.

11 March 1990
Best night's sleep for ages. Riggs and security.

12 March 1990
Tariq and Howard. V. good. Picture from Tariq replaces Hockney to Riggs' delight. Rewrites around Simple Soviet Woman and the people. *The Mother* as model.

13 March 1990
RSC telex to Svob. yesterday. No from Hopkins. Fool!

14 March 1990
Consider Jacobi, Thaw, Woodward, Finney. Phone RSC re their list of 'stars'.
Wrong injection at 6. Idiot! Concentrate! Glum night.

15 March 1990
Howard & Tariq, tea and talk about actors. Push for David Calder as Gorbachev.

18 March 1990
To Great Sampford. Wonderful day and wonderful house.
Riggs phoned this morning – *Parade* set up for the Châtelet 1991/92.

19 March 1990
Howard, Tariq & Casting Department. Good meeting. David Calder as No. 1.
Siobhan Brack [RSC Casting Director] good value. Howard and Tariq are the only authors I have ever worked with who are secure enough to set about writing a play with me in mind.

20 March 1990
Waiting.

21 March 1990
Waiting.

Howard & Tariq rang. Literary Department good news – forget Hands.

22 March 1990
In again for the 'Eight day package deal'.

23 March 1990
D-Day?

Epilogue

*A few days after the obituary he
wrote appeared in the Daily Telegraph,
Michael Gambon received the
following letter:*

28 March 1990

I have followed John's career since we were demobbed,
noting with pleasure his considerable success in British theatre
productions, and I have read with some surprise and considerable sorrow John's obituary.

John and I were incarcerated in a British Army hospital
together, and I can remember to this day John's efforts to get his
legs working again after his polio attack. As I was similarly
disabled we both felt we had to make the effort to exercise. In
John's case he would stand up on his bed and try out a few ballet
exercises. This usually ended with him flopping down and
cursing over his lack of control. We shared weeks in adjoining
beds before being shipped back home via Port Said on the SS
Aba.

I can remember with some amusement John's words to me as
we were lifted aboard the 'blighty' boat by POW's of the Africa
Corps. He sat up on his stretcher like some Roman emperor,
turned to me and said, clutching the bearer's biceps: 'With – like
this how did we win the desert war?'

His anecdotes on theatre life and his interest in theatre was
obvious even in those days, and I sometimes wondered how
much of it was fiction. He was a true Thespian, and I'm sure the
theatre will be saddened by his passing.

Yours sincerely,

John Kirk

Ex 6th Airborne Division

Letter from Diana Rigg
Darling Riggs,
As I drove away from Portland Road I heard myself say 'Oh God, John, *why* did you have to die?' And then, 'Well, all right, I'll just keep you inside me.' Which means for the rest of my life his standards are the benchmark. What would he say to this or that – would he approve? etc., etc. Not easy to live up to, but having known and loved him the only alternative. And now to you – I care passionately that you are taken care of and all right. Please telephone *any time* while I am away, for *any* reason with whatever request. I shall be there to do it.
Love you,
Diana

John Dexter – Chronology of Work

1957
Appointed Associate Director of
the English Stage Company

1957
9 June: Royal Court Theatre,
London (Sunday Night)
Yes – and After by Michael
Hastings
Cast included:
Alan Bates
Anthony Carrick
Jimmy Carroll
Olivia Irving
Patricia Lawrence
Graham Pyle
Heather Sears
Robert Stephens

1957
22 July: Royal Court Theatre,
London (after opening at the
Devon Festival)
Purgatory by W.B. Yeats
Design: Jocelyn Herbert
Cast list not available

1957
28 October: Royal Court Theatre,
London
Look Back in Anger by John
Osborne [First Revival]
Design: Alan Tagg
Cast included:
Clare Austin

Willoughby Gray
Alec McCowen
Gary Raymond
Anna Steele

1958
23 March: Royal Court Theatre,
London (Sunday Night)
Each His Own Wilderness by Doris
Lessing
Cast included:
Philip Bond
Patricia Burke
Colin Jeavons
Ewen MacDuff
Sarah Preston
Vernon Smythe
Valerie Taylor

1958
14 July: Royal Court Theatre,
London (after opening at the
Belgrade Theatre, Coventry)
Chicken Soup with Barley by
Arnold Wesker
Design: Michael Richardson
Cast included:
Richard Briers
Patsy Byrne
Charmian Eyre
Frank Finlay
Alfred Lynch
Henry Manning
Richard Martin
Cherry Morris

Anthony Valentine
Jacqueline Wilson

1959
10 November: Lyric Theatre,
Hammersmith, London
Last Day in Dreamland
by Willis Hall
Design: Sean Kenny
Cast included: Jill Bennett
Paul Daneman
John Ferguson
Peter Gill
Gordon Gostelow
Pamela Hewes
Roy Hines
Philip Ingram
Charles Leno
Daniel Moynihan
Alex Murray
Brian Murray
Charles Workman
Ken Wynne

A Glimpse of the Sea
by Willis Hall
Design: Sean Kenny
Cast included:
Jill Bennett
Paul Daneman
Pamela Lane
Vivian Pickles

1959
23 March: Grand Theatre,
Croydon
No Concern of Mine by Jeremy
Kingston
Design: John Dinsdale
Cast included:
John Briggs
John Dane
Valerie Dunlop
David Maloney

Bridget Panet
Betty Romaine

1959
13 April: Cambridge Theatre,
London
The Hidden River by Ruth and
Augustus Goetz
Design: Roger Ramsdell
Costume: Beatrice Dawson
Marianne Benet
Leo Genn
Catherine Lacey
Alan MacNaughtan
Ralph Michael
John Stratton

1959
30 June: Royal Court Theatre,
London (after opening at the
Belgrade Theatre, Coventry).
Roots by Arnold Wesker
Design: Jocelyn Herbert
Patsy Byrne
Frank Finlay
Alan Howard
Charles Kay
Richard Martin
Gwen Nelson
Patrick O'Connell
Brenda Peters
Joan Plowright
Jack Rodney

(Transferred Duke of York's, 30
July 1959)

1959
6 September: Royal Court
Theatre (Sunday Night)
The Kitchen by Arnold Wesker
Design: Jocelyn Herbert

Cast included:
Kenneth Adams
Tarn Bassett
Anne Bishop
James Bolam
John Briggs
Cecil Brock
Patsy Byrne
Anthony Carrick
James Culliford
Tenniel Evans
Peter Gill
Ida Goldapple
Alan Howard
Charles Kay
Ann King
Alfred Lynch
Mary Miller
Sandra Miller
Gwen Nelson
Patrick O'Connell
Brenda Peters
Jack Rodney
David Ryder
Christopher Sandford
Jennifer Wallace
Jeanne Watts

1960
7 June: Royal Court Theatre,
London
Chicken Soup with Barley by
Arnold Wesker
Design: Jocelyn Herbert
Cast included:
Patsy Byrne
Mark Eden
Frank Finlay
Alan Howard
Charles Kay
Ruth Meyers
Kathleen Michael
Cherry Morris
David Saire

1960
28 June: Royal Court Theatre,
London
Roots by Wesker [Revival]
Design: Jocelyn Herbert
Cast included:
Patsy Byrne
John Colin
Frank Finlay
Anthony Hall
Alan Howard
Charles Kay
Cherry Morris
Joan Plowright

1960
27 July: Royal Court Theatre,
London
I'm Talking About Jerusalem by
Arnold Wesker
Design: Jocelyn Herbert
Cast included:
Mark Eden
Frank Finlay
Alan Howard
Charles Kay
Ruth Meyers
Kathleen Michael
Cherry Morris
Terry Palmer
Michael Phillips
Jessie Robins

1960
10 November: Piccadilly Theatre,
London
Toys in the Attic by Lillian
Hellman
Design: Howard Bay
Costume: Motley
Cast included:
Ian Bannen
Coral Browne
Wendy Hiller

Desmond Jordan
Judith Stott
Diana Wynyard

1960
20 October: Vaudeville Theatre,
London
This Year, Next Year by Jack
Ronder
Design: Neil Hobson
Cast included:
Pamela Brown
Brenda Bruce
Michael Gough
David Langton
Anne Lawson
Terence Stamp

1961
7 April: Lyric Hammersmith,
London
South by Julien Green
Design: Disley Jones
Cast included:
Nadia Catouse
Barbara Cavan
Denholm Elliott
Ronald Etienne
Tommy Eytle
William Fox
Jemma Hyde
Clifton Jones
James Land
Bessie Love
Randolph Mackenzie
Felicity Peel
Robin Phillips
Heather Sears
Charles Workman

1961
27 June: Royal Court Theatre,
London

The Kitchen by Arnold Wesker
Design: Jocelyn Herbert
Cast included:
Dimitri Andreas
Tarn Bassett
Alison Bayley
Martin Boddey
André Bolton
Shirley Cameron
Sandra Caron
Gladys Dawson
Tommy Eytle
Ida Goldapple
Reginald Green
Harry Landis
Andreas Lysandrou
Andreas Markos
Marcos Markou
Jane Morrow
Patrick O'Connell
Wolf Parr
Ken Parry
Mary Peach
Brian Phelan
Jessie Robins
Charlotte Selwyn
Robert Stephens
Rita Tushingham
Jeanne Watts
Arnold Yarrow

1961
21 August: Royal Court Theatre,
London
The Kitchen by Arnold Wesker
Design: Jocelyn Herbert
Dimitri Andreas
Mai Bacon
Tarn Bassett
Alison Bayley
Steven Berkoff
Jeremy Brett
Shirley Cameron
Sandra Caron

Gladys Dawson
Rodney Douglas
Ida Goldapple
Reginald Green
Glenda Jackson
Panayiotis Jacovou
Harry Landis
Andreas Lysandrou
Michael McKevitt
Andreas Markos
Jane Morrow
Patrick O'Connell
Wolf Parr
Ken Parry
Charlotte Selwyn
Martin Sterndale
Rita Tushingham
Jeanne Watts
Arnold Yarrow

1961
25 September: Royal Court
Theatre, London
The Kitchen by Arnold Wesker
Design: Jocelyn Herbert
Same cast as 21 August 1961

1961
22 November: Royal Court
Theatre, London
The Keep by Gwyn Thomas
Design: Ken Calder
Music: Dudley Moore
Cast included:
Windsor Davies
Jessie Evans
David Garfield
Denys Graham
Mervyn Johns
Dudley Jones
Glyn Owen
Aubrey Richards
Graham Suter

1962
13 February: Comedy Theatre
My Place by Elaine Dundy
Designer: Voytek
Cast included:
Diane Cilento
Annette Crosbie
Guy Deghy
Barry Foster
Betty Hare
Barbara Hicks
Robert Hollyman
Tristram Jellinek
Mary Jones
Kate Lansbury
Janet Milner
Dandy Nichols
John Rees
Harry Towb

1962
20 February: Royal Court
Theatre, London
The Keep by Gwyn Thomas
Design: Ken Calder
Cast included:
Windsor Davies
Jessie Evans
Tenniel Evans
Denys Graham
David Garfield
Mervyn Johns
Dudley Jones
Glyn Owen
Aubrey Richards
Graham Suter

(Transferred Piccadilly Theatre,
27 March 1962)

1962
27 April: Royal Court Theatre,
London
Chips with Everything by Arnold
Wesker

Design: Jocelyn Herbert
Music: Colin Farrell
Cast included:
Laurie Asprey
Alexander Balfour
Michael Blackham
Martin Boddey
Robert Bruce
John Bull
Colin Campbell
Michael Craze
Colin Farrell
Frank Finlay
Hugh Futcher
Michael Goldie
Roger Heathcott
Bruce Heighley
George Innes
John Kelland
Peter Kelly
Ronald Lacey
Corin Redgrave
Alan Stevens

(Transferred Vaudeville Theatre,
13 June 1962)

1962
7 May: Princes Theatre, London
England, Our England, a revue by
Keith Waterhouse and Willis
Hall
Design: Alan Tagg
Music: Dudley Moore
Choreography: Gillian Lynne
Cast included:
Arthur Blake
Peter Brett
Carmel Cryan
Liz Henry
Barrie Ingham
David Jackson
Roy Kinnear
Alison Leggatt

Murray Melvin
Gavin Reed
Billie Whitelaw

1962
19 July: Royal Court Theatre,
London
The Blood of the Bambergs by John
Osborne
Design: Alan Tagg
Music: John Addison
Cast included:
Norman Allen
Alan Bennett
Tony Caunter
Robin Chapman
James Cossins
Graham Crowden
Avril Elgar
Jimmy Gardner
Barbara Keogh
Charles Lewsen
Constance Lorne
John Maynard
John Meillon
Glyn Owen
Vivian Pickles
Anton Rodgers
Billy Russell

(One half of an Osborne
double-bill called *Plays for
England*)

1962
18 December: Royal Court
Theatre, London
Squat Betty and *The Sponge Room*
by Keith Waterhouse/Willis Hall
Design: Ken Calder
Cast included:
Jill Bennett
George Cole
Robert Stephens

1963
Appointed Associate Director of
the National Theatre

1963
1 February: Royal Court Theatre,
London
Jackie the Jumper by Gwyn
Thomas
Design: Michael Annals
Music: Alun Hoddinott
Cast included:
Graham Crowden
Graham Curnow
Frank Davies
Sian Davies
Anne Edwards
Peter Forest
David Garfield
John Gill
Michael Gough
Branwen Iorwerth
Dudley Jones
Anne Lakeman
Jeanne Lé Bars
Ronald Lewis
Raymond Llewellyn
Judith Lloyd Thomas
William McAllister
Bernard Martin
Maureen Morelle
Vernon Morris
Arthur Parry
Gaynor Rees
Talfryn Thomas
Meg Wynn Owen

1963
21 March: Cambridge Theatre,
London
Half a Sixpence
Music and Lyrics: David Heneker
Design: Loudon Sainthill
Choreography: Edmund Balin

Cast included:
Anna Barry
Brian Beaton
Marie Betts
Arthur Blake
Anne Briley
Arthur Brough
John Bull
Susan Dawn
Colin Farrell
James Grout
Jeff Hall
Henrietta Holmes
Helen Hurst
Jessica James
Cheryl Kennedy
Diana Landor
Sheila Reid
Roy Sone
Tommy Steele
Anthony Valentine
Marti Webb
Ian White
David Williams
Charles Workman

1963
15 August: Royal Court Theatre,
London
Chips with Everything by Arnold
Wesker [Revival]
Design: Jocelyn Herbert
Cast included:
Norman Allen
Gary Bond
Edward Burrell
Tony Caunter
Howard Marion Crawford
Alan Dobie
Patrick Ellis
Barry Evans
Derek Fowlds
Robert Hewitt
George Innes

Ronald Lacey
John Lane
George Layton
John Levitt
James Luck
Gerald McNally
John Noakes
Corin Redgrave
Michael Standing
Terence Taplin
Christopher Timothy
Frank Wylie

1963

30 October: National Theatre at the Old Vic, London. (First presented at the Chichester Festival Theatre)
Saint Joan by George Bernard Shaw
Design: Michael Annals
Cast included:
Max Adrian
Colin Blakely
Martin Boddey
Peter Cellier
Raymond Clarke
Lewis Fiander
Frank Finlay
Richard Hampton
Roger Heathcott
Derek Jacobi
Terence Knapp
Robert Lang
Keith Marsh
Trevor Martin
Dan Meaden
James Mellor
· Anthony Nicholls
Joan Plowright
John Rogers
Ann Rye
Robert Stephens

John Stride
Michael Turner

1964

7 January: National Theatre at the Old Vic, London
Hobson's Choice by Harold Brighouse
Design: Motley
Cast included:
Elizabeth Burger
Christopher Chittell
Raymond Clarke
Frank Finlay
Reginald Green
Jeanne Hepple
Terence Knapp
Harry Lomax
Enid Lorimer
Mary Miller
Anthony Nicholls
Joan Plowright
Michael Redgrave
Alan Ridgway
Jean Rogers

1964

21 April: National Theatre at the Old Vic, London
Othello by William Shakespeare
Design: Jocelyn Herbert
Music: Richard Hampton
Fights: William Hobbs
Cast included:
Martin Boddey
Edward Caddick
Frank Finlay
Neil Fitzpatrick
Roger Heathcott
Edward Hardwicke
William Hobbs
George Innes
Derek Jacobi

Peter John
Tom Kempinski
Terence Knapp
Harry Lomax
Kenneth Mackintosh
Keith Marsh
Mary Miller
Laurence Olivier
Edward Petherbridge
Joyce Redman
Michael Rothwell
Maggie Smith

1964
8 December: National Theatre at
the Old Vic, London
The Royal Hunt of the Sun by
Peter Shaffer
Produced by John Dexter and
Desmond O'Donovan
Design: Michael Annals
Music: Marc Wilkinson
Movement: Claude Chagrin
Cast included:
Colin Blakely
Peter Cellier
Neil Fitzpatrick
Michael Gambon
Edward Hardwicke
Roy Holder
Derek Jacobi
Caroline John
Peter John
Tom Kempinski
Robert Lang
Kenneth Mackintosh
Trevor Martin
Dan Meaden
James Mellor
Edward Petherbridge
Louise Purnell
Robert Russell
Robert Stephens

Christopher Timothy
Michael Turner
Frank Wylie

(Opened at the Anta
Theatre, New York, 26
October 1965, starring
Christopher Plummer, David
Carradine and George Rose.)

1965
18 March: 46th Street Theatre,
New York
Do I Hear a Waltz?
Music: Richard Rodgers
Lyrics: Stephen Sondheim
Book: Arthur Laurents
Design: Beni Montresor
Choreography: Herbert Ross
Cast included:
Elizabeth Allen
Carol Bruce
Stuart Damon
Fleury D'Antonakis
James Dybas
Sergio Franchi
Jack Manning
Julienne Marie
Madeleine Sherwood
Christopher Votos

1965
5 July: Chichester Festival
Theatre
Armstrong's Last Goodnight by
John Arden
Directed by John Dexter and
William Gaskill
Later produced on 12 October by
the National Theatre at the Old
Vic, London (re-directed for the
proscenium theatre by Albert
Finney)
Design: Rene Allio

Cast included:
Chloe Ashcroft
Michael Byrne
Alan Collins
Paul Curran
Albert Finney
Neil Fitzpatrick
Kay Gallie
John Hallam
Jennie Heslewood
Derek Jacobi
Gerald James
Caroline John
Carolyn Jones
Roger Kemp
Geraldine McEwan
Ron Pember
Edward Petherbridge
Malcolm Reynolds
David Ryall
John Savident
Robert Stephens
Pauline Taylor
James Wilson
Frank Wylie
Michael York

1966
6 June: National Theatre at the
Old Vic, London
A Bond Honoured by John
Osborne
Adapted from *La Fianza Satisfecha*
by Lope de Vega
Design: Michael Annals
Cast included:
Chloe Ashcroft
Michael Byrne
Graham Crowden
Paul Curran
Hugo d'Alton
Janina Faye
Neil Fitzpatrick

John Hallam
Gerald James
Claude Lintott
Piero Matte
Laurie Morgan
Robert Stephens
Frank Wylie

followed by

Black Comedy by Peter Shaffer
Design: Alan Tagg
Cast included:
Michael Byrne
Wynne Clark
Graham Crowden
Paul Curran
Derek Jacobi
Louise Purnell
Maggie Smith
Robert Stephens

(Previously presented with
Miss Julie on 8 March)

1966
18 October: National Theatre at
the Old Vic, London
The Storm by Alexander
Ostrovsky
Adapted by Doris Lessing
Design: Josef Svoboda
Costume: Ruth Myers
Cast included:
Alan Adams
David Bailie
Petronella Barker
David Belcher
Jill Bennett
Peter Cellier
Oliver Cotton
Margo Cunningham
Barry Evans
Frank Finlay
Michael Gambon

Reginald Green
Mary Griffiths
Edward Hardwicke
Luke Hardy
David Hargreaves
Barbara Hicks
Roy Holder
Anthony Hopkins
William Hoyland
Caroline John
Lewis Jones
Kate Lansbury
Beatrix Lehmann
Harry Lomax
John McEnery
Kenneth Mackintosh
Peter Penry-Jones
Ronald Pickup
Frederick Pyne
Sheila Reid
Malcolm Reynolds
Maggie Riley
John Stride
Christopher Timothy
Michael Turner
Jeanne Watts
Richard Winter

1966
15 December: Covent Garden,
London
Benvenuto Cellini by Hector
Berlioz
Conductor: John Pritchard
Design: Beni Montresor
Choreography: Claude Chagrin
and Peter Clegg
Cast included:
Nicolai Gedda
Yvonne Minton
Elizabeth Vaughan

1967
12 February: Ethel Barrymore
Theatre, New York
Black Comedy and *White Lies*: Two
plays by Peter Shaffer
Design: Alan Tagg

Cast included:
White Lies
Michael Crawford
Donald Madden

Black Comedy
Camila Ashland
Peter Bull
Michael Crawford
Pierre Epstein
Donald Madden
Michael Miller
Geraldine Page
Lynn Redgrave

1967
6 July: Vivian Beaumont Theatre,
New York
The Unknown Soldier and His Wife
by Peter Ustinov
Design: Motley
Music: David Shire
Cast included:
Andrew R. Amic-Angelo
Gary Barton
Brian Bedford
Bernard Berger
W. B. Brydon
Howard Da Silva
B. J. DeSimone
Bob Dishy
William Dolive
M'El Dowd
Irwin Farberman
Andrew Johns
William Kirby
Alan Mixon

Melissa C. Murphy
Robert Rogers
Marco St. John
Don Scardino
James Storm
Larry Swanson
Christopher Walken

1967
10 October: Wyndham's Theatre,
London
Wise Child by Simon Gray
Design: Motley
Cast included:
Alec Guinness
Gordon Jackson
Cleo Sylvestre
Simon Ward

1968
Columbia Pictures and Carl
Foreman
The Virgin Soldiers, screenplay by
John Hopkins (from the novel by
Leslie Thomas)
Cast included:
Hywel Bennett
Nigel Davenport
Nigel Patrick
Lynn Redgrave

1969
4 May: Hamburg State Opera
I Vespri Siciliani by Giuseppe
Verdi; *Libretto* by E. Scribe & C.
Duveyrier, *adapted by* Kurt
Honolka
Conductor: Nello Santi
Design: Josef Svoboda
Costume: Jan Skalicky
Choreography: Isabella Vernici
Cast included:
Jürgen Förster

Franz Grundheber
Willy Hartmann
Wieslaw Ochman
David Ohanesian
Wilfried Plate
Carl Schultz
Hans Sotin
Vera Soukupova
Felicia Weathers
William Workman

1969
18 June: Presented by the
American Shakespeare Festival
and Academy at Stratford,
Conn.
Hamlet by William Shakespeare
Design: Karl Eigsti
Costume: Jane Greenwood
Music: Conrad Susa
Cast included:
Brian Bedford
Martin Broomfield
Morris Carnovsky
Charles Cioffi
Barry Corbin
Danny Davis
Herb Davis
Robert Foxworth
Mervyn Haines, Jr.
William Hickey
Tom Klunis
Joseph Maher
Riggs O'Hara
Edwin Owens
Michael Parish
Anthony Passantino
Wyman Pendleton
Kate Reid
Ellis Richardson
Frederick Rivera
Robert Scogin
Carl Strano

Kristoffer Tabori
Toby Tompkins
Maria Tucci
Tony van Bridge

1970
The Sidelong Glances of a Pigeon Kicker, screenplay by Ron Whyte
Cast included:
Jordan Christopher
Boni Enten
Melba Moore
Lois Nettleton
Jill O'Hara
William Redfield
Kate Reid
Elaine Stritch
Robert Walden

1970
Granada TV
Twelfth Night by William Shakespeare
Design: Carl Toms
Cast included:
Adrienne Corri
Alec Guinness
John Moffatt
Riggs O'Hara
Joan Plowright
Gary Raymond
Sheila Reid
Ralph Richardson
Tommy Steele

1971
6 April: National Theatre at the Old Vic, London
A Woman Killed with Kindness by Thomas Heywood
Design: Jocelyn Herbert
Cast included:
Tom Baker
Frank Barrie

Dai Bradley
Paul Curran
Derek Jacobi
Anthony Hopkins
Joan Plowright
Louise Purnell

1971
20 July: The National at the New Theatre, London
Tyger, a celebration of William Blake by Adrian Mitchell
Directed by John Dexter and Michael Blakemore
Design: Jocelyn Herbert and William Dudley
Music by Mike Westbrook
Cast included:
Sarah Atkinson
Anthony Barnett
Norman Beaton
Jean Boht
Ian Burford
Ray Callaghan
Peter Duncan
Bill Fraser
Bernard Gallagher
Mary Griffiths
John Gulliver
James Hayes
David Henry
Hazel Hughes
Alan Jackson
Gerald James
David Kincaid
Tony Leary
Maureen Lipman
Isabelle Lucas
John Moffatt
Anthony Nicholls
Riggs O'Hara
Denis Quilley
Louie Ramsay

Malcolm Reid
Maggie Riley
David Ryall
Peter Smart
Michael Turner
Jane Wenham
Dave Wintour

1971
9 December: National Theatre at
the Old Vic, London
The Good-Natured Man by Oliver
Goldsmith
Design: William Dudley
Music: Marc Wilkinson
Cast included:
Sarah Atkinson
Jim Dale
Bill Fraser
Bernard Gallagher
James Hayes
Hazel Hughes
Maureen Lipman
Desmond McNamara
David Ryall

1972
30 January: Hamburg State
Opera
*Z Mrtvého Domo (From the House
of the Dead)* by Leoš Janáček
Libretto by the composer after
Dostoevsky
Conductor: Rafael Kubelik
Design: Josef Svoboda
Costume: Jan Skalicky
Cast included:
Roberto Bañuelas
Heinz Blankenburg
Willy Caron
Richard Cassilly
Herbert Fliether
Jürgen Förster

Peter Haage
Tom Krause
Heinz Kruse
Kurt Marschner
Helmut Melchert
Norman Mittelmann
David Ohanesian
Martin Schomberg
Peter Schuba
Carl Schultz

1972
I Want What I Want
Screenplay by Gillian Freeman
from the novel by Geoff Brown
Music composed and conducted by
Johnny Harris
Cast included:
Harry Andrews
Jill Bennett
Michael Coles
Anne Heywood
Paul Rogers

1972
2 May: Hamburg State Opera
Billy Budd by Benjamin Britten
Libretto: E. M. Forster and Eric
Crozier
Conductor: Gary Bertini
Design: William Dudley
Cast included:
Roberto Bañuelas
Heinz Blankenburg
Harald Ek
Herbert Fliether
Hajo Fouquet
Franz Grundheber
Peter Haage
Louis Hendrikx
Hans-Otto Kloose
Heinz Kruse
Noël Mangin

Kurt Marschner
David Ohanesian
Carl Schultz
Werner Shürmann
Richard Stilwell
Ernst Wiemann
Horst Wilhelm

1972
28 September: Hamburg State
Opera
Boris Godunov by Modest P.
Mussorgsky
Musical Score by Dmitri
Shostakovich
Libretto by Alexander S.
Pushkin and Nikolai Karamsin
Conductor: Horst Stein
Design: Josef Svoboda
Costume: Jan Skalicky
Cast included:
Cvetka Ahlin
Roberto Bañuelas
Toni Blankenheim
Ursula Boese
Willy Caron
Mignon Dunn
Jürgen Förster
Herbert Fliether
Franz Grundheber
Helmut Grundmann
Peter Haage
Ude Krekow
Heinz Kruse
Noël Mangin
Regina Marheineke
Kurt Moll
Wieslaw Ochman
Anna Ringart
Carl Schultz
Martti Talvela
Hans Wilpert

1972
8 August: Royal Court Theatre,
London
The Old Ones by Arnold Wesker
Design: Douglas Heap
Cast included:
Amelia Bayntun
Terry Burns
Patience Collier
Susan Engel
Leonard Fenton
Stephen Grives
James Hazeldine
Rose Hill
George Pravda
Wanda Rotha
Martin Skinner
George Tovey
Max Wall

1973
22 February: National Theatre at
the Old Vic, London
The Misanthrope by Molière;
English version by Tony
Harrison
Design: Tanya Moiseiwitsch
Music: Marc Wilkinson
Cast included:
Gillian Barge
Nicholas Clay
Robert Eddison
Gawn Grainger
Alec McCowen
Peter Needham
Louie Ramsay
Diana Rigg
Albert Roffrano
Daniel Thorndike
Stephen Williams

(Toured the John F. Kennedy
Centre, Washington, 10
February 1975, and the St

James's Theatre, New York, 10
March 1975
Revived at the Old Vic 9 July
1975)

1973
30 March: Hamburg State Opera
*Un Ballo in Maschera (A Masked
Ball)* by Giuseppe Verdi
Libretto: Antonio Somma
Conductor: Nello Santi
Design: Julia Trevelyan Oman
Cast included:
Roberto Bañuelas
Ursula Boese
Peter Haage
Noël Mangin
Regina Marheineke
Kurt Marshner
Sherrill Milnes
Luciano Pavarotti
Orianna Santunione
Ernst Wiemann

1973
26 July: National Theatre at the
Old Vic, London
Equus by Peter Shaffer
Design: John Napier
Music: Marc Wilkinson
Cast included:
Gillian Barge
Nicholas Clay
Peter Firth
Doran Godwin
David Healy
Alan MacNaughtan
Alec McCowen
Louie Ramsay
Keith Skinner
Jeanne Watts

(Revived at the Old Vic 21

August 1974, transferred to West
End (Albery) 20 April 1976.
Opened Plymouth Theatre, New
York, 24 October 1974, starring
Anthony Hopkins and Peter
Firth)

1973
27 September: Duchess Theatre,
London
In Praise of Love: Two plays by
Terence Rattigan
Design: Desmond Heeley

Cast included:
Before Dawn
Don Fellows
Joan Greenwood
Donald Sinden
Richard Warwick

After Lydia
Cast: the same

1973
1 November: Sadlers Wells
Company at the London
Coliseum
The Devils of Loudon by Krzysztof
Penderecki
Conductor: Nicholas Braithwaite
Design: John Napier
Cast included:
Josephine Barstow
Harold Blackburn
Geoffrey Chard
Paul Crook

1973
20 December: National Theatre
at the Old Vic, London
The Party by Trevor Griffiths
Design: John Napier

Cast included:
Sarah Atkinson
Gillian Barge
Anna Carteret
Rachel Davies
Frank Finlay
Doran Godwin
Gawn Grainger
Ram John Holder
Desmond MacNamara
Laurence Olivier
Ronald Pickup
Denis Quilley
John Shrapnel
Harry Waters

1974
Appointed Director of
Productions at the Metropolitan
Opera House, New York

1974
31 January: Metropolitan Opera
House, New York
I Vespri Siciliani by Giuseppe
Verdi
Conductor: James Levine
Design: Josef Svoboda
Costume: Jan Skalicky
Cast included:
Montserrat Caballé
Justino Diaz
Nicolai Gedda
Sherrill Milnes

1974
3 April: Théâtre National de
l'Opéra, Paris
I Vespri Siciliani) by Giuseppe
Verdi
Libretto: H. Scribe and C.
Duveyrier
Conductor: Nello Santi

Design: Josef Svoboda
Costume: Jan Skalicky
Cast included:
Martina Arroyo
Placido Domingo
Peter Glossop
Wieslaw Ochman
Ruggero Raimondi
Roger Soyer

1974
16 May: Albery Theatre, London
Pygmalion by George Bernard
Shaw
Design: Jocelyn Herbert and
Andrew Sanders
Cast included:
Sarah Atkinson
Hilda Fenemore
Dennis Handby
Bob Hoskins
Simon MacCorkindale
Alec McCowen
Jack May
Anthony Naylor
Melanie Peck
Ellen Pollock
Diana Rigg
Margaret Ward

(Transferred Ahmanson Theatre,
Los Angeles, 20 April 1979,
starring Roberta Maxwell, Milo
O'Shea, Maureen O'Sullivan,
Robert Stephens)

1975
Tony Award – Best Director of a
Drama – *Equus*

1975
17 January: Metropolitan Opera
House, New York

La Forza del Destino by Giuseppi
Verdi
(Reworking of the Eugene
Berman Production)
Conductor: James Levine
Cast included:
Martina Arroyo
Cornell MacNeil
Jon Vickers

1975
2 May: Théâtre National de
l'Opéra, Paris
La Forza del Destino (*The Force of
Destiny*) by Giuseppe Verdi
Libretto: Francesco Maria Piave
Conductor: Julius Rudel
Design: Jocelyn Herbert and
Andrew Sanders
Cast included:
Martina Arroyo
Gabriel Bacquier
Jules Bastin
Huguette Brachet
Fiorenza Cossotto
Placido Domingo
Fernand Dumont
Norman Mittelmann
Michel Sénéchal
Jean-Louis Soumagnas
Martti Talvela

1975
9 September: National Theatre at
the Old Vic, London
Phaedra Britannica by Tony
Harrison (after Jean Racine)
Design: Tanya Moiseiwitsch
Cast included:
Ishaq Bux
Robert Eddison
Michael Gough
Talat Hussain

Jagdish Kumar
Ilona Linthwaite
Albert Moses
Diana Quick
Diana Rigg
Alaknanda Samarth
Daniel Thorndike
David Yelland

1976
3 February: Metropolitan Opera
House, New York
Aida by Giuseppe Verdi
Libretto: Antonio Ghislanzoni
Conductor: James Levine
Design: David Reppa
Costume: Peter J. Hall
Choreography: Louis Johnson
Cast included:
Charles Anthony
Marcia Baldwin
Bonaldo Giaiotti
Marilyn Horne
Cornell MacNeil
James McCracken
James Morris
Leontyne Price

Principal dancers:
William Badelato
Jack Hertzog
Stanley Perryman

1977
18 January: Metropolitan Opera
House, New York
Le Prophète by Giacomo
Meyerbeer
Libretto: Eugène Scribe
Conductor: Henry Lewis
Design: Peter Wexler
Choreographer: Stuart Sebastian
Cast included:
Charles Anthony

Richard Best
Gene Boucher
Nico Castel
Raimund Herincx
Jerome Hines
Marilyn Horne
Frank Little
Shirley Love
James McCracken
Morley Meredith
Renata Scotto
Alma Jean Smith

1977
5 February: Metropolitan Opera
House, New York
Dialogues of the Carmelites by
Francis Poulenc
Conductor: Michel Plasson
Design: David Reppa
Costume: Jane Greenwood
Cast included:
Charles Anthony
Richard Best
Gene Boucher
Nico Castel
Régine Crespin
Russell Christopher
William Dooley
Mignon Dunn
Maria Ewing
Jon Garrison
Raymond Gibbs
Batyah Godfrey
Jean Kraft
Betsy Norden
Shirley Verrett

1977
18 March: Metropolitan Opera
House, New York
Lulu by Alban Berg
Libretto by the composer based

on Frank Wedekind's *Earth Spirit*
and *Pandora's Box*
Conductor: James Levine
Design: Jocelyn Herbert
Cast included:
Richard Best
Lenus Carlson
Nico Castel
Carole Farley
Andrew Foldi
Raymond Gibbs
Donald Gramm
William Lewis
Cynthia Munzer
Peter Sliker
Tatiana Troyanos

1977
31 October: Metropolitan Opera
House, New York
Rigoletto by Giuseppe Verdi
Libretto: Francesco Maria Piave
Conductor: James Levine
Design: Tanya Moiseiwitsch
Cast included:
James Atherton
Philip Booth
Ileana Cotrubas
Ariel Bybee
Justino Diaz
Loretta di Franco
Placido Domingo
Robert Goodloe
Isola Jones
Sherrill Milnes
Vern Shinall
Peter Sliker
Alma Jean Smith

1977
16 November: Plymouth
Theatre, New York. Opened 6
September 1977 in Philadelphia,

30 September 1977 at the
Kennedy Center, Washington
The Merchant by Arnold Wesker
Design: Jocelyn Herbert
Cast included:
John Clements
Julie Garfield
Gloria Gifford
Jeffrey Horowitz
Leib Lensky
Joseph Leon
Roberta Maxwell
Everett McGill
Riggs O'Hara
John Seitz
William Roerick
Marian Seldes
Nicolas Surovy
Boris Tumarin
Angela Wood

1978
Awarded Shakespeare Prize in
Hamburg.

1978
19 September: Metropolitan
Opera House, New York
Billy Budd by Benjamin Britten
Libretto: E. M. Forster and Eric
Crozier
Conductor: Raymond Leppard
Design: William Dudley
Cast included:
James Atherton
Gene Boucher
John Carpenter
Michael Carter
Nico Castel
John Cheek
John Davies
Andrew Foldi
Mark Freiman

Peter Glossop
Robert Goodloe
Morley Meredith
James Morris
Robert Nagy
Jeremy Pearce
Peter Pears
Godehard Rau
Scott Rigby
Andrew Smith
Richard Stilwell
Andrea Velis
David Ward

1978
25 October: Metropolitan Opera
House
Prodaná Nevešta (*The Bartered
Bride*) by Bedřich Smetana
Libretto: K. Sabina
Translated by Tony Harrison
Conductor: James Levine
Design: Josef Svoboda
Costume: Jan Skalicky
Choreography: Pavel Smok
Nicolai Gedda
Cast included:
Teresa Stratas
Jon Vickers

1978
7 December: Metropolitan Opera
House, New York
Don Pasquale by Gaetano
Donizetti
Libretto: Giovanni Ruffini and the
composer
Conductor: Nicola Rescigno
Design: Desmond Heeley
Cast included:
Gabriel Bacquier
Nico Castel
Nicolai Gedda

Håkan Hagegård
Beverly Sills

1979
5 February: Metropolitan Opera
House, New York
Don Carlo by Giuseppe Verdi
Libretto: Francois Joseph Méry
and Camille du Locle
Conductor: James Levine
Design: David Reppa
Costume: Ray Diffen
Cast included:
Charles Anthony
John Cheek
Nicolai Ghiaurov
Giuseppe Giacomini
Marilyn Horne
Robert Manno
Sherrill Milnes
Leona Mitchell
James Morris
Betsy Norden
Dana Talley
Renata Scotto

1979
1 August: Olivier, National
Theatre, London
As You Like It by William
Shakespeare
Design: Hayden Griffin
Costume: Peter J. Hall
Music: Harrison Birtwistle
Cast included:
Michael Bryant
Selina Cadell
Simon Callow
Anna Carteret
Oz Clarke
Dermot Crowley
Andrew Cruickshank
Anthony Douse

Greg Hicks
Brian Kent
Sara Kestelman
Harry Lomax
Robin Meredith
David Morris
Peter Needham
John Normington
Adam Norton
Nicholas Selby
Louis Selwyn
William Sleigh
Daniel Thorndike
Martyn Whitby
Marjorie Yates

1979
12 October: Metropolitan Opera
House, New York
Die Entführung aus dem Serail (*The
Abduction from the Seraglio*) by
Mozart
Libretto: Gottlieb Stephanie
Conductor: James Levine
Design: Jocelyn Herbert
Cast included:
Norma Burrowes
Nicolai Gedda
Werner Klemperer
Kurt Moll
Edda Moser
Norbert Orth

1979
16 November: Metropolitan
Opera House, New York
*Aufstieg und Fall der Stadt
Mahagonny* (*The Rise and Fall of
the City of Mahagonny*) by Kurt
Weill
Libretto: Bertolt Brecht
Translators: David Drew and
Michael Geliot

Conductor: James Levine
Design: Jocelyn Herbert
Cast included:
Michael Best
Richard Cassilly
Nico Castel
Cornell MacNeil
Paul Plishka
Arturo Sergi
Vern Shinall
Teresa Stratas
Ragnar Ulfung
Astrid Varnay

1980
13 August: Olivier, National
Theatre, London
The Life of Galileo by Bertolt
Brecht
Translator: Howard Brenton
Design: Jocelyn Herbert
Costume: Jocelyn Herbert and
Stephen Skaptason
Music: Hanns Eisler
Cast included:
Melvyn Bedford
Michael Beint
Nigel Bellairs
Edmund Bennett
Marc Brenner
Yvonne Bryceland
Selina Cadell
Simon Callow
Elliott Cooper
Andrew Cruickshank
Peter Dawson
Mark Dignam
Sandra Fehr
Michael Gambon
Roger Gartland
Peter Harding
James Hayes
Basil Henson

Robert Howard
Brian Kent
Peter Land
Harry Lomax
Kenneth Mackintosh
Peggy Marshall
Artro Morris
Peter Needham
Adam Norton
Timothy Norton
Robert Oates
Robert Ralph
Norman Rutherford
Nicholas Selby
William Sleigh
Adam Stafford
Jill Stanford
David Stone
Michael Thomas
Daniel Thorndike
Gordon Whiting
Glenn Williams

1980
28 October: Nederlander
Theatre, New York
One Night Stand by Herb
Gardner
Design: Pat Zipprodt
Music by Jule Styne
cast list not available

1981
20 February: Metropolitan Opera
House, New York
Parade: Parade
          Les Mamelles de Tirésias
          L'Enfant et les Sortilèges
Conductor: Manuel Rosenthal
Design: David Hockney
Choreographer: Stuart Sebastian

Parade by Erik Satie
Text by Jean Cocteau

Choreographer: Gray Veredon
With Gary Chryst and the
Metropolitan Opera Ballet

Les Mamelles de Tirésias by Francis
Poulenc
Text by Guillaume Apollinaire
Cast included:
James Atherton
Christian Boesch
Nico Castel
John Darrenkamp
Geraldine Decker
Andrij Dobriansky
Joseph Frank
David Holloway
Jean Kraft
Shirley Love
Catherine Malfitano
Allan Monk

L'Enfant et les Sortilèges by
Maurice Ravel
Text by Colette
Cast included:
Gene Boucher
Gwendolyn Bradley
Therese Brandson
Ariel Bybee
Claudine Carlson
James Courtney
Loretta di Franco
Joseph Frank
Hilda Harris
David Holloway
Isola Jones
Shirley Love
Robert Nagy
Betsy Norden
Florence Quivar
Julien Robbins
Gail Robinson
Andrea Velis
Ruth Welting

1981
19 June: Olivier, National
Theatre, London
The Shoemakers' Holiday or *The
Gentle Craft* by Thomas Dekker
Design: Julia Trevelyan Oman
Music: Dominic Muldowney
Choreography: David Busby
Cast included:
Michael Beint
Nigel Bellairs
Marc Brenner
Brenda Bruce
Selina Cadell
Elliott Cooper
Andrew Cruickshank
Nicholas Geake
Stephen Hattersley
Peter Løvstrøm
Alfred Lynch
Peggy Marshall
Emily Morgan
Peter Needham
John Normington
Norman Rutherford
John Salthouse
Nicholas Selby
Adam Stafford
Michael Thomas
Daniel Thorndike
Janet Whiteside
David Yelland

1981
3 November: Metropolitan
Opera House, New York
Stravinsky: triple-bill of
Le Sacre du Printemps (*The Rite of
Spring*), *Le Rossignol* (*The
Nightingale*) and *Oedipus Rex*
Conductor: James Levine
Design: David Hockney

Le Sacre du Printemps

Choreographer: Jean-Pierre
Bonnefous
Dancers:
Linda Gelinas
Christopher Stocker

Le Rossignol
Libretto by Stravinsky and Stepan
Mitusov
Choreographer: Frederick Ashton
Dancers:
Anthony Dowell
Natalia Makarova
Singers included:
Ara Berberian
Gwendolyn Bradley
Claudia Catania
John Cheek
Lili Chookasian
Philip Creech
Morley Meredith

Oedipus Rex
Libretto by Stravinsky and Jean
Cocteau
Cast included:
Charles Anthony
Richard Cassilly
Anthony Dowell
John Macurdy
Franz Mazura
Tatiana Troyanos

1982
17 February: Mermaid Theatre,
London
The Portage to San Cristobal of AH
adapted for the stage by
Christopher Hampton from the
novel by George Steiner
Design: Jocelyn Herbert and
Andrew Sanders
Cast included:
Graham Callan
Norman Chancer

Laura Davenport
Bernard Kay
Harry Landis
Alec McCowen
Stella Maris
Francisco Morales
John Salthouse
John Savident
Sebastian Shaw
Morgan Sheppard
Barry Stanton
David Sumner
Jeffrey Vanderbyl
Benjamin Whitrow

1982
17 May: Chichester Festival
Theatre
Valmouth by Sandy Wilson, from
the novel by Ronald Firbank
Design: Andrew and Margaret
Brownfoot
Choreography: Lindsay Dolan
Cast included:
Marcia Ashton
June Bland
Simon Butteriss
Judy Campbell
Terence Conoley
Richard Evans
Fenella Fielding
Richard Freeman
Doris Hare
Cathryn Harrison
Robert Helpmann
Liza Hobbs
Cheryl Kennedy
H. Lockwood West
Robert Meadmore
Bertice Reading
Frank Shelley
Femi Taylor
Paula Tinker

Jane Wenham
Sue Withers
Mark Wynter

1983
10 March: Theatre Royal,
Haymarket, London
Heartbreak House by George
Bernard Shaw
Design: Jocelyn Herbert
Cast included:
Paul Curran
Doris Hare
Rosemary Harris
Rex Harrison
Mel Martin
Frank Middlemass
Charles Rea
Diana Rigg
Simon Ward
Paxton Whitehead

1983
19 September: Royal Opera
House, Covent Garden, London
Le Rossignol (The Nightingale)
L'Enfant et les Sortilèges
Conductor: David Atherton
Design: David Hockney

The Nightingale
Russian Text: Igor Stravinsky and
Stepan Mitusov
After the Fairy Tale by Hans
Christian Andersen
Music by Igor Stravinsky
Cast included:
Kim Begley
Phyllis Bryn-Julson
Dorothy Dorow
Anthony Dowell
Francis Egerton
Stuart Harling

Alfreda Hodgson
Anne Howells
Philip Langridge
Natalia Makarova
Maria Moll
Patricia Parker
Joseph Rouleau
Richard Van Allan
David Wilson-Johnson

L'Enfant et les Sortilèges
Text by Colette
Music by Maurice Ravel
Cast included:
Kim Begley
Suzan Bingemann
Anne Collins
Meryl Drower
Sandra Dugdale
Francis Egerton
Alfreda Hodgson
Anne Howells
Della Jones
Fiona Kimm
Philip Langridge
Maria Moll
Ann Murray
Patricia Parker
Elizabeth Robson
Joan Rodgers
Joseph Rouleau
David Wilson-Johnson

1984
13 September: Lyric Theatre,
Hammersmith, London
The Devil and the Good Lord by
Jean-Paul Sartre
Translator: Frank Hauser
Design: Jocelyn Herbert
Cast included:
Stephen Boxer
Gerard Murphy
Simon Ward

1985
25 July: Derby Opera House,
Buxton Festival
La Buona Figliola by Niccolo
Piccinni
Libretto by Carlo Goldoni (after
Samuel Richardson's novel
Pamela)
Performed in an English
translation by Geoffrey Dunn
Conductor: Anthony Hose
Design: Brien Vahey
Cast included:
Miriam Bowen
Nan Christie
Rita Cullis
Pamela Geddes
Mark Holland
Nigel Robson
Janine Roebuck
Gordon Sandison

1985
17 September: Lyric Theatre,
London
Gigi
Book and Lyrics: Alan Jay Lerner
Music: Frederick Loewe
Design: Jocelyn Herbert
Cast included:
Jean-Pierre Aumont
Geoffrey Burridge
Sian Phillips
Beryl Reid
Amanda Waring

1986
12 June: Opernhaus, Zürich
Nabucco by Giuseppe Verdi
Conductor: Nello Santi
Design: Josef Svoboda
Costume: Jan Skalicky
Cast included:

Zsuzsa Alfoldi
Giorgio Aristo
Franco Bordoni
Lorenza Canepa
Piero Cappuccilli
Silvano Carroli
Ezio di Cesare
Ghena Dimitrova
Stefan Elenkov
Timo Korsa
Susan Maclean
Alfred Muff
Maria Noto
Rene Rohr
Olivia Stapp
Eduard Tumagian

1986
28 July: Phoenix Theatre,
London, after opening Theatre
Royal, Bath
The Cocktail Party by T. S. Eliot
Design: Brien Vahey
Cast included:
Sheila Allen
Stephen Boxer
Robert Eddison
Sheila Gish
Rachel Kempson
Alec McCowen
Simon Ward

1987
11 August: Savoy Theatre,
London (after opening at
Malvern)
Portraits by William Douglas
Home
Design: Brien Vahey
Cast included:
Stephen Boxer
Pamela Lane
Keith Michell

Simon Ward
Richard Wordsworth

1988
20 March: Eugene O'Neill
Theatre, New York
M. Butterfly by David Henry
Hwang
Design: Eiko Ishioka
Music: Giacomo Puccini
Lucia Hwong
Cast included:
Lori Tan Chinn
Lindsay Frost
John Getz
Rose Gregorio
Jamie H. J. Guan
John Lithgow
Alec Mapa
George N. Martin
Chris Odo
B. D. Wong

1988
Tony Award – Best Director – *M. Butterfly*

1988
19 October: Haymarket Theatre,
Leicester
Julius Caesar by William
Shakespeare
in repertory with
Creon, adapted from Sophocles
Theban plays by Stephen
Spender
Design: Jocelyn Herbert
Cast included:
Delaval Astley
Robert Blythe
Stephen Boxer
Philip Brook
Jacqueline Dankworth

Cathy Finlay
Robert Flemyng
Janet Key
William Key
Duncan Law
Peter Løvstrøm
Joseph Marcell
Martin McKellan
Tamsin Olivier
Gil Superman
Richard Williams

1989
25 March, Leicester Haymarket
M. Butterfly by David Henry
Hwang
Design: Eiko Ishioka
Music: Giacomo Puccini
Lucia Hwong
Cast included:
Darren Chan
Tsai Chin
Don Fellows
Lynn Farleigh
G. G. Goei
Anthony Hopkins
Johnny Lyon
Catherine McQueen
Ian Redford
Tom Wu

(Transferred to the Shaftesbury
Theatre, London, and opened 14
April 1989. There were further
productions in Italy and Japan.)

1989
4 November: Lunt-Fontanne
Theatre, New York
Die Dreigroschenoper (*The
Threepenny Opera*) by Bertolt
Brecht
Music: Kurt Weill

Design: Jocelyn Herbert
Cast included:
Georgia Brown
Kim Crisswell
Suzanne Douglas

Alvin Epstein
Larry Marshall
Maureen McGovern
Josh Mostel
Sting

Index